THE GUIDE TO
ACADEMIC
TRAVEL

Other *ShawGuides*:
- *The Guide to Cooking Schools*
- *The Guide to Writers Conferences*
- *The Guide to Photography Workshops*
- *The Guide to Arts & Crafts Workshops*

If *ShawGuides* are not available at your local bookseller, you can order directly from us. Include the book's title with a check or money order for $16.95 (includes shipping and handling) and mail to:

Shaw Associates
625 Biltmore Way, Dept. 1406U
Coral Gables, FL 33134

FIRST EDITION

THE GUIDE TO ACADEMIC TRAVEL

SHAW ASSOCIATES, Publishers
625 Biltmore Way, Suite 1406
Coral Gables, Florida 33134
(305) 446-8888

Please note that the information herein has been obtained from the listed schools, organizations, and individuals and is subject to change. The editors and publisher accept no responsibility for inaccuracies. Sponsors should be contacted prior to sending money and/or making travel plans.

Library of Congress Catalog Card Number 90-61178
ISBN 0-945834-07-1

Printed by R. R. Donnelley & Sons Company

INTRODUCTION

The Guide to Academic Travel is the first comprehensive source of information about adult vacation-study programs throughout the world. Compiled for all who are interested in expanding their knowledge of the arts, humanities, sciences, and nature, *The Guide* contains detailed descriptions of hundreds of courses, tours, and programs sponsored by 258 colleges, universities, museums, educational and cultural organizations, travel companies, and individuals.

The programs listed in *The Guide* span a broad range of subjects, including anthropology, archaeology, art history, architecture, astronomy, botany, culture, current and world affairs, ecology, environment, folklore, geology, history, literature, marine life, military history, music, ornithology, paleontology, performing arts, philosophy, political science, religion, sociology, and zoology.

Many programs focus on a specific topic while others cover a range of topics that pertain to a certain geographic region. These often consist of daily sessions devoted to an in-depth study of the culture and history of the region, complemented by excursions to course-related sites, opportunities to become acquainted with local residents, and other activities geared toward enriching the travel experience. Those who want their children to share in vacation learning will find more than 30 sponsors of educational programs for the whole family, with a variety of courses for different ages and interests. More than 20 listings contain descriptions of research projects and expeditions that involve participants as active, contributing members of the research team.

Each listing contains such specific details as the average length and number of programs offered each year, approximate dates, maximum number of participants, type and scope of academic content, itinerary or schedule, faculty and credentials, availability of academic credit, and costs, payment, and refund policies. Those programs that are ongoing or repeated each year are highlighted in bold type. Listings for sponsors that vary their offerings from year to year include "typical" or "representative" program descriptions. While the exact course, tour, or destination may not be currently available, the program subject and format are likely to be similar.

The **Appendix** contains three indexes to assist the reader in finding programs suited to a particular need or interest: A **Geographic Index of Sponsors**, a **Geographic Index of Programs**, and a **Specialty Index** of research projects, family programs, and eight subject categories.

The content of *The Guide* is based on factual information obtained from questionnaires, brochures, catalogs, and personal interviews with program sponsors. Each listing was sent to the sponsor for verification prior to publication. The length of a listing depends largely on the amount of information provided by the sponsor and is not intended to reflect the merit of its faculty or curriculum. The programs are not endorsed by the publisher nor do sponsors pay for their listings. Although every effort has been made to ensure accuracy, changes in prices and programs do occur. Sponsors request that you phone, fax, or write to them for a current brochure or catalog before sending money or making travel plans.

We thank the program sponsors for their cooperation and assistance. Readers are invited to let us know about their academic travel experiences and to submit names and addresses of sponsors and/or sources of additional listings for future editions. Comments and suggestions are also welcome.

We wish you pleasure in your pursuit of knowledge.

The Editor

CONTENTS

I

PROGRAMS

ADIRONDACK MOUNTAIN CLUB (ADK)
Lake Placid, New York

One and two-day summer workshops

Founded in 1922, this nonprofit membership organization, dedicated to the preservation and enjoyment of the Adirondack and Catskill Parks, sponsors a variety of field natural history programs that include workshops, free evening lectures, and outdoor activities. Typical titles include Birds of the Adirondacks, an introduction to many of the region's birds and their habitats, with emphasis on identification through markings and song and the use of field guides; Ferns & Non-Flowering Plants, a discussion/field trip that focuses on the identification, life history, habitat, and ecology of such varieties as clubmosses and horsetails; and Forest Types and Forest Management, an advanced workshop for recreationists that emphasizes forest ecology, commercial management, and habitat relationships of tree species.

Specialties: Field natural history.

Faculty: Staff and guest naturalists.

Costs, Accommodations: Workshop fees range from $10 to $55 ($8 to $50 for members) and payment should accompany application. Cancellations received three weeks prior to course receive a full refund less $5 handling fee; within three weeks 50% of the fee is refundable. Meals and lodging are additional. Participants are encouraged to stay on the workshop site at the Adirondack Loj, a rustic lodge offering family-style meals, or at the more remote John Brook Lodge.

Location: New York's Adirondack Park, established in 1892, encompasses six million acres of diverse landscape and terrain and is the largest national park outside Alaska. It contains a variety of habitats, from marshes and bogs to hardwood forests and alpine areas, as well as numerous recreational opportunities.

Contact: Adirondack Mountain Club, P.O. Box 867, Lake Placid, NY 12946; (518) 523-3441.

ADULT EDUCATION STUDY TOURS
Faversham, Kent, England

Weekend to three-week tours worldwide

Established in 1980, Adult Education Study Tours offers about 40 itineraries annually that cover the fields of art, archaeology, architecture, contemporary life, and wildlife and ecology. Groups range from 15 to 35 participants. Many tours are held in conjunction with colleges and universities.

Archaeology of Southern Italy features guided visits to both popular and lesser known sites as well as preparatory lectures by a Roman specialist. Life in the USSR includes planned visits and meetings with Soviet people. Weekend tours of Gerald Durrell's Jersey Wildlife Preservation Trust provide an opportunity to learn about its captive breeding program and overseas work and look behind the scenes at this zoo.

Specialties: Art, archaeology, architecture, contemporary life, and wildlife and ecology.

Faculty: Co-owners are Dr. Harold Goodwin, BA, Diploma in Adult and Continuing Education. All tour leaders are established adult educators with a relevant special interest.

Costs, Accommodations: Costs range from £200 to £2,500, including shared lodging, ground transportation, and some meals. Deposits vary and full refund is granted written cancellations received at least 56 days prior.

Location: Includes Africa, China, England, France, Greece, Holland, India, Indonesia, Ireland, Italy, the U.S., and the U.S.S.R.

Contact: Adult Education Study Tours Ltd., Granville House, 49 The Mall, Faversham, Kent ME13 8JN, England; (44) 795-539744, Fax (44) 795-533738.

ADVENTURES IN IDEAS
University of North Carolina Vacation Colleges and Weekend Seminars
Chapel Hill, North Carolina
Weekend and six-day programs

Since 1981, the University of North Carolina-Chapel Hill has sponsored **Adventures in Ideas**, a series of programs that consists of year-round **Weekend Seminars** and summer **Vacation Colleges** on the University's campus in Chapel Hill. Enrollment is usually limited to 60 participants and teacher renewal credit is available.

The ten or so **Weekend Seminars**, which run from Friday evening to Saturday afternoon, explore cultural, moral, and social topics from the perspective of the humanities. Lectures form the basis of each session, followed by group discussion. Representative titles include The Impressionists: Colors of a Changing Culture; Ancient Egypt; Bloomsbury: Ideas and Arts in Early Twentieth Century England; The Struggle for Democracy and Capitalism in China; Art, Politics, and Censorship; and Heresy and the Origins of Christianity.

The **Vacation Colleges**, four six-day summer theme programs of lectures, discussions, movies, and social events, also examine a variety of topics from the perspective of the humanities. Two courses are held concurrently during each of two sessions, usually during the last week in June and July. Typical themes include France and the Two Napoleons, which focuses on the interaction between these famous leaders and the nations they led — with emphasis on society, politics, art, literature, and music; Russian Revolutions: From Lenin to Gorbachev, which explores the cultural, political, and economic aspects of these two pivotal events in Russian history and also offers an optional post-seminar travel program to Russia; Number One? The Ascendancy of Contemporary Japan, an in-depth study of Japan today and what it may become; and Folklife in the South, a study of the region's traditional beliefs, tales, crafts, music, religion, and its work and play.

Specialties: A variety of cultural, moral, and social topics viewed from the perspective of the humanities.

Faculty: University of North Carolina-Chapel Hill faculty members.

Costs, Accommodations: Weekend Seminar tuition ranges from $60 to $65. Refund, less $10 fee, is granted cancellations until the day of the seminar. Vacation College registration fees are $240 to $250. Lodging may be arranged in the college dormitories or at local inns. A nonrefundable $30 deposit must accompany application with balance due on the first day of class. Credit cards (VISA, Mastercard) are accepted.

Contact: Humanities Program, CB #3420, Abernathy Hall, UNC-Chapel Hill, NC 27599-3420; (919) 962-1106.

ADVENTURES IN NEW OLD SPAIN
Pasadena, California

Two-week travel programs to Spain

James A. Person organizes cultural and historical travel programs to Spain. A typical itinerary, The Path of St. James, explores such cities as Pamplona, Burgos, Leon, and Santiago and includes an excursion to the entrance of the Path of Pilgrims into Spain and tours of historic sites, shrines, chapels and cathedrals. Other tours include Discovering Columbus, which visits locales where the explorer lived and worked, and the Gardens of Spain.

Specialties: Cultural travel programs to Spain.

Faculty: Tour hosts include Cultural Director and University of Southern California (USC) Professor Ramon Araluce, who earned his Ph.D. in philology and medieval literature, and Administrative Director James Person, who has planned tours for USC, conducted Los Angeles-area choirs, and organizes concert tours of Europe.

Costs, Accommodations: The $3,390 cost includes airfare, deluxe or first class double occupancy hotel lodging (single supplement $455), two meals daily, and ground transportation. A $500 deposit must accompany application with $900 due five months prior to departure, $1,100 four months prior, and balance three months prior. Full refund is granted cancellations at least four-and-a-half months prior; thereafter a $100 fee is charged until 60 days prior, when nonrecoverable costs are also assessed.

Contact: James A. Person, Travel, P.O. Box 90034, Pasadena, CA 91109; (818) 794-8558.

THE AEGEAN SCHOOL OF CLASSICAL STUDIES AND PHILOSOPHY
Arcata, California

17 and 36-day summer programs in Greece and Turkey

Since 1980, The Aegean School of Classical Studies & Philosophy has offered a 36-day mid-summer Greek travel program for adults (18 and over) that focuses on the Greek concept of the structure of society and its culture being the highest form of art. Study begins on Crete with a survey of the main philosophical issues in ancient Greek thought, from pre-Classical art and mythology through the Classical and Hellenistic periods to Byzantine times. Participants have the opportunity to become familiar with Greek geography and antiquities and explore the ways various philosophies, mythologies, literature, drama, art, and architecture contributed to ancient Greek and Byzantine life. A nine-day period of study on the island of Paros consists of informal seminars, discussions, and site explorations supplemented by lessons in modern Greek language and culture, with part of each day set aside for swimming and visits to local attractions. The remainder of the program is spent traveling to important archaeological sites and museums throughout the country. Travel is somewhat rigorous and applicants are expected to be in good physical condition in order to endure hiking in the warm climate. A short bibliography of required reading is sent to registrants and each is asked to prepare two oral reports in conjunction with visits to the sites. At the close of the program, those who desire a school certificate, which may qualify for college credit, can elect to take an examination and submit a written report.

The 17-day June program in Turkey, first offered in 1990, features lectures, seminars, and a cruise.

The Aegean School, founded in 1966 by the artist Brett Taylor, also sponsors a year-round fine arts program on Paros. Each eight-week study session consists of work in small groups or tutorial settings and focuses on the individual's art objectives and experience.

Specialties: Archaeological, artistic, and literary aspects of ancient and Byzantine Greek life; study in Turkey.

Faculty: Sessions are conducted by School Director and tour leader Professor Philip L. Drew, Jr., a Ph.D. in the History of Philosophy and Assistant Professor of Philosophy at California State University-Humboldt. Additional talks are given by resident excavation directors/archaeologists.

Costs: Tuition of $1,100 for the Greek program includes reservation fees and local transportation while in Greece. Airfare, room, and board are additional. A $500 deposit is required upon acceptance and no refunds are granted after March 1. Students are accommodated in local hotels, pensions, and/or rooming houses; the School receives special rates at these lodgings. The cost of the Turkey program is approximately $1,700.

Contact: Prof. Philip L. Drew, Jr., Director, Aegean School of Classical Studies & Philosophy, 946 "A" St., Arcata, CA 95521; (707) 822-9668.

ALABAMA AT OXFORD
Capstone International Program Center
University of Alabama
Tuscaloosa, Alabama

Four weeks in July-August

Since 1978, the University of Alabama has sponsored a summer term at Oxford University, England, that is open to both students and interested adults. Participants must enroll in two of nine three-credit courses that are offered in English, history, political science, and music. Afternoon field trips are scheduled to Shakespeare's birthplace and the Memorial Theatre in Stratford-Upon-Avon, Blenheim Palace, Stonehenge and Salisbury, and Berkeley Castle and Gloucester. An optional five-day excursion to the Lake District is offered during the term and a five-day optional Paris extension follows the program.

Typical course titles include A Survey of English Literature since 1800, devoted to readings of British authors from the Romantic period to the present; Modern British Literature, a study of important contemporary poets and novelists of England, Wales, and Ireland; Shakespeare, an introduction to six of Shakespeare's plays, viewed as literary texts and performance scripts; England in the Middle Ages, which explores England's religious, political, intellectual, and socio-economic development from the Anglo-Saxon invasions to the 15th century; Britain in the Great War, a study of the British experience from 1914 to 1918; Introduction to Listening, which focuses on the forms, styles, and history of European music with emphasis on critical listening and discussions; and Modern British Politics, a survey from the end of World War II through the Thatcher Revolution.

Specialties: English literature, history, music, political science, culture.

Faculty: Includes University of Alabama faculty members William D. Barnard, Associate Professor and Chairman of the Department of History; Dwight Eddins, Professor of English; Eugenia Kiesling, Assistant Professor of History; David B. McElroy, Associate Professor of History; and Dennis Monk, Professor of Music; Oxford University faculty members Andrew Adonis and Martin Holmes; Auburn University Associate Professor of History Joseph Kicklighter; and University of Newcastle-Upon-Tyne Lecturer Gordon McMullen.

Costs, Accommodations: Comprehensive fee of $2,950 includes tuition for six course hours, private room, weekday meals, airport transfers, and field trips. Excursion to the Lake District and Edinburgh is $300, Paris excursion is $435. A $200 deposit, refundable until March 1, must accompany application with balance due 90 days prior. Participants are housed in single rooms at Wadham College and meals are taken in the College Hall.

Facilities: The College, founded in 1613, offers playing fields, gardens, and a common room. Bicycles, boats, and athletic equipment are available.

Contact: Alabama at Oxford, C.I.P.C., Box 870254, University of Alabama, Tuscaloosa, AL 35487-0254; (205) 348-5256.

AMERICAN MUSEUM OF NATURAL HISTORY DISCOVERY TOURS
New York, New York

One-week to one-month domestic and international tours

The Discovery Tours program of New York's American Museum of Natural History, established in the late 1970's, offers more than 25 travel programs throughout the year, about evenly divided between land expeditions, limited to 15 to 30 participants, and luxury cruises, limited to about 120. A lecture program is part of each trip.

A representative domestic tour, Archaeology and Natural History of the Colorado Plateau, explores the Grand Canyon, Monument Valley, the San Juan River, and Mesa Verde. An archaeologist and a naturalist lead the program and conduct informal lectures and group discussions relating to the sites visited. A typical international tour, French Caves and Castles, features the prehistoric caves and rock shelters of the Dordogne with special permission to enter the original cave of Lascaux. Visits to Giverny and the home and gardens of Claude Monet are also included.

Specialties: Tours with a natural history and art focus.

Faculty: All tours are accompanied by members of the Museum's curatorial staff as well as scholars and specialists in the regions visited.

Costs, Accommodations: All-inclusive land (cruise) costs range from $2,095 to $2,890 for domestic trips, from $2,900 to $6,390 for international trips. Deposit and refund policies vary. Museum membership (not required for tour participation) begins at $22 for an individual, $45 for a family, which includes a subscription to *Natural History* magazine and other benefits.

Location: In addition to the above, locations may include Alaska, Costa Rica, Egypt, Japan, Scotland, Norway, and Denmark, Spain and Portugal, the Yucatan Peninsula, the Soviet Union, and various regions of East Africa.

Contact: Discovery Tours, American Museum of Natural History, Central Park West at 79th St., New York, NY 10024-5192; (800) 462-8687 *or* (212) 769-5700.

ANDANTE TRAVELS
Salisbury, Wiltshire, England

One-week international travel study programs

Established in 1985, Andante Travels offers four to six week-long programs each year that visit both little and well-known cultural and historical sites. Typical tours, which are limited to 25 to 34 participants, include Stone Age Cave Paintings of the Dordogne; Pompeii, Herculaneum, and the Territory of the Samnites; Southern Germany and the Danube; and Roman and Carthaginian Tunisia. Informal lectures are a part of each program.

Specialties: Historical and cultural tours.

Faculty: Director Annabel Lawson, who holds a Ph.D. in Roman Provincial Archaeology, and other specialists in their fields of study.

Costs, Accommodations: Prices, which include lodging and some meals, range from £435 to £487; single supplement is available on some trips. A nonrefundable £60 deposit must accompany registration with balance due two months prior to travel. Full refund less deposit is granted cancellations more than two months prior; thereafter penalty ranges from 30% of total price (28 days to two months prior) to 60% (15 to 27 days prior); no refunds less than 15 days prior.

Contact: Andante Travels, Grange Cottage, Gaters Lane, Winterbourne Dauntsey, Salisbury, Wiltshire SP4 6ER, England; (44) 980 610979.

ANDOVER FOUNDATION FOR ARCHAEOLOGICAL RESEARCH (AFAR)
Andover, Massachusetts

Domestic and international archaeological projects of one week or more

Founded in 1984 as a nonprofit scientific organization, the Andover Foundation for Archaeological Research (AFAR) provides opportunities for students and the interested public to participate in archaeological expeditions. No previous experience is needed and volunteers (Friends of the Foundation), who usually work a five-day week, receive on-site training and are involved in all aspects of the project including field excavation and laboratory studies.

Typical projects include the Maya site of Kichpanha in Belize, where students uncover such objects of trade as stone tools, ceramics, and animal bones (food remains); Fort Bliss, New Mexico, where a newly discovered unlooted rock shelter is searched for such items of subsistence as preserved plant remains and perishable artifacts; the Southwest, an investigation into the origins of agriculture and early man in the Las Cruces, New Mexico area; the St. Lawrence Iroquois, excavation of a palisaded village near Watertown, New York; and a search for the Little Spanish Armada, reportedly sunk in the lagoon off St. George Cay in Belize.

Specialties: Archaeological expeditions.

Faculty: Includes AFAR founder Dr. Richard (Scotty) MacNeish and other experienced specialists.

Costs, Accommodations: Tax-deductible contribution to Friends of the Foundation, which usually includes food, lodging, and ground transportation, ranges from $1,120 for one week to $2,000 for one-month, and special group rates are available for longer periods. A nonrefundable $200 to $300 deposit must accompany application.

Contact: Andover Foundation for Archaeological Research, 1 Woodland Rd., Box 83, Andover, MA 01810; (508) 470-0840.

ANTICHITÀ
St. Catharines, Ontario, Canada
Two to three-week Mediterranean summer cruises and expeditions

Established in 1985 to conduct educational cruises and tours to Greece and other Mediterranean countries, Antichità (the Italian word for antiquity) offers an annual two-week Aegean cruise and three-week archaeological research expeditions to Cyprus. The Aegean Argosy cruise, limited to 24 physically and intellectually active individuals, focuses on the archaeology, history, and culture of the sites visited. Destinations, which change each year, include Crete, the Cycladic islands, the Peloponnesos, and the southwestern and southern coasts of Turkey and Greece. Participants receive a set of books on Greek archaeology, art, architecture, and history and a briefing pamphlet.

The purpose of the Antichità Archaeological Research Teams, established in 1990, is to recruit volunteers for the Vasilikos Valley Project and other excavations working in Cyprus and to teach inexperienced individuals the basic principles and methods of field archaeology. The teams are open to upper-level high school students, college students, educators, and interested adults. Ten-member teams, are instructed in field techniques and procedures, recording archaeological data, taking measurements, drawing plans and sections, and the preliminary cleaning and processing of finds. Experienced volunteers are given more challenging projects and responsibilities. The program includes lectures on the history and research problems encountered at the site, major artifact types recovered, and the archaeology and history of Cyprus. Day trips are scheduled to selected major archaeological sites, other excavations, and museums in the southern part of the island.

Specialties: Archaeology, history, and culture of Greece, Cyprus, and the Mediterranean area.

Faculty: Antichità was founded by Dr. David W. Rupp and his wife, Elizabeth. Dr. Rupp is a Professor of Classical Art and Archaeology at Brock University in St. Catharines, Ontario. He has excavated in Italy, Greece, Cyprus, and Israel and was the principal investigator and organizer of the Canadian Palaipaphos Survey Project in the Paphos District of Cyprus. Elizabeth H. Rupp teaches Latin and English at Ridley College.

Costs, Accommodations: Cost of the Aegean Argosy is $3,195, which includes double occupancy lodging (single supplement $600), most meals, ground transportation, and scheduled activities. A $500 deposit secures reservation with balance due 60 days prior to departure. Cancellation penalty ranges from $150 (more than 60 days prior) to 75% of cruise fee (less than one week prior). Cost of the Antichità Archaeological Research Teams is $1,795, which includes simple dormitory-style lodging (or rooms for couples), most meals, instruction and reading materials, and some excursions. A $100 deposit must accompany application with $500 due two months prior and balance due one month prior. Cancellation penalty ranges from $50 (more than two months prior) to $900 (three to thirty days prior).

Contact: David W. Rupp, President, Antichità, P.O. Box 156, St. Catharines, ON L2R 6S4, Canada; (416) 682-8124, Fax (416) 684-8875.

APPALACHIAN MOUNTAIN CLUB (AMC)
Gorham, New Hampshire

Two-day to two-week seminars in the Appalachian Mountains and abroad

Appalachian Mountain Club, the nation's oldest mountaineering/conservation organization and the largest in the Northeast, offers more than 50 workshops, programs, and travel seminars on a broad range of topics with emphasis on natural history and ecology. Academic credit is available for many programs through the University of New Hampshire School for Lifelong Learning.

Representative titles include Mountain Weather, which combines a moderate hike up Mt. Washington with a study of local weather patterns and microclimates and how certain plants and animals adapt to the harsh mountain-top environment; Spring in the Mountains, a series of lectures and field trips that explore the flora and fauna of the Mt. Washington area; Backcountry Birdwatching, a naturalist excursion that visits three diverse habitats to observe and discuss the distribution of a variety of spring warbler species; Plants of the Presidentials, which focuses on the identification, distribution and ecology of plant life in the southern Presidential Mountains; Bushwacking, a series of classroom and field sessions that cover map reading skills, using a compass, triangulation, dealing with obstacles, and interpreting the terrain; Forest Ecology, a study of forest history and the components of the diverse habitats that make up the northern forests; and Wild Mushroom Hunting, which focuses on collecting and identifying field and woodland mushrooms, what to eat and what not to eat, and such fundamentals as identification keys and observable important field characteristics. **International Timberline Seminars** are conducted to scenic areas, such as the mountains of North Wales and the Highlands of Scotland. Daily field trips focus on sites of archaeological and natural interest.

Established in 1876 to encourage the wise use and preservation of our natural areas, the more than 30,000-member AMC is active in conservation, education, research, and backcountry management throughout the Northeast. Members participate in trips and programs and receive club publications.

Specialties: Natural history and ecology.

Faculty: Includes AMC staff naturalists and visiting specialists.

Costs, Accommodations: Workshop fees, including lodging and meals, range from $170 ($180 for members) to $350 ($375); and from $65 ($60) to $80 ($70), course fee only. Timberline costs vary. Membership dues are $40 individual, $65 family. Full fee must accompany application for one and two-day workshops; otherwise a $75 deposit is required. Fees are refundable for cancellations received at least three weeks prior or if space can be filled. Nightly room rate ranges from $28.50 to $34.50 ($23.50 to $29.50) and a deposit of $20 per person per night is required. Housing is provided at Pinkham Notch Camp in two to four-bunk rooms. AMC also operates a system of eight backcountry huts that are located at intervals of one day's hike and sleep from 36 to 90 persons. Tuition is charged for college credit.

Location, Facilities: Pinkham Notch Camp, located 2 1/2 miles below treeline in the heart of the White Mountain National Forest, is eight miles north of Jackson on NH Rte. 16 at the eastern base of Mt. Washington. Nearby scenic attractions include Tuckerman Ravine and the Alpine Gardens. Bus service is available from Boston's Logan Airport and from Portland, ME, or Burlington, VT. Facilities include common living room, library, rathskeller, conference rooms, and a trading post that sells hiking supplies and equipment.

Contact: Appalachian Mountain Club, P.O. Box 298, Gorham, NH 03581; (603) 466-2727.

APPALACHIAN STATE UNIVERSITY
SUMMER STUDY ABROAD
Boone, North Carolina

Three to four-week study programs in Europe

Appalachian State University offers a series of annual summer study programs abroad for students and interested adult learners. Academic credit is offered.

Summer in Lugano, Switzerland, a four-week program sponsored by the Department of Art, combines residency study and focused weekend travel to Florence, Arles, and Venice and throughout the area surrounding Lugano. The program of study includes such credit courses as Modern European Landscape Masters, an exploration of the development of modern landscape approaches plus weekend trips to areas painted by selected masters; Culture and Consciousness, an examination of the integration of culture, environment, and personal space; and Art, Creativity, & Personal Growth, an opportunity for students to integrate experiences of viewing and analyzing art with the making of art and writing. Six semester hours of credit are available.

Bards and Balladeers of Brittania, a three-week travel-study program sponsored by the English Department, begins with a series of three pre-trip lecture/seminar classes. The program focuses on major British works and folk traditions in their cultural and historical contexts and includes folk and dramatic performances, visits to museums and homes of literary figures, and visits with performers and crafters. The itinerary includes England, Scotland, Ireland, and Wales.

Specialties: European study programs with emphasis on arts and humanities.

Faculty: Appalachian State University faculty members.

Costs, Accommodations: Program costs, which include round-trip airfare, tuition, lodging, some meals, and excursions, range from approximately $2,450 to $2,850. Deposit and refund policies vary.

Contact: Office of International Studies, Appalachian State University, Boone, NC 28608; (704) 262-2046.

THE ARCHAEOLOGICAL CONSERVANCY TOURS
Santa Fe, New Mexico
Seven to ten-day domestic and foreign tours

Since 1984, The Archaeological Conservancy has offered four to six tours annually to ruins of past cultures, Conservancy preserves, and developed and undeveloped archaeological sites. Groups are limited to 30 participants.

Representative itineraries include The 450th Anniverary Coronado's Trail Tour, which traces the Trail from Phoenix to view ancient Indian ruins and study the early Spanish explorers and colonizers of the American Southwest; Cliffdwellers Tour, focusing on such Indian cultures as the ancient Sinagua and Anasazi and the modern Hopi and Navajo and visits to the great ruins at Mesa Verde and Canyon de Chelly and the cliffdwellings at Betatakin and Walnut Canyon; Sonoran Desert Tour, an exploration of this southern Arizona and northern Mexico desert and the ancient people who colonized it, including the Hohokam and early European settlers; and Mayan Adventure, devoted to the study of this advanced civilization that appeared on the Yucatan Peninsula sometime before A.D. 250.

Specialties: Archaeological tours.

Faculty: Stewart L. Udall (Coronado's Trail Tour), former Secretary of the Interior and Conservancy Board Chairman, author of *To the Inland Empire: Coronado and Our Spanish Legacy*; Mayan scholar Dr. Peter Harrison (Mayan Adventure); Conservancy President Mark Michel; and Conservancy Southwest Regional Director Jim Walker. Several prominent archaeologists join tours as special guest guides for one or two-day periods.

Costs, Accommodations: Tour costs, which include a $100 tax-deductible contribution, first class hotel accommodations, lunches, and local travel, range from $1,295 to $1,595. A $150 deposit must accompany application with balance due 60 days prior to departure. Cancellations more than 60 days prior are charged a fee of $100 per person; from 7 to 59 days prior a 50% fee is charged unless space can be filled; no refunds thereafter.

Contact: The Archaeological Conservancy, 415 Orchard Dr., Santa Fe, NM 87501; (505) 982-3278.

ARCHAEOLOGICAL TOURS
New York, New York
14 to 25-day tours year-round in the U.S. and abroad

Established in 1969, Archaeological Tours offers approximately 27 tours annually in addition to special tours for museums, universities and cultural institutions. Each tour is limited to 22 to 30 participants, depending upon the destination. Typical itineraries include Anasazi Four Corners, a study of the ancient Anasazi people with a visit to the University of Arizona's excavation at Grasshopper Pueblo; Caves and Castles of Northern Spain & Southern France, an exploration of the major prehistoric caves plus visits to Roman and medieval villages and castles; Egypt & Israel, focusing on the ancient connection between the countries with an in-depth study of Jerusalem; and Greece, Crete & Santorini, featuring the classical sites of the Peloponnese, Athens, and seldom-visited archaeological sites on the island of Santorini.

Specialties: Archaeological tours.

Faculty: All tours are conducted by distinguished scholars who stress the historical, anthropological, and archaeological aspects of the areas visited.

Costs, Accommodations: Land costs range from $2,300 to $3,770, which includes double occupancy lodging (single supplement available), most meals, ground transportation, and all scheduled activities. A $400 to $500 deposit must accompany booking with balance due eight to ten weeks prior to departure. Cancellations at least 12 weeks prior receive full refund less $50; thereafter penalty ranges from $200 (10 to 12 weeks prior) to $1,300 plus nonrecoverable costs (less than 10 weeks prior).

Location: In addition to the above, tours are scheduled to southern India, the Himalayas, Indonesia, Thailand and Nepal, northern Thailand and southwestern China, Sicily and southern Italy, Great Britain, Etruscan Italy, Turkey, Guatamala, Tunisia, and Malta, Sardinia, and Corsica.

Contact: Archaeological Tours, 30 E. 42nd St., #1202, New York, NY 10017; (212) 986-3054.

ARCHAEOLOGY FIELD SCHOOL AT MOUNT INDEPENDENCE
The University of Vermont
Burlington, Vermont

Six-week summer program in Orwell, Vermont

Mount Independence, considered to be one of the most intact military sites of the Revolutionary War Period, is part of a long-term research and interpretive plan that includes construction of a visitors' center. College students, teachers, and interested adults began excavations at the site in 1989, with extensive mapping and archaeological testing into soldiers' cabins, barracks, and a blockhouse.

Continued study of the ordinary living areas — soldiers' cabins — helps the State of Vermont in its preparation of exhibits and in designing new visitor trails. During the six-week program, from late June to early August, a maximum of 40 participants are instructed in field and laboratory techniques, mapping, conservation methods, and historical research. They dig at the site from 9 am until 5 pm and spend the evenings cleaning and sorting their finds and attending public lectures by noted authorities. Six credits are available.

Specialties: Archaeological exploration at a Revolutionary War site.

Faculty: Dr. David Starbuck is experienced in excavating sites of the Revolutionary War and other historic and prehistoric periods. He is assisted by a teaching assistant, trained avocationals, and visiting scholars.

Costs, Accommodations: Registration fee is $10, tuition is $114/credit hour for Vermont residents, $285/credit hour for nonresidents. Six weeks' housing (meals) at Orwell Elementary School is $180 ($108).

Contact: Archaeology Field School, Continuing Education, The University of Vermont, 322 South Prospect Street, Burlington, VT 05401-3505; (802) 656-2085.

THE ART INSTITUTE OF CHICAGO
Chicago, Illinois
One to seventeen-day local, domestic and international tours

The Art Institute of Chicago offers its members and friends a variety of programs with an art and/or architecture focus, including day-long bus tours, three to four-day domestic trips, and 10 to 17-day international tours. Bus tours, including the annual New Buildings of Chicago tour, focus on the art and architecture of various areas of the city, including the cemeteries, the North Shore, ethnic neighborhoods, and private collections.

Domestic trips, planned four times a year to such art centers as Los Angeles, Boston, and Santa Fe, feature guided architectural tours and behind-the-scenes museum visits, as well as opportunities to view private collections. International tours and cruises to a variety of destinations were first offered in 1984 and are now scheduled approximately eight times a year. Typical itineraries include The Legendary World of the Aegean, Inspirations in Modern Art: Provence and the Côte D'Azur, A Journey on the Danube, The Island World of Japan, A Tour of Southern Italy and Sicily, and Scandinavia & the British Isles.

Specialties: Tours with an art focus.

Faculty: All trips are accompanied by curators and/or study leaders who are experts in their fields.

Costs, Accommodations: Day-long bus tours are $50 ($48 members); domestic trips range from $750 to $1,850 all-inclusive, which include a $150 contribution to the Art Institute; costs of international tours range from approximately $3,500 to $6,500, all-inclusive, which include a $250 to $400 contribution. Payment and refund policies vary. Annual membership dues begin at $25 student, $35 individual, $45 family.

Contact: The Art Institute of Chicago, Membership Programs, Michigan Ave. at Adams St., Chicago, IL 60603; (312) 443-3917.

ARTS ABROAD
School of Visual Arts
New York, New York
Three-week summer program in Greece

Since 1989, the School of Visual Arts has offered a three-week summer Humanities program, open to all, that focuses on the art and archaeology of ancient Greece. Designed as an archaeological exploration rather than a workshop, students travel with an expert to visit the country's historic sites and museums. The program includes stops in Corinth, Mycenae, Nauplia, Epidaurus, Sparta, Mystra, the Olympia Grounds, Patras, and Delphi; a series of lectures in Athens; and three days in Mykonos. Three credit hours are available. The School also sponsors summer programs abroad in the practical and graphic arts for advanced students and professionals.

Specialties: The archaeology of Ancient Greece.

Faculty: Includes In-Residence Director Joel Garrick, School of Visual Arts' Public Information Director and a former National Endowment for the Arts panelist; on-tour lecturer Persephone Kourboubeti, a University of Athens Guide; Charilaos Sotiropoulos, Assistant in the Chair of Architecture, Ecole Speciale d'Architecture, Paris; and Yannis Stavrakakis, Director, Parthenon Restoration Technical Office.

Costs, Accommodations: Cost of $2,700 includes round-trip airfare, tuition, superior or first class double occupancy hotel accommodations (single supplement available), most meals, and land transfers. A nonrefundable $25 fee must accompany application, a $900 down payment is due on acceptance, a second $900 payment is due six weeks prior to departure, and balance is due ten days prior. Full refund less $150 fee is granted cancellations more than four weeks prior; recoverable costs less $150 are refunded thereafter; no refunds within one week of departure.

Contact: Office of International Studies, School of Visual Arts, 209 E. 23rd St., New York, NY 10010-3994; (212) 679-7350.

THE ASIMOV SEMINAR
OF THE RENSSELAERVILLE INSTITUTE (TRI)
Rensselaerville, New York

Five-day annual summer seminar

Since 1972, The Rensselaerville Institute has sponsored a simulation inquiry, headed by Isaac Asimov, into a topic critical to science, technology, and the survival of life on Earth. The program is limited to 60 participants, who need no specific knowledge but should have an interest in the subject and a strong willingness to join in freewheeling discussion and decision-making sessions and to work in small task groups in roles suggested by the simulation.

In a 1990's simulation, the giant space station "Asimovia" is in high earth orbit in the year 2000. The job of its crew (the program participants) is to monitor the effects of global warming and to recommend ethical responses to the growing crisis on Earth in the face of conflicting national interests.

Specialties: Simulation inquiry into a topic critical to survival.

Faculty: Isaac Asimov and his close scientist/writer friends: Mark Chartrand III, telecommunications consultant and vice-president of the National Space Institute; M. Mitchell Waldrop, senior writer for *Science* magazine; and Joseph Leary, television producer for GTE.

Costs, Accommodations: The cost of $550 per person, $1,000 for a couple includes program fees, all meals, and lodging. A $100 deposit must accompany registration with balance due on arrival. No refunds are granted within two weeks of program.

Location, Facilities: The interior of "Asimovia" is a replica of the rural campus of The Rensselaerville Institute, an independent educational center overlooking the northern Catskill Mountains of upstate New York, 27 miles from Albany. Formerly a family estate, the Institute's turn-of-the-century buildings share the campus with modern residence and meeting spaces and a restaurant in a converted carriage house. Facilities, which are handicapped accessible, include 100 acres of meadows, flower gardens, and woods, with tennis and volleyball courts and a swimming lake nearby.

Contact: Mary-Ann Ronconi, Program Coordinator, The Asimov Seminar of The Rensselaerville Institute, Rensselaerville, NY 12147; (518) 797-3783.

THE ASPEN INSTITUTE
Queenstown, Maryland

Weekend to two-week programs in Queenstown, Aspen, and five countries overseas

Established in 1950, The Aspen Institute is an international organization whose programs are designed to enhance the ability of leaders in business, government, the nonprofit sector, academia, and the media to understand and act upon the issues that challenge the national and international community. The Institute's method is to gather approximately 20 participants around a table to explore the world's great literature and relate it to contemporary society. The two major programs are the tuition-paying Seminars, and the Policy Programs, which are sustained by grants and attended by individuals chosen for their expertise. Seminars include the one to two-week **Executive Seminar** and **Justice and Society Seminar** and one-week and weekend seminars on a variety of related topics. Seminar reading materials are sent to participants in advance.

The **Executive Seminar,** the core of the Institute's program, is designed for senior-level management and other decision-makers. Offered approximately a dozen times a year for a period of seven, nine, or fourteen days, the program focuses on the writings of great thinkers on such questions as justice, freedom, property, democracy, and ethical conduct on the private, corporate, and state levels. The **Justice and Society Seminar,** offered about three times a year, is open to executives, judges and lawyers, journalists, corrections officials, academics, and others interested in the justice system. The program offers participants the opportunity to examine the meaning of justice through reading and discussion of classical writings on justice, works of creative literature, and contemporary cases.

One-week seminars, offered about a half dozen times a year, cover such topics as Communications and Society, an assessment of the changes in society resulting from advances in communications and information technologies; Corporation in Contemporary Society, an exploration of the history of the modern corporation and its present and future challenges; Major Ethical

Problems, an examination of the things we value, such as pleasure, virtue, and learning, and their purpose in life; and The Mind and Its Powers, which addresses major controversial issues in psychology.

Two and three-day **Weekend Seminars**, offered six to eight times a year, cover such topics as U.S.-Soviet relations, law and literature, capitalism and communism, U.S.-Japan relations, and the corporation and public education. These programs usually begin on a Thursday or Friday evening and conclude with lunch on Sunday.

Specialties: Round-table discussion of universal human questions, including justice, freedom, property, democracy, and ethical values.

Faculty: Seminar moderators include Supreme Court justices, federal and state court judges, and academics.

Costs, Accommodations: Costs, which include tuition, lodging, meals, and reading materials, range from $4,500 to $4,800 for two-week seminars ($2,700 for participating guest, $1,200 for auditing guest); $3,000 to $4,000 for seven to nine-day seminars ($1,800 to $2,500 for participating guest, $800 to $1,000 for auditing guest), and from $600 to $1,000 for weekend seminars ($150 to $800 for participating/auditing guest). A 50% deposit must accompany application with balance due 90 days prior to seminar. Cancellations more than 30 days prior forfeit 50% of fee unless space can be filled; no refunds within 30 days. Membership in the Society of Fellows ranges from $1,750 to $5,000. Benefits include reduced seminar fees, auditing at no cost, invitations to special programs and events, and Aspen Institute publications.

Location: Fall, winter, and spring programs are conducted at the Wye Center on Maryland's Eastern Shore in the Chesapeake Bay area, about an hour's drive from Washington, D.C. Recreational opportunities include hiking, bicycling, swimming, and tennis. Summer programs are held in Aspen, Colorado. Institute affiliates are situated in Berlin, Rome, Oxford, France, and Japan.

Contact: Seminar Administration Office, The Aspen Institute, Wye Center, P.O. Box 222, Carmichael Rd., Queenstown, MD 21658; (301) 827-7168, Fax (301) 827-9295.

THE ATHENS CENTRE
Athens, Greece

Three to six-week summer sessions

The Athens Centre, a nonprofit educational organization founded in 1969, sponsors summer sessions in Greece in affiliation with American colleges and universities. These programs, which are limited to 35 university students, teachers, and interested adults, consist of seminars, lectures, and field trips that focus on the history, literature, art, and archaeology of Classical, Byzantine, and Modern Greek civilization. Academic credit is available. Participating institutions include The College of Wooster, San Diego State University, and Broward College. The Centre also sponsors university-affiliated semesters in Greece and such other programs as fine arts, performing arts, language study, and cultural events.

Specialties: Greek history, culture, art, and archaeology.

Faculty: Faculty members of sponsoring institutions, archaeologists working in Greece, and other qualified instructors.

Costs: Costs range from approximately $1,600 to $2,400. Payment and refund policies are set by the individual institutions. Participants are usually housed in centrally-located hotels.

Location: The Centre, a neo-classical building surrounded by a quiet garden courtyard, is located in a residential area of central Athens.

Contact: The Athens Centre, 48 Archimidous St., 116 36 Athens, Greece; (30) 701-5242/2268, Fax (30) 701-8603. Dr. Thomas Falkner, Dept. of Classical Studies, The College of Wooster, Wooster, OH 44691; (216) 264-1234. Charles Smith, CAWS, P.O. Box 3494, Anaheim, CA 92803; (714) 956-2067. Dr. Jeff Mitchiner, Social Sciences Dept., Broward Community College, Central Campus, 3501 S.W. Davie Rd., Davie, FL 33314; (305) 475-6500.

THE BALTIMORE MUSEUM OF ART
Baltimore, Maryland
One to twelve-day domestic and international trips

The Baltimore Museum of Art sponsors one or two travel programs each year that are designed for those with an interest in art. The trips, which accommodate from 10 to 40 participants, are sometimes accompanied by a member of the Museum's curatorial staff. They range from single day excursions to nearby locales, such as New York City, to ten to twelve days abroad. Although anyone is eligible to register for the programs, a contribution to the Museum is required. Arrangements are handled by reputable group tour operators.

Contact: Programs Office, The Baltimore Museum of Art, Art Museum Dr., Baltimore, MD 21218; (301) 396-6314.

BAYLOR IN THE BRITISH ISLES
Baylor University
Waco, Texas
Thirty three-day summer study-travel program in London

First offered in 1982, this 33-day mid-July to mid-August program is limited to 175 participants, most of whom are students who enroll for course credit. Approximately 20 courses in history, psychology, biology, finance, religion, communication, English, economics, and philosophy are offered, including such titles as British Philosophy and Culture, Western World Literature: Masterpieces in Translation, Twentieth Century British Poetry, and England Since 1603. The weekday schedule includes lectures, seminars, and travel, with classes from 8 to 10 am and the rest of the day devoted to faculty-escorted excursions to such locations as Stonehenge, Salisbury, Winchester, Tintern Abbey, and cities in Ireland, Wales, and Scotland.

Specialties: Courses in history, psychology, biology, finance, religion, communication, English, economics, and philosophy, most with emphasis on Great Britain.

Faculty: All courses are taught by Baylor University faculty. Permanent faculty includes Dr. James Vardaman, Dr. Ann V. Miller, Dr. William D. Hillis, Dr. Lewis M. Barker, and Dr. Terry S. Maness.

Costs, Accommodations: The basic program cost is $2,399 ($2,499 noncredit), which includes dormitory room, breakfast and dinner, ground transportation, access to faculty, and passes to many museums and monuments. Students who register for academic credit pay regular tuition (by June 1). A $200 deposit, nonrefundable after February 1, must accompany reservation with balance due by March 15.

Location: The program is based at Westminster School, where students live, attend classes, and have breakfast and dinner. Part of Westminster Abbey, the school is reserved exclusively for students and faculty of the Baylor program. Following study in England, students travel to Berlin and Poland and optional extension trips continue to Israel or Italy.

Contact: James Vardaman, Ph.D., Dept. of History, Baylor University, B.U. Box 7306, Waco, TX 76798-7306; (817) 755-2667.

BEAR TREKS
California Alumni Association Travel Program
Berkeley, California
Ten-day to three-week domestic and foreign trips

The California Alumni Association sponsors approximately 20 Bear Treks travel programs each year. Some trips, where appropriate, may include an accompanying faculty lecturer, visits to research sites, and special events. Typical destinations include India and Nepal, Asia, Switzerland, Soviet Union, Antarctica, New Zealand, Canada, Maine Coast, and New Mexico.

Costs, Accommodations: Costs, which include round-trip airfare from San Francisco and Los Angeles, range from $1,745 to $7,650. A $400 deposit must accompany application. Lodging and meal arrangements vary.

Contact: BEAR TREKS, California Alumni Association, Alumni House, Berkeley, CA 94720; (415) 642-3717.

BICYCLE AFRICA
International Bicycle Fund (IBF)
Bellevue, Washington
15 to 31-day programs in Kenya, West Africa, and Tunisia

Established in 1982, the nonprofit International Bicycle Fund assists economic development projects utilizing bicycles and sponsors four to six educational bicycle tours in Africa annually, each limited to 12 participants accompanied by two leaders. The program provides an opportunity for Westerners who are in good physical and mental health to learn more about Africa on a personal level, focusing on its culture, history, economy, and physical diversity. Cycling difficulty is moderate, with occasional challenging sections, and daily distances range from 20 to 60 miles, with an average of 40. Separate tours are planned to west, central, and east Africa, each visiting areas that are seldom on tour itineraries. Academic credit is available for some programs

West Africa: People-to-People, a series of four 15-day tours to Burkina Faso, Togo, Benin, and Ghana, offers participants the opportunity to meet traditional villagers, village chiefs, craftsmen, educators, university students, government officials, missionaries, and diplomats. Tunisian Odessey, a 23-day tour, features exploration of the Teboursouk Mountains, Tunis, and Carthage, and visits to archaeological sites in Makthar and Sbeitla. Other programs include a three-week tour of Kenya's Rift Valley, Maasai Mara National Park, Lakes Victoria and Baringo, Nakuru, and Nairobi, and a one-month Zimbabwe Sojourn in conjunction with Evergreen State College.

Specialties: Educational bicycle tours of Africa.

Faculty: Program Director and tour leader David Mozer, an accomplished cyclist, bicycle activist, African scholar, collector of African art, and educator, served as a Peace Corps volunteer to Liberia, directed an educational extension program in West Africa, and administered a grant program for village development. Assistant leaders have a broad knowledge of the culture, history, natural science, politics, social development, and economic activity of the program area.

Costs, Accommodations: Costs, which are partly tax-deductible and include accommodations, two meals daily, and admission fees, range from $895 to $2,225. Airfare from/to the U.S., which is additional, must be booked through Bicycle Africa (a $100 supplement is charged those who make their own air arrangements). Accommodations may include camping, village housing, makeshift dormitories, and simple hotels. Participants furnish their own bicycles (all-terrain bikes are recommended). A $300 deposit (which includes $50 nonrefundable registration fee) must accompany registration, which should be submitted at least 90 days prior to departure. Full payment is due 60 days prior.

Contact: International Bicycle Fund, 4887 Columbia Dr. South, Seattle, WA 98108-1919; (206) 628-9314.

BIOLOGICAL JOURNEYS
McKinleyville, California
Five to nineteen-day trips in the U.S. and abroad

Established in 1981, Biological Journeys offers almost 50 whale watching and natural history trips annually to areas known for their wildlife and natural beauty. Most trips are limited to ten participants, who live on board a small cruise vessel. Informal lectures are given during the day and evenings are often devoted to video and slide presentations and discussions of the day's events. Some tours offer photographic instruction.

Specialties: Natural history, with emphasis on whales.

Faculty: Ronn Storro-Patterson has been a whale consultant and biologist, a member of the Scientific Committee of the International Whaling Commission, and co-founded the nonprofit Whale Center, which is devoted to conservation, research, and education. Ron LeValley taught natural history and birdwatching classes and served as regional editor for *American Birds*. Other guides include marine mammalogist Jeff Jacobsen, naturalist John Kipping, and humpback whale authority Mason Weinrich.

Costs, Accommodations: Costs range from $550 to $6,500, which includes instruction, meals, accommodations, and transportation during the program. Participants live aboard small cruise vessels, each equipped with small skiffs for excursions and a library stocked with natural history books. A $200 deposit must accompany reservation with balance due 60 days prior to departure. Cancellations more than 60 days prior receive full refund less $50; thereafter refund is granted only if space can be filled.

Location: Several tours focus on the whales of Baja California, Alaska's Inside Passage, Washington's Puget Sound, and the Galápagos Islands. Other itineraries include British Columbia, Costa Rica, Antarctica, and Australia.

Contact: Biological Journeys, 1696 Ocean Dr., McKinleyville, CA 95521; (800) 548-7555, (707) 839-0178 (Ron LeValley), *or* (415) 527-9622 (Ronn Storro-Patterson).

BIRDS & BIRDERS NATURE TOURS
The Netherlands

Four to ten-day birding tours to The Netherlands, Belgium, Germany, Denmark, and Sweden

Birds & Birders specializes in year-round birdwatching tours for both beginning and experienced birders. Groups are limited to 16 participants, who are taught how to find, identify, and understand a variety of European birds as well as the culture and natural aspects of the countries visited.

Specialties: Birdwatching.

Faculty: Tour Directors Ib S.O. Huysman and Reinko van der Laan both have BA degrees in Biology and English and speak fluent English, Dutch, and German. Both are bird specialists and involved in the national bird survey of The Netherlands. They teach field classes in coastal biology of the Northsea and the Waddensea.

Costs, Accommodations: Costs range from $375 to $1,500, which includes double occupancy accommodations (single supplement available), all meals, ground and ferry transportation from Amsterdam, and entrance fees.

Location: Depending upon the season, tours are offered to national parks, wildlife refuges, and other sites of natural interest in The Netherlands, Belgium, Germany, Denmark, and Sweden.

Contact: Birds & Birders, P.O. Box 737, 9700 AS Groningen, The Netherlands; (31) 5952-280, Fax (31) 50-144717.

BRANDYWINE RIVER MUSEUM TRAVEL PROGRAM
Brandywine Conservancy
Chadds Ford, Pennsylvania

The Brandywine River Museum sponsors day trips to nearby cities. Typical programs include New York Theatre and Washington, D.C.'s National Gallery of Art. Costs range from approximately $50 to $100, which includes transportation, theatre tickets, entrance fees, and a $7 donation.

Contact: Travel Program, Brandywine River Museum, P.O. Box 141, Chadds Ford, PA; 19317; (215) 388-7601.

BUDDHIST PILGRIMAGE TO INDIA AND NEPAL
Insight Travel
Yellow Springs, Ohio
Three-week January-February program

Since 1987, Insight Travel has operated an annual three-week pilgrimage to India and Nepal that focuses on the sites associated with the life of Shakyamuni Buddha. The program, which is limited to 15 participants, includes visits to ancient monuments and modern monasteries, complemented by daily group meditation and opportunities to meet traditional Buddhist teachers. A series of lectures on the history and development of Buddhism in India provide the group with background information and a focus for discussion.

Specialties: Buddhism.

Faculty: Group Leader is Robert Pryor, Director and co-founder of Antioch University's Buddhist Studies Program and a student of Buddhism since 1971. He has been leading groups to India since 1979. Teachers with whom participants meet include archaeologist Dr. Mukunda Raj Aryal of Tribhuvan University, Cho Kyi Nyima Rinpoche, abbot of Karma Thargey Chunkorling Monastery, Tara Rinpoche, abbot of the Galugpa Tibetan Monastery in Bodhgaya, and Dr. V.P. Mishra, Mahant of the Sankat Mochan Temple.

Costs, Accommodations: Cost of $3,750 includes round-trip airfare from San Francisco to Kathmandu, double occupancy lodging (single supplement $235) in first class hotels or guesthouses with breakfast and lunch or dinner, ground and air transportation in India and Nepal, and all planned activities. A $300 deposit must accompany reservation with balance due five weeks prior to departure.

Location: The itinerary includes Bodh Gaya, Sarnath, Varanasi, Kushinagar, Lumbini, and Kathmandu.

Contact: Insight Travel, 502 Livermore St., Yellow Springs, OH 45387; (513) 767-1102.

BUFFALO MUSEUM OF SCIENCE
Buffalo, New York

One to twelve-day trips in the U.S.

Each year the Museum conducts several day trips, some weekend trips, and a few longer tours to places of historical and natural interest in the U.S. Most tours are limited to 10 to 20 participants and many are open to youngsters age 12 and over. Day trips include a cruise on Lake Erie and the Niagara River and exploration of the inner and outer harbor areas; a visit to local bogs to experience the "quaking" phenomenon; a field trip to Mendon Ponds Park to study topographic features associated with Pleistocene glaciation; and a walk along Shale Creek to learn about stream and forest ecology and view a waterfall with a natural gas leak. Regional and national trips are scheduled to Allegheny National Forest, Independence National Historical Park in Philadelphia, historic sites along the Hudson River, and Chaco Canyon, Canyon de Chelly, and Mesa Verde in the U.S. Southwest.

Specialties: Tours with a natural science or history focus.

Faculty: Tours are led by museum staff and knowledgeable specialists.

Costs: Day and weekend trips range from $6 ($5 member) to $22 ($18). Longer trips range from $400 to $1,700. Payment must accompany registration and refunds are granted written cancellations received at least five business days prior to departure. Credit cards (MasterCard, VISA) accepted. Museum membership begins at $20 individual, $30 family.

Contact: Buffalo Museum of Science, 1020 Humboldt Parkway, Buffalo, NY 14211-1293; (716) 896-5200.

CAMP DENALI/NORTH FACE LODGE
Denali National Park, Alaska

Two to seven-day programs from June-September

North Face Lodge and Camp Denali, vacation lodges located in the heart of Denali National Park, offer programs that focus on the Park's natural history. On arrival day, guests are met at the park entrance and escorted by naturalist/drivers on a 90-mile introduction to the area's plants, animals, birds, geology, and history. Subsequent days' field activities, which may vary at each lodge, include guided hiking and wildlife observation and scheduled evening interpretive programs of slides, films, and discussions that focus on such topics as wildflowers, nesting birds, nature photography, and the Aurora Borealis.

Specialties: The natural history of Denali National Park.

Faculty: Staff naturalist-guides and guest leaders in various fields of natural history.

Costs, Accommodations: All-inclusive costs are $450 (two nights) or $675 (three nights) at North Face Lodge and range from $585 (three nights) to $1,230 (seven nights) at Camp Denali. North Face Lodge is a modern 15-room country inn with private baths. Camp Denali, a rustic wilderness complex, consists of a centralized living/dining room and bathroom/shower facilities and 18 individual log or frame cabins. A deposit of $200 per person must accompany reservation with balance due 30 days prior to arrival. Full refund is granted cancellations prior to April 1; thereafter 50% of deposit is refunded only if space can be filled.

Location: The 5.7 million-acre Denali National Park, home to a wide variety of birds and wildflowers and 35 species of mammals, contains 150 miles of the permanently snow-capped Alaska Range, including Mt. McKinley, North America's highest peak. Camp Denali and North Face Lodge are situated in the center of the park, within view of Mt. McKinley.

Contact: Camp Denali/North Face Lodge, P.O. Box 67, Denali National Park, AK 99755; (907) 683-2290 (June-Sept.) *or* P.O. Box 216, Cornish, NH 03746; (603) 675-2248 (Sept.-June).

CAMP SHAKESPEARE
Utah Shakespearean Festival
Southern Utah State College
Cedar City, Utah
Five days in August

Camp Shakespeare, a five-day program open to college and advanced high school students, teachers, and the general public, is offered by Southern Utah State College in conjunction with the summer-long Utah Shakespearean Festival. Interaction between the students and members of the Festival professional company is emphasized in daily class sessions, which run from 9:30 am to noon and 2 to 5 pm and feature lectures and discussions of the ongoing productions. Activities also include attendance at four or five performances, a backstage tour, and a "Renaissance Feaste". Three quarter units of credit (two semester units) are available.

The ten-week Utah Shakespearean Festival, begun in 1962, sponsors six theatrical productions in three theaters, production and literary seminars, backstage tours, and various workshops.

Specialties: The works of William Shakespeare.

Faculty: Camp Program Director is Dr. Michael Flachmann, Professor of English at California State University-Bakersfield, dramaturg for the Festival, and author of four books and more than 30 articles on Shakespeare. Instruction is also provided by members of the professional company, including actors, directors, designers, stage technicians, and Shakespeare scholars.

Costs, Accommodations: The $375 tuition fee includes dormitory lodging, meals at the student center, college credit, theater tickets, and special activities. A $50 deposit must accompany application with balance due five weeks prior to the session.

Location: Cedar City, in the heart of the Utah National Parks, is 260 miles south of Salt Lake City and 165 miles north of Las Vegas.

Contact: Camp Shakespeare, The Office of Continuing Education, Braithwaite 203, Southern Utah State College, Cedar City, UT 84720; (801) 586-1994, Fax (801) 586-1944.

CANADIAN NATURE TOURS
Federation of Ontario Naturalists (FON)
Don Mills, Ontario, Canada
Five-day to two-week trips in the Western Hemisphere

Canadian Nature Tours, operated by the FON since 1976, is a service to the members of the Federation of Ontario Naturalists and the Canadian Nature Federation (CNF), Canada's two foremost conservation groups. Approximately 50 nature tours, canoe trips, and backpacking trips are offered year-round in a variety of locations, primarily the U.S and Canada. Group size ranges from 6 to 15 participants, age 16 to 86, who must be members of either FON or CNF.

Typical tours include Spring in the Arctic, which features the migration of the Bathurst Inlet caribou herd, the largest herd of migrating mammals in the world. Participants become acquainted with members of an Inuit (eskimo) community and participate in their daily activities. Bird in the Hand offers participants the opportunity to play an active part in scientific research through bird banding, daily censuses, and other population monitoring techniques. Canoe trips, usually limited to ten participants and two leaders, are rated according to skill level, from novice to advanced.

Specialties: Natural history and wildlife.

Faculty: All tours are conducted by experienced naturalists.

Costs, Accommodations: Costs, which include accommodations and meals and may include airfare, range from C$320 to C$4,050. Nonrefundable $100 to $500 deposit must accompany application with balance due eight weeks prior to tour and nonrefundable thereafter. Accommodations, which are rustic, range from tents to motels. Credit cards (VISA, MasterCard) accepted. Annual FON membership dues are $28 individual, $35 family, $21 student, $22 seniors. All profits are used for conserving the natural environment in Canada.

Location: Includes Cuba, Galápagos, and a variety of scenic locales in the U.S. and Canada.

Contact: Canadian Nature Tours, Federation of Ontario Naturalists, 355 Lesmill Rd., Don Mills, ON M3B 2W8, Canada; (416) 444-8419, Fax (416) 444-9866.

CANYONLANDS ED VENTURES
Canyonlands Field Institute (CFI)
Moab, Utah
One to seven-day programs from February-October

Established in 1984 to continue the legacy of the late Bates Wilson, the "father" of Canyonlands National Park, this educational nonprofit organization specializes in outdoor instruction on the Colorado Plateau. Canyonlands Ed Ventures are limited to groups of 10 to 15 people and include seminars, van tours, backcountry trips, and photography workshops. Programs provide an insider's view of Arches and Canyonlands National Parks and the Four Corners Area — where Arizona, New Mexico, Colorado, and Utah meet. CFI also sponsors a Desert Writer's Workshop, seminars specifically for teachers and naturalists, and week-long Elderhostel programs. International programs with a nature focus are planned, including one on the Rock Art of Baja. Many of the programs grant one or two graduate or undergraduate credits from Utah State University or Brigham Young University.

Ten to fifteen one-day weekend seminars are scheduled annually. Ecology of the Black Bear studies food habits, wintering, reproductive rates, and such field techniques as radio telemetry and live trapping; Literary Landscapes of Canyonlands offers readings and discussions of 19th and 20th century Western writers; and Hooting With the Owls examines the life history of the owl with a nighttime field trip to "hoot" (call out) the birds. Three or four van tours are planned annually to the Hopi and Navajo reservations to explore their ancient and modern cultures. Navajo Trading Posts, a three-day tour, includes visits to a variety of trading posts with lectures on Navajo history, lifeways, trading practices, and considerations for purchasing Native American art. Enduring Seeds: Native Farming on the Colorado Plateau visits contemporary and prehistoric farming sites on the reservations. Participants meet with elderly and young farmers, explore the revival of culinary interest in native foods, and dine on a traditional Hopi meal. Backcountry trips, scheduled a half-dozen times a year, explore the heartlands by backpacking. Grand Gulch Archaeology offers an in-depth look at Anasazi culture with four days of hiking in Grand Gulch Primitive Area, noted for colorful rock formations and cultural sites representing several stages of prehistoric development. Photography workshops, geared to the intermediate to advanced photographer, offer the opportunity to work with professionals who specialize in canyon country lighting and landscape.

Specialties: Natural history, wildlife, ecology, and culture of the Colorado Plateau.

Faculty: Accomplished naturalists, biologists, ecologists, geologists, astronomers, anthropologists, writers, photographers, and other experts who have studied the canyonlands.

Costs, Accommodations: Most one-day seminars are $35 ($10 deposit); multi-day seminars range from $100 to $300 ($30 to $60); van tours range from $475 to $565 ($150); backcountry trips range from $160 to $685 ($70 to $200); and photography workshops range from $125 to $215 ($50 to $80).

Fee, which is payable by credit card (VISA, MasterCard), includes lodging, some meals, transportation, and instruction. Cost per academic credit ranges from $30 to $75. Refund policy varies. Members of CFI receive newsletters and other publications and a discount on program fees. Annual dues begin at $15 individual, $25 family.

Location: The canyonlands are located in southeast Utah, one day's drive from Grand Canyon and Bryce, Zion, and Mesa Verde National Parks. Most CFI programs begin and end in Moab, Utah, which is just south of I-70 and a two-hour drive from the airport in Grand Junction, Colorado.

Contact: Canyonlands Field Institute, P.O. Box 68, Moab, UT 84532; (801) 259-7750.

CARETTA RESEARCH PROJECT
Savannah Science Museum
Savannah, Georgia
One-week research sessions from May-October

Since 1973, the Savannah Science Museum, in cooperation with the U.S. Fish and Wildlife Service and the Wassaw Island Trust, has conducted a hands-on research and conservation program involving the endangered loggerhead sea turtle (*Caretta caretta*). The program's purpose is to learn more about population levels and trends and nesting habits of loggerheads, to enhance the survival of eggs and hatchlings, and to involve the public in these efforts. Each week during the egg laying and hatching season, a maximum of eight volunteers are needed to assist with the Project. During the egg laying season (mid-May through mid-August), volunteers, who need no experience but must be age 15 or older, spend most of each night patrolling the Island's beaches in search of female turtles that have crawled out of the sea to nest. They tag and measure the turtles, record other pertinent data, transplant some nests to safety, and protect others with screen. During the hatching season (late July through early October) volunteers monitor the nests, escort hatchlings to the sea, and record data on unhatched eggs. Daytime activities may include monitoring the beach for dead turtles, maintaining the Project's vehicles, and sharing housekeeping and cooking duties. Volunteers also receive instruction in research techniques and learn about sea turtles and the progress of related projects.

Specialties: Research into saving the endangered loggerhead sea turtle.

Faculty: Win Seyle, Project Director and Island Leader, helped begin the Project in 1973. Other faculty includes Bobby Moulis, who has seven years' experience, and John Crawford, who directed the Project for four years.

Costs, Accommodations: Tax deductible registration fee, which includes dormitory-style lodging in rustic cabins, meals, leadership/instruction, and transportation from/to the museum and on the island, is $375 per week from May through August, $300 per week in September. Full payment must accompany application. Full refund, less $25 penalty, is granted cancellations at least 60 days prior to departure and thereafter if space can be filled. Academic credit may be available.

Location: Wassaw Island, one of Georgia's coastal barrier islands and a National Wildlife Refuge, has 20 miles of dirt roads and seven miles of beach. The island is situated about ten miles south of Savannah and is accessible only by boat.

Contact: Win Seyle, Director, Caretta Research Project, Dept., G, Savannah Science Museum, 4405 Paulsen St., Savannah, GA 31405; (912) 355-6705.

CEDAR RAPIDS MUSEUM OF ART
Cedar Rapids, Iowa

Since 1981, The Cedar Rapids Museum of Art has offered a series of travel opportunities for its members. Now housed in a new facility, the Museum is planning a variety of trips to such locales as Chicago, Minneapolis, and Kansas City. Programming is led by the Museum's curator or local experts.

Costs: Annual membership dues range from $15 for students and seniors to $35 for a family. Benefits include a quarterly newsletter, special lectures, docent tours, teacher workshops, and studio classes taught by local artists.

Contact: Education Department, Cedar Rapids Museum of Art, 410 Third Ave. S.E., Cedar Rapids, IA 52401; (319) 366-7503.

CENTER FOR AMERICAN ARCHEOLOGY
Kampsville Archeological Center
Kampsville, Illinois

Five-day summer field schools

Since the early 1960's, the Center for American Archeology has incorporated interested students of all ages in its excavation and analysis of the more than 5,000 documented archaeological sites of the lower Illinois River Valley. Each summer, Adult Field Schools are offered to people with little or no archaeological experience. A typical session includes orientation and training, on-site excavation work, and assisting in the laboratory with the washing, sorting, and cataloging of artifacts. Evenings are devoted to activities such as an ecological tour, lectures, and a visit to a reconstructed Indian village where students participate in a series of replicative experiments of prehistoric dwellings, stone tools, and ceramics.

Specialties: Archaeology.

Faculty: Archaeologists and investigators, including Dr. Jane E. Buikstra, President of the Center for American Archeology and Professor of Anthropology at the University of Chicago.

Costs, Accommodations; Tuition, which includes meals and dormitory housing, is $350 per week. A $50 nonrefundable deposit must accompany application with balance due 30 days prior to program. A 50% refund is granted cancellations more than 14 days prior, a 25% refund thereafter.

Location: Kampsville is situated 60 miles north of St. Louis, Missouri, and 80 miles southwest of Springfield, Illinois. No public transportation service is available to the area, however the Center can provide pick-up service for participants arriving via Amtrak in Alton, Illinois, or at the St. Louis Lambert Airport. Novices work at Twin Ditch, a significant archaeological site that is buried beneath dense floodplain soil; more experienced students are assigned to Mound House, a National Register Historic Place that is both a village and a mortuary site.

Contact: Center for American Archeology, Kampsville Archeological Center, Box 366, Kampsville, IL 62053; (618) 653-4316.

CENTER FOR THE FINE ARTS
Miami, Florida

One-day to two-week domestic and international trips

Miami's Center for the Fine Arts offers occasional art-oriented trips for members. Day trips to nearby locales and two to four-day weekend trips, scheduled to such cities as Philadelphia and Richmond/Williamsburg/Norfolk, focus on current museum exhibitions and often include visits to private collections and artists' studios. Typical trips abroad include such titles as The Art Treasures of the Lowlands (Brussels, Ghent, Brugge, Antwerp, Amsterdam, The Hague), European Masters (Rome, Florence, Paris), and The Orient Express (Munich, Vienna, Paris).

A three-day excursion to Philadelphia includes tours of an artist's home, the Barnes Foundation, Winterthur Museum, and curator-guided viewings of specific works at the The Philadelphia Museum of Art, as well as visits to important Main Line art collections. The Richmond/Williamsburg/Norfolk itinerary consists of visits to the Shirley and Berkeley Plantations and guided tours of the Virginia Museum of Art, Abby Aldrich Rockefeller Folk Art Museum, Chrysler Museum, and DeWitt Wallace Decorative Arts Center.

Specialties: Trips with an art focus.

Faculty: Usually local docents and curators.

Costs: Day trips are approximately $50. Costs, which include round-trip airfare, lodging, and most meals, range from $385 to $1,400 for two to four-day weekend trips, $2,195 to $4,099 for travel abroad. The price of most trips includes a $100 to $200 donation to the Center. Deposit, which must accompany reservation, ranges from full payment for day trips to $400 for two-week tours. Museum membership ($100 or $1,000 level, depending on trip) is required for participation. Cancellation and refund policies vary.

Contact: Center for the Fine Arts, 101 W. Flagler St., Miami, FL 33130; (305) 375-3000.

THE CENTER FOR GLOBAL EDUCATION TRAVEL SEMINARS
Augsburg College
Minneapolis, Minnesota
Ten-day to three-week study seminars to Central and South America, the
Philippines, Israel and the Occupied Territories, and Hawaii

Founded at Augsberg College in 1982 to help citizens expand their world
view and deepen their understanding of international issues, The Center for
Global Education offers more than 40 experiential travel programs each year
that are designed to introduce participants to the realities of poverty and
injustice, to examine the root causes of these conditions, and to encourage
reflection on the role and responsibility of North Americans in working for
social and political change. Participants meet with a wide range of representatives in government, business, church, and grassroots communities and visit
relief and development projects. Typical itineraries include Mexico; Israel &
the Occupied Territories; and Guatemala, Nicaragua, Honduras, and El
Salvador. The center also sponsors semester-long undergraduate academic
study programs based in Mexico and Central America, Spanish language
courses, and a series of seminars, primarily for civic leaders and elected public
officials, that focus on the nature of regional conflicts and the impact of U.S.
foreign policy.

Specialties: Social issues.

Faculty: Program staff and service personnel of the Center.

Costs: Costs range from $1,295 to $1,995.

Location: Mexico, Central and South America, the Philippines, Israel and
the Occupied Territories, and Hawaii. Trips depart from a number of different
cities throughout the U.S.

Contact: The Center for Global Education, Augsburg College, 731 21st
Ave. South, Minneapolis, MN 55454; (612) 330-1159.

CHAUTAUQUA INSTITUTION
Chautauqua, New York
Weekend and one-week sessions in spring, summer, and fall

Established in 1874, Chautauqua Institution is an international center for
continuing education for all ages, offering more than 150 courses in a variety
of subjects, a series of theme week lectures, programs for older adults, and
such cultural events as concerts, operas, theater, and popular performers.
Most of the Institution's activities are scheduled during the nine-week period
from the end of June to the end of August but special weekend and one-week
programs are also offered during the off-season.

During the summer, more than 2,000 participants enroll in the **Special
Studies** program of courses that include art, dance, music, contemporary
issues, literature and writing, and special interest subjects such as handicrafts,
foreign languages, and family and personal development. College credit is
available for some courses through the State University of New York at

Fredonia. Courses change from week to week, with most sessions scheduled for 60 to 90 minutes daily, Monday through Friday. Each week is devoted to a different theme and features a morning and afternoon theme-related lecture by a distinguished personality. Themes include Business, Social Issues, Communications, Education, Arts and Humanities, Religion, and National Affairs. Evenings are reserved for performances by the Chautauqua Symphony Orchestra, the Chautauqua Opera Company, and contemporary performers. The "55 Plus" weekends for older adults present a current events topic through discussion, workshops, lectures, films, cassette tapes, and other means. Cultural programs are planned for Saturday evenings. The **Residential Week for Older Adults** offers lectures, music, recreation, and drama.

Specialties: A variety of topics relating to the arts, education, religion, recreation, and current events.

Faculty: The more than 200-member faculty consists of educators and experts in their fields.

Costs, Accommodations: Admission to the Chautauqua Institution is by gate pass, which is $125 for one week and $110 to $120 for each additional week and entitles holder to move freely on the grounds, attend theme lectures, evening concerts, and participate in other activities. Course fees average $35 to $70 per week. A free Visitor's Guide and Accommodations Directory lists lodging available on the grounds.

Location: Chautauqua is a lakeside community in the southwest corner of New York State, midway between Buffalo and Erie and 16 miles north of Jamestown. Ground transportation is available to and from the airports in Jamestown, Buffalo, and Erie.

Contact: Chautauqua Institution, Box 1098, Chautauqua, NY 14722; (716) 357-6200.

CHICAGO-EUROPE LANGUAGE CENTER
Chicago, Illinois
Day tours

This tour organization specializes in tours that emphasize specific facets of Chicago culture. The Center's multilingual staff can accommodate groups of from 2 to 500 people, in 30 different languages. While customized programs are available, planned tours include Architectural Tours of Chicago, which highlights 20th century architecture from Frank Lloyd Wright homes to new structures; Chicago City Highlights, including Chinatown, other ethnic neighborhoods, museums, and jazz clubs; Gospel Music Tour, featuring gospel music and dining at a soul food restaurant; and the Al Capone Tour, which includes a show on the roaring '20s and visits to speakeasy sites. Tours outside the Chicago area can be arranged to visit American Indian reservations, the Amish country, and Wisconsin farms.

Specialties: Architectural and cultural tours of Chicago.

Faculty: All tour leaders are English speaking or multilingual and many are Chicago natives.

Costs: Costs for each tour are $40 per hour, with a four hour minimum.

Contact: Michael LaRusso-Reis, Director, Chicago-Europe Language Center, 180 N. LaSalle St., Ste. 2510, Chicago, IL 60601; (312) 276-6683, Fax (312) 358-1044.

CHINA ADVOCATES
San Francisco, California

Eighteen-day to three-week June-September programs in China

This private cultural organization, created to help Americans study in China, sponsors a variety of in-depth summer programs in culture, archaeology, music, painting and sculpture, language, medicine, and the culinary arts.

Chinese Culture, Medicine, and Fine Arts, a three-week program of lectures, demonstrations, and Saturday excursions, examines how these disciplines express the Chinese character and soul. One week is spent at each of three institutions: Beijing University, the Academy of Traditional Chinese Medicine, and the Academy of Fine Arts. **Beijing Life & Culture With Tour** — eleven days in Beijing followed by a seven-day tour of culturally important cities — is designed to bring participants into direct contact with Chinese people from all walks of life. The schedule in Beijing includes morning lectures/demonstrations, afternoon and evening excursions, and special Saturday trips to such sites as the Ming Tombs and the Great Wall. **Chinese Archaeology With Silk Road Tour** — an eight-day seminar with field trips in Beijing followed by a ten-day tour along the Silk Road — affords a first-hand view of excavations, methods, artifacts, and interpretations of the Chinese archaeological world.

Traditional & Western Music in China With Tour — ten days in Beijing followed by a seven-day cities tour — examines the convergence of Western and Chinese music and their continuing evolution. The Beijing program focuses on experiencing music through rehearsals and performances, lectures on its theoretical and historical development, demonstrations of Chinese instruments, and a full day studying the Beijing Opera in preparation for an evening performance. Participants spend three days at the Central Academy of Music, where they meet with and observe distinguished soloists and music teachers, and three days with noted composers who are creating works that combine Chinese and Western traditions.

Specialties: Chinese culture, fine arts, archaeology, music.

Faculty: Includes faculty of the local institutions. Traditional & Western Music in China is accompanied by Professor Bob Greenberg, Chairman of the Music History Department at the San Francisco Music Conservatory and lecturer at UC Berkeley.

Costs, Accommodations: Program fees, which include tuition, round-trip airfare, double-occupancy dormitory room, all meals, and weekend excursions, range from $2,080 to $2,570. A $400 deposit must accompany application with balance due 75 days prior to start of program. Penalty ranges from $200 for cancellations more than 75 days prior to 40% of program cost plus airline cancellation charges less than 15 days prior.

Contact: China Advocates, 1635 Irving St., San Francisco, CA 94122; (800) 333-6474 or (415) 665-4505.

CINCINNATI ART MUSEUM (CAM) TRAVEL PROGRAM
Cincinnati, Ohio
One-day to two-week domestic and international tours

The Cincinnati Art Museum Travel Program, established in 1963 for museum members, now offers approximately ten itineraries annually, with most trips weekend excursions to art centers in the U.S. and the others to destinations abroad. Group size ranges from 20 to 30 participants. The tours are planned by a volunteer standing committee of the museum, known as Travel Planners, who develop itineraries that are compatible with the museum collection and the interests of membership. Tour highlights include visits to current museum exhibitions and architectural landmarks and opportunities to meet local artists and artisans.

Specialties: Tours with an art focus.

Faculty: Domestic tours are accompanied by a member of the Travel Planners and a travel agency escort. Some international tours are accompanied by art scholars.

Costs, Accommodations: All-inclusive costs range from $370 to $713 for domestic weekend tours, approximately $3,300 to $5,500 for international tours. Deposit and refund policies vary. Museum membership dues begin at $15 student, $27.50 individual, $35 family.

Location: Typical domestic tour destinations include Washington, D.C., Chicago, Indianapolis, St. Louis, Toledo, and New York City. International destinations may include Portugal, Costa Rica, and Scandinavia and the British Isles.

Contact: Travel Planners, Cincinnati Art Museum, Eden Park, Cincinnati, OH 45202; (513) 721-5204.

CINCINNATI ZOO TRAVEL PROGRAMS
Cincinnati, Ohio
Ten to seventeen-day international tours

The Cincinnati Zoo offers escorted travel programs to such destinations as Antarctica, Kenya and Tanzania, Namibia-Botswana-Zimbabwe, Costa Rica, and the Galápagos Islands.

Specialties: Tours with a natural history focus.

Faculty: Tour leaders include such staff personnel as Executive Director Edward Maruska; Dr. Betsy Dresser, Director of Research; Thane Maynard, Assistant Curator of Education; and Curator Bob Lotshaw.

Costs, Accommodations: Costs, which include airfare, accommodations, and most meals, range from $2,100 to $8,000. Some tours include a tax deductible donation of $100 to $250. Deposit and cancellation policies vary with each program.

Contact: Provident Travel, 2800 Atrium Two, 221 E, Fourth St., Cincinnati, OH 45202; (800) 543-2120 *or* (513) 621-4900.

THE CLEARING
Ellison Bay, Wisconsin
Five-day to one-week courses from May-October

Built in 1935 by Jens Jensen, a distinguished landscape architect and friend of Frank Lloyd Wright, The Clearing offers more than 40 courses annually in the arts, nature, and humanities. One-week courses begin with supper on Sunday and end with breakfast the following Saturday.

Changing Attitudes About Nature, a "shared-inquiry" discussion of the works of authors, artists, and composers who have expressed their relationship with nature, includes text readings, musical tape experiences, and art slide presentations. Identification and Natural History of Flowering Plants focuses on learning the major plant groups, the use of wildflower guides and plant identification manuals, the role of various species in the environment, and the problems of preserving biodiversity. The Beauty of the Earth, a series of natural history field trips, is an introduction to regional birds, trees, and wildflowers combined with readings and a study of how writers, artists, and scientists react to beauty in nature. Art and Nature consists of morning readings of poetry by Robert Frost and other nature-inspired poets with evenings devoted to musical works — primarily those of Ravel and Debussy — that attempt to imitate the beauty of the natural world. Music Appreciation, a course that coincides with the Peninsula Music Festival, features guided listening, lectures, and discussions of the elements and concepts of music combined with attendance at evening performances. Environmental Geology focuses on the causes and solutions for such geological problems as earthquakes, landslides, floods, waste disposal, acid rain, and the greenhouse effect, with field trips to examine the geology of the Door County.

Specialties: Arts, humanities, and natural history.

Faculty: The faculty includes university and college professors and other practicing professionals.

Costs, Accommodations: The one-week course cost, which includes dormitory (twin-bedded) room and all meals except Thursday supper, is approximately $395 ($420). A $75 deposit must accompany registration with balance due one month prior to course. Cancellations at least 20 days prior receive full refund less $25; deposit is forfeited thereafter. Dormitory and double room lodgings are in log and stone cabins.

Location: The Clearing is situated in Wisconsin's Door County woods, on Green Bay.

Contact: The Clearing, P.O. Box 65, Ellison Bay, WI 54210; (414) 854-4088.

CLEMSON UNIVERSITY ALUMNI ASSOCIATION TRAVEL PROGRAM
Clemson, South Carolina
Seven to twelve-day international trips

Since 1975, Clemson University has offered approximately six study tours annually, most held during the summer months and limited to 15 to 40 members and other interested adults. Typical programs include Clemson in the Caribbean, a seven-day trip to Dominica that emphasizes study of the area's tropical foliage and over 100 species of birds as well as a visit to the natural rainforest at Clemson University's Archbold Tropical Research Center; Medieval and Renaissance Architecture of Italy, an educational study tour based in Genoa at Clemson's Charles E. Daniel Center for Building Research and Urban Studies; and Legends of the Nile, which includes a stay in London, visits to important sites in Egypt, and a Nile Cruise, supplemented by enrichment lectures.

Specialties: Study tours that cover a variety of subjects.

Faculty: Clemson University faculty members, including Dr. Joseph Arbena, Professor of Latin American History; Dr. Charles Jennett, Dean of Engineering; Dr. Steven Hill, Curator of the Herbarium; Professors Harold Cooledge and Dale Hutton of the College of Architecture; Robert Waller, Dean of Liberal Arts; and Judy Melton, Head of the Language Department.

Costs, Accommodations: Tour costs range from $1,300 to $3,500, which includes round-trip airfare from/to Atlanta, double occupancy first class accommodations (single supplement available), most meals, and scheduled activities. Deposit and refund policies vary.

Location: In addition to the above, destinations may include Europe, Russia, South and Central America, and Asia.

Contact: Clemson University Alumni Association Travel Program, Alumni Center, Clemson, SC 29634-5603; (803) 656-2345.

THE COLONIAL WILLIAMSBURG FOUNDATION
Williamsburg, Virginia
One, two, and five-week summer sessions

The Colonial Williamsburg Foundation offers two archaeological programs for students and adults: **Learning Weeks in Archaeology**, first offered in 1987, and College of William and Mary/Colonial Williamsburg

Archaeological Field School, first offered in 1985. No previous archaeological experience is required, however participants must be able to perform such physical tasks as shoveling soil and pushing wheelbarrows.

Learning Weeks in Archaeology, a two-week program (one-week option available) offered four times each summer and limited to four to eight participants, is an introduction to the goals and methods of archaeological research at Colonial Williamsburg. Hands-on experience excavating a site in the Historic Area, taking field notes, mapping finds, identifying artifacts associated with colonial daily life, and analyzing site remains, supplemented by tours, lectures, and special events, provide participants with an understanding of how scholars reconstruct the life of Virginia's colonial capital and translate discoveries into interpretive programs.

The Department of Archaeological Research at Colonial Williamsburg, in conjunction with the Anthropology and History Departments of the College of William and Mary, offers two five-week **Archaeological Field Schools** each summer. Approximately 15 participants are introduced to the methods and theory of historical archaeology and learn basic excavation and recording skills, laboratory procedures, and identification of artifacts associated with 17th and 18th century American sites. A variety of modern techniques for data recovery are taught, including the use of microcomputers for landscape reconstruction and the analysis of spatial patterning. Sessions are scheduled from 8 am to 4:30 pm, Monday through Friday, and are supplemented by weekly lectures on various aspects of archaeology. The program grants undergraduate or graduate credit in anthropology (six credits) or history (three credits). Those desiring credit in history must enroll in a reading seminar that meets once weekly.

Specialties: Archaeological research at Colonial Williamsburg.

Faculty: Director of Archaeological Research Marley R. Brown III and Staff Archaeologists Gregory J. Brown, David F. Muraca, and Meredith Moodey of the Department of Archaeological Research, Colonial Williamsburg Foundation; Professor James P. Whittenburg of the College of William and Mary.

Costs, Accommodations: Learning Weeks registration, payable in advance, is $350 for a one-week session, $550 for two weeks. The fee includes lectures, tours, welcoming reception, one or two dinners, and tickets to all Historic Area attractions. Other meals and lodgings are not included. Full refund is granted cancellation at least two weeks prior to session. Archaeological Field School registration, which includes tuition and dormitory accommodations on the campus of William and Mary, is approximately $845 for in-state students, $1,799 for out-of-state students. Part and full scholarships may be available.

Contact: Dr. Marley R. Brown III, Dept. of Archaeological Research, Colonial Williamsburg Foundation, P.O. Box C, Williamsburg, VA 23187; (804) 220-7336.

COLORADO RIVER & TRAIL EXPEDITIONS
Salt Lake City, Utah
Nine-day Grand Canyon Colorado River trips in August and September

This river rafting company, founded in 1971, offers a variety of expeditions, mainly in the Colorado Plateau Country, that include a geology river expedition and a natural history river trip in Grand Canyon National Park.

Grand Canyon Geology Expedition covers such topics as history of the rocks and their erosion, volcanic activity and evidence for former canyons in the western part of the Canyon, the area's living geology as manifested in rapids and side canyons, an overview of the river and the canyon as a system, and the effects of dams on the system. **Grand Canyon Natural History River Trip** emphasizes the overall ecology of the region and an appreciation of the intricate balance of climate, environment, flora, fauna, and human impact in the Grand Canyon.

Specialties: Geology and natural history of the Grand Canyon.

Faculty: Geologist Duncan Foley and naturalist Terry Tempest Williams.

Costs, Accommodations: The fee of $1,295 for each trip includes round-trip transportation from/to Las Vegas, meals, and camping gear. A $100 deposit must accompany reservation with balance due 30 days prior to departure. Cancellations more than 30 days prior receive full refund less $25 fee; no refunds thereafter unless space can be filled.

Contact: Colorado River & Trail Expeditions, Inc., P.O. Box 7575, 5058 South 300 West, Salt Lake City, UT 84107; (801) 261-1789, Fax (801) 268-1193.

COLORADO STATE UNIVERSITY
STUDY ABROAD PROGRAM
Office of International Programs
Fort Collins, Colorado
Four-week December-January tour of India

Professors James W. Boyd and Ron G. Williams of the Colorado State University Philosophy Department conduct a four-week study tour of India during the interim period between fall and spring semesters. The goal of the program, which offers four credits and is open to both college students and interested adults, is to provide a guided introduction to the people, culture, philosophy, and religion of contemporary India. Participants are provided with a list of readings to be completed prior to travel, class readings during the program, and those enrolled for credit are required to complete a 20-page term paper (due two months later), pass examinations, and keep a "reflective" journal that integrates the materials being learned with daily experiences. Students travel during the first and last weeks of the trip and spend the middle two weeks in Banaras, where most of the formal lectures, study, and journal writing take place. Lectures and discussions focus on such topics as the Indian World View, Indian Poetry, Rasa Theory, Bhakti Hinduism, Indian Buddhist

Thought, and A Comparison of Indian and Modern Western Art. Students have time for individual travel and field study and opportunities to meet Indian scholars at Banaras Hindu University and attend museum exhibitions, concerts, and films.

Specialties: The people, culture, philosophy, and religion of India.

Faculty: Professor James W. Boyd is an Indologist; Professor Ron G. Williams is a specialist in the philosophy of art. Both have traveled together in India and collaborate closely on research and teaching.

Costs, Accommodations: Cost, which includes round-trip airfare from/to Denver, meals, lodging, and tuition, is $3,350.

Location: The itinerary includes visits to Old and New Delhi, the Taj Mahal and Agra, two weeks in Banaras with a city tour of Kathmandu, the Khajuraho Temples, and Calcutta.

Contact: Dr. Richard Price, Office of International Programs, 315 Aylesworth Hall, Fort Collins, CO 80523; (303) 491-5917, Fax (303) 491-5501.

COLUMBIA UNIVERSITY'S
ALUMNI TRAVEL/STUDY PROGRAMS
New York, New York
One to two-week international tours

Columbia University's Alumni Federation sponsors a variety of tours with academic emphasis that are open to alumni and other interested adults. Approximately ten tours are scheduled annually, including such itineraries as A Journey Through Switzerland by Boat and Alpine Train, Alaska's Coastal Wilderness, The Canadian Rockies and Vancouver, England's Stately Homes and Gardens, Splendors of Antiquity, Western Mediterranean Odyssey, The Island World of Japan, and a family voyage, Mythical Lands.

Specialties: Culturally oriented tours with academic input.

Faculty: Informal lectures are provided by distinguished Columbia University faculty members, including Professor of Geological Sciences James D. Hays (Alaska's Coastal Wilderness); Professor of History Alden T. Vaughan (England's Stately Homes); Professor of Japanese History Paul Varley (Japan); James P. Shenton, Professor of History (Canadian Rockies/Vancouver); James Beck, Chairman of the Art History Department (Western Meditterean); Professor of German Inge D. Halpert (Switzerland); and J.A MacGillivray, Assistant Professor of Art History and Archaeology (Splendors of Antiquity).

Costs, Accommodations: Land/cruise costs, which include first-class accommodations, some meals, and a $100 to $250 tax-deductible contribution, range from $2,400 to $6,300. Deposit and refund policies vary with each itinerary.

Contact: The Alumni Federation of Columbia University, Inc., Box 400, CMR, Columbia University, New York, NY 10027; (212) 854-3237.

CONSERVATION SUMMITS
National Wildlife Federation (NWF)
Washington, D.C.

One-week summer programs in the U.S.

Since 1970, the National Wildlife Federation has sponsored week-long outdoor learning vacations — Conservation Summits — that offer NWF members the opportunity to discover the natural history of a particular area. Approximately four Summits are held each summer and are attended by 350 to 500 participants, including singles, couples, families, and seniors. The program allows adults to design their own schedules by choosing from approximately 20 different classes and field trips that range from plant and wildlife ecology, geology, and environmental issues to all-day nature hikes, birdwatching, astronomy, and outdoor photography. Separate programs are offered for teens, youth, and pre-schoolers with child care available. Special afternoon and evening activities, open to all attendees, include square dancing, sing-alongs, slide shows on local natural history, and cookouts. One Summit each year is specifically designed to meet the needs of educators and provides the latest in nature education curricula and activities.

Specialties: Natural history field trips, outdoor recreation, and conservation issues.

Faculty: Each class or field trip is led by qualified naturalists, many of whom are university faculty members or freelance experts.

Costs, Accommodations: Adult program fee is $200; educator/teacher fee is $175; youth and teen fees range from $70 to $140. Accommodations and meals range from $230 single occupancy ($194 double) to $411 ($306). A $100 deposit (plus membership fee) must accompany registration with balance due 60 days prior to Summit. Credit cards (VISA, MasterCard) accepted. Penalty is $50 for cancellations postmarked more than 60 days prior, $100 for cancellations 11 to 60 days prior, no refunds thereafter. Choice of lodging ranges from university dormitories, suites, and rustic inns to newer lodges and apartment buildings. Annual NWF membership dues are $15, which includes a bimonthly magazine subscription.

Location: Includes Estes Park, in the heart of the Colorado Rockies at the gateway to Rocky Mountain National Park; the University of Vermont at Burlington, near the shore of Lake Champlain; Black Mountain, in North Carolina's Blue Ridge Mountains; and Bellingham, Washington, between the Cascade Mountain range and the San Juan Islands.

Contact: Conservation Summits, National Wildlife Federation, 1400 Sixteenth St., N.W., Washington, DC 20036-2266; (800) 432-6564 or (703) 790-4363.

COOPER-HEWITT MUSEUM
New York, New York

One-day to two-week domestic and international tours

The Cooper-Hewitt Museum, the Smithsonian Institution's National Museum of Design, offers three to four day trips and one domestic study tour each semester and one international tour each year. Group size is limited to 30 participants.

Typical day trips include East/West Gardens, which includes tours of public gardens on Long Island's North Shore and culminates with a traditional tea ceremony in the John P. Humes Japanese Stroll Garden; Winterthur Museum and Gardens, a private tour of this decorative arts collection, which is showcased in nearly 200 period room settings; and Connecticut Architecture and Gardens: From Colonial to Colonial Revival, which includes tours of the Hill-Stead Museum and the 1720 Stanley-Whitman House.

Domestic study tours visit such art centers as Chicago, Newport, Rhode Island and Albuquerque, Taos, and Santa Fe, and focus on their art, architecture, and culture. Museum tours, visits to historical sites, and receptions with private collectors are usually a part of the program. A typical international tour, The Splendors of Ornament: Architecture and the Applied Arts of Russia, offers an exploration of the decorative arts and architectural monuments from the oldest wooden churches of Suzdal to the lavish Winter and Summer Palaces in Leningrad to Moscow's Kremlin and Red Square. In addition to seeing the monuments of the Czars and the collections of the Hermitage and other museums, participants study Art Nouveau residential architecture in Moscow and observe Constructivist experiments in the company of a practicing Soviet architect.

Specialties: Tours with an architecture and design focus.

Faculty: A study tour leader, usually a scholar who has done extensive work in the area visited, accompanies the group.

Costs, Accommodations: Day trips range from $90 to $100 ($75 to $85 for members); domestic travel programs range from $850 to $1,995 ($875 to $1,895 for members), which includes double occupancy deluxe accommodations (single supplement available), some meals, and a tax-deductible contribution (amount varies with each tour). Costs of international trips and deposit and refund policies vary. Annual Cooper-Hewitt membership dues begin at $20 student, $35 individual, and $50 family.

Contact: Programs Office, Cooper-Hewitt Museum, 2 E. 91 St., New York, NY 10128-9990; (212) 860-6868.

COOPERSMITH'S ENGLAND
Tours of Fine Gardens, Country Inns, and Stately Homes
Oakland, California
Twelve to fifteen-day excursions from May-September

Established in 1984, Coopersmith's England offers several tours each year that focus on British and European history, architecture, gardens, and fine arts. Typical programs, each limited to 20 to 25 participants, include England's Enchanted Gardens: The West Country, which visits the homes and haunts of such British literary notables as Samuel Taylor Coleridge, Thomas Hardy, and Jane Austen; England's Enchanted Gardens: The Southeast, which concentrates on the gardens and estates of the Cotswolds, Kent, and Sussex; Gardens & Chateaux of France, a tour of the Loire Valley, Fontainbleu, Versailles, and Monet's garden at Giverny; and English Autumn: Foliage, Antiques, & Theatre, which features gardens known for their autumn foliage, several evenings of theater, and antique shopping.

Specialties: British and European history, architecture, gardens, fine arts.

Faculty: Distinguished English landscape designer and gardener Penelope Hobhouse, well-known English garden writer Rosemary Verey, and tour manager Inga Stone.

Costs, Accommodations: Costs, including airfare, double occupancy first class or deluxe accommodations (single supplement available), breakfasts and some other meals, and deluxe ground transportation, range from $3,600 to $3,950. A $400 deposit must accompany reservation with balance due 90 days prior. Full refund, less $200 fee, is granted cancellations more than 90 days prior to departure; cancellations 30 to 90 days prior and within 30 days, if space can be filled, incur a 25% fee.

Contact: Coopersmith's England, 6441 Valley View Rd., Oakland, CA 94611; (415) 339-2499.

CORNELL'S ADULT UNIVERSITY (CAU)
Ithaca, New York
Weekend to three-week programs on-campus, in the U.S., and abroad

Established in 1968, Cornell's Adult University offers a variety of programs for adult and family vacation study, including a four-week on-campus summer program consisting of 28 different one-week workshops and courses; fall, winter, and spring weekend seminars at retreat locations in the U.S.; and year-round study tours throughout the world. The programs are open to all, with enrollment ranging from 12 participants in workshops to 40 or more in courses, study tours, and seminars.

The summer program, held from early July to early August, offers a choice of seven workshops and courses during each of four weeks. Typical topics include Africa: cultures, political systems, economic and social change; High Art in the Low Countries: the Flemish painters from Rubens to Rembrandt; Cayuga Lake Archaeology and Paleobiology: field trips to explore history and prehistory; and Acting Shakespeare: a participatory workshop for lovers

of theater and acting. Sessions meet mornings and afternoons from Monday
through Friday, with lectures, plays, and special events scheduled in the
evenings. A fully-supervised youth program for 3 to 16-year-olds features
activities and courses geared to five age groups.

More than 20 off-campus study programs are offered annually, ranging
from weekend retreats to three-week international trips. Typical retreat topics
include Communism at the Crossroads, an assessment and discussion of
developments in the Soviet Union and Eastern Europe, and Eyes on Latin
America, an exploration of the resurgence of democracy. Five to seven-day
domestic travel programs focus on the nature and ecology of such locations
as Florida's Everglades, Georgia's Sapelo Island, Arizona's Sonoran Desert,
New Mexico's Sangre de Cristo Mountains, and the Isles of Shoals, Maine.
Trips abroad, most two to three weeks long, emphasize the social and natural
history, culture, art and architecture of such regions as England, Turkey,
Australia, Kenya and Tanzania, and Ecuador and the Galápagos Islands.
International study programs are often planned as a follow-up to a summer on-
campus program.

Specialties: A variety of topics, including history, current events, ecology,
art and architecture, music, and literature.

Faculty: All programs are taught by Cornell University faculty members.

Costs, Accommodations: Cost of the summer program is approximately
$600 per week for adults and $200 to $300 for children, which includes
tuition, double occupancy dormitory lodging (single supplement available),
16 meals, and planned activities. Materials fees are additional. A $25
nonrefundable deposit reserves a space with balance due 30 days prior to
program. Per person costs range from $325 to $400 for weekend retreats,
from $600 to $1,000 for domestic trips, and from $2,000 to $4,500 for travel
abroad, which includes tuition, double occupancy lodging (single supplement
available), most meals, and planned activities. Deposits, which may be
partially refundable, range from $25 to $400. Cancellations within 30 days
of domestic programs or 60 days of foreign travel are charged nonrecoverable
costs if space cannot be filled. Credit cards (MasterCard, VISA) accepted.

Contact: Cornell's Adult University, 626 Thurston Ave., Ithaca, NY 14850-
2490; (607) 255-6260.

COWBOY ARTISTS OF AMERICA (CAA) MUSEUM
Kerrville, Texas

Two-day workshops

Opened in 1983, the Cowboy Artists of America Museum offers workshops on the art, history, folklore, and music of America's West. Most
courses are limited to 20 participants and scheduled as two-day sessions.
Representative titles include The Tragedy of Bobwire and Pickup Trucks:
Folklore of the West, which focuses on the changing character of the West
through stories that cover such subjects as grizzly bears, gunfighters, cowboy

humor, and the cowboy as a hero figure; Cowboyography, a survey of the books, films, and music that have attempted to portray the cowboy as America's folk hero; From Trail Songs to Radio Rhythms, an exploration of the history of western ballads, folk music, and poetry; Mountain Man History, an overview of both the Upper Missouri Period (1800-1821) and the Fur Trade Rendezvous Era (1822-1840) with emphasis on the impact of such notables as Lewis and Clark and Kit Carson; and Origins of Cowboy Art: The Historical Context, an examination of the artistic representation of the cowboy's role from both a modern and historical perspective.

Dedicated to educating the public to a better understanding and appreciation of America's Western heritage, the CAA Museum hosts art workshops for serious students, displays works of cowboy and historic Western artists, serves as a repository of information about each artist's life work, and houses a library of Western Americana with special emphasis on the history of the range cattle industry.

Specialties: Art, history, folklore, and music of the American West.

Faculty: Includes folklorist and storyteller Jim Garry; Don Hedgpeth, a freelance writer whose books include *The Texas Breed* and *Horses and Wars;* folklorist/performer Justin Bishop, who has been sponsored on numerous tours by the U.S. Information Agency's Arts America Program; Dr. Fred Gowans, professor of Western American History at Brigham Young University and author of *Mountain Man and Grizzly* and *Rocky Mountain Rendezvous*; and Susan H. McGarry, editor-in-chief of *Southwest Art.*

Costs, Accommodations: Two-day workshop fee is $55 ($45 for members). An 80% refund is granted cancellations more than one month prior (members receive full refund less $5 cancellation fee); thereafter only if space can be filled, however credit may be applied to a future class. Accommodations are available at area motels, RV parks, and camping facilities. Annual Museum memberships begin at $30 individual and $50 family.

Location: Located in the Texas Hill Country, Kerrville is 65 miles northwest of San Antonio and 100 miles west of Austin and has bus service and a municipal airport. Facilities are handicapped accessible.

Contact: Cowboy Artists of America Museum, P.O. Box 1716, Kerrville, TX 78029-1716; (512) 896-2553.

CROW CANYON ARCHAEOLOGICAL CENTER
Cortez, Colorado
One-day to four-week programs in the U.S. Southwest

Since 1984, the Crow Canyon Archaeological Center has offered a variety of research and culturally-oriented programs for adults, students, and families. Day programs, offered every Tuesday through Thursday from June through August, feature such activities as a visit to an archaeological site, a lesson in the use of ancient Anasazi tools, and an opportunity to examine artifacts and reconstruct the lifeways they represent. One-week (Sunday-

Saturday) programs include **Adult Research in Excavation, Adult Research in Archaeobotany, Cultural Explorations** that focus on Native American traditions, **Southwest Seminars** that travel to important archaeological sites, and fall lab programs for adults. Two-week winter lab programs are open only to alumni of the Adult Research Programs. The Center also offers a four-week summer **High School Field School** for 40 students, a nine-day summer **Teachers' Workshop** that grants three hours of graduate credit, and three to five-day school group programs year-round.

The **Adult Research Excavation Program**, offered from the end of May until mid-October and limited to 60 participants per week, is an introduction to the Anasazi culture as well as the process of archaeological research. Undergraduate credit is available from Fort Lewis College in Durango, Colorado. Participants begin the week by examining artifacts, reconstructing the lifeways they represent, and determining their chronological sequence. They then spend a day in the lab where they wash, sort, analyze, and catalog artifacts. Subsequent days are devoted to working with archaeologists in the field and learning such techniques as digging with a trowel, mapping artifact locations, and removing artifacts for analysis; participating in a hike to explore the natural environment; and trying out such prehistoric technologies as fire-starting, corn grinding, and spear throwing with an atlatl. Evening lectures and programs expand on the day's activities. **Alumni Weeks,** conducted twice each summer for previous participants, feature more time for excavation and field trips to unique archaeological sites. **Family Week,** offered once each summer for families with children in fourth grade or higher, provides special programs for each age group as well as the whole family.

The **Adult Research Archaeobotany Program,** offered for eight weeks during July through October and limited to 20 participants per week, examines plant communities, monitors seasonality, and provides information on how a plant community changes over time. The format is similar to that of the excavation program, with emphasis on the identification of the region's plants and their use by Native Americans. Participants learn the parts of a plant, trace centers of origin, help develop a complete list of all the plants that grow in the region, and provide observations on the evolution of plant communities.

Fall lab programs for adults, offered during late October, are scheduled to process and analyze artifacts that have accumulated during the field season. Participants are exposed to a wide range of artifacts and work on a more independent basis. Two-week winter lab programs, offered in February for alumni, provide participants with a working knowledge of ceramic analysis.

Cultural Explorations, offered approximately once a month throughout the year and limited to 20 participants, include hands-on experience in spinning, dyeing, and weaving with traditional Navajo weavers and a textile historian; study and construction of ancient and modern ceramics with visits to collections and trading posts; exploration of the southwestern Colorado cultures with archaeologists and historians; and in-depth study of such Native American tribes as the Navajos and the Zuni Pueblos.

Southwest Seminars are designed to reconstruct, through on-site discussions, the unique character of ancient sites. Titles include Four Corners

Seminar, focusing on major archaeological sites; Rio Grande Field Seminar, which explores the Spanish influence on Pueblo Indian culture; San Juan River Rock Art & Archaeoastronomy, a rafting trip on the San Juan River with visits to archaeological sites; and Art and Archaeology Seminar, which includes visits to the homes of leading Native American artisans.

Specialties: Archaeology, archaeobotany, and cultural exploration of the U.S. Southwest.

Faculty: Research programs are conducted by the Center's 14-member research and education staff. Cultural Explorations are conducted by Native American scholars and other specialists in archaeology and related fields.

Costs, Accommodations: Costs of the Research Excavation and Archaeobotany Programs are $690 per week (alumni $620, college students $420, children in family program $300 to $350), deposit $150 to $250; lab programs are $425 per week, deposit $150 to $250; Cultural Explorations range from $950 to $1,095, deposit $250 to $350; day programs $25 for adults, $12.50 for children, which includes lunch (24 hour advance notice required); Southwest Seminar costs vary. Off-peak season and Excavation/Exploration package discounts are available. Fees cover tuition, food, dormitory-style lodging in Crow Canyon lodge, and transportation after arrival at Cortez airport. College credit is additional. Deposit must accompany reservation with balance due 30 days prior to program. Cancellations more than 45 days prior forfeit $100; no refunds thereafter. Credit cards (VISA, MasterCard, American Express) accepted. Participants in research programs may be able to deduct out-of-pocket costs. Handicapped persons are welcome.

Location: Crow Canyon is situated at an altitude of 6,000 feet, four miles from Cortez, ten miles from Mesa Verde National Park, and 400 miles southwest of Denver.

Contact: Crow Canyon Archaeological Center, 23390 County Rd. K, Cortez, CO 81321; (800) 422-8975 *or* (303) 565-8975.

CULTURAL TOURS TO TURKEY
Cultural Folk Tours International
San Diego, California

Two to three-week tours from April-September

Established in 1979, Cultural Folk Tours International offers more than 20 tours each year to Turkey, some with visits to Hungary, Spain, and Yugoslavia. Four or five tours begin with a four-day seminar that includes folk dancing and singing as well as lectures on Turkey's history, tradition, government, and daily life. Visits to museums and historic sights are also featured. All tours are limited to 30 participants.

Specialties: Turkish culture.

Faculty: Tour director and seminar leader Bora Ozkok is an architect, author, musician, and teacher of Turkish folk dance, music, and culture. Other tour leaders include teachers, folklorists, dancers, and musicians who are knowledgeable about Turkish culture.

Costs, Accommodations: Land costs range from $1,300 to $2,000, which includes double occupancy lodging in first-class hotels, two to three meals daily, ground transporation, and planned activities. Airfare is approximately $900 and enrollment in the four-day seminar alone is $330. A $15 deposit must accompany application with balance due 60 days prior to departure. Full refund is granted written cancellations at least 90 days prior, thereafter a $75 fee is charged.

Location: Turkey, Spain, Hungary, and Yugoslavia.

Contact: Cultural Folk Tours International, 10292 Gumbark Pl., San Diego, CA 92131; (800) 448-0515 *or* (619) 566-5951.

DARTMOUTH ALUMNI COLLEGE
Dartmouth College
Hanover, New Hampshire

Twelve-day on-campus summer program and ten-day to three-week tours abroad

Since 1964, Dartmouth College has offered an adult summer college devoted to a different theme each year and, since 1978, six to eight foreign study travel programs a year. These are part of the Alumni Continuing Education offerings and are open to Dartmouth alumni, parents, and friends of the College.

The 12-day **Dartmouth Alumni College** (students may enroll for five or seven days) is limited to approximately 250 participants who receive a set of books and articles for advance reading. The program features two morning theme-related lectures followed by small, faculty-led group discussions or a faculty panel, with afternoons at leisure or reserved for special instruction such as optional language classes. Scheduled evening activities include films, special lectures, and cultural events. A Junior Program, tailored for ages 9 through 14, combines recreational activities with learning sessions. Representative themes include Perestroika, Glasnost, and the Lessons of History, which examines the dramatic changes taking place in the Soviet empire and offers an optional Russian language course and post-program study tour to Russia; China: Old and New, an exploration of the country's historical, religious, literary, and cultural roots, with opportunity for language study and an optional follow-up journey to China; and The Environment.

The **Alumni Colleges Abroad**, a series of faculty-led tours that are sometimes offered in cooperation with another university, may include such itineraries as Antarctica, the Aegean Sea, The Leeward Islands, Egypt, Vienna to Istanbul, Waterways of Holland and Belgium, and Alaska.

Specialties: A variety of academic topics.

Faculty: Members of the Dartmouth College faculty.

Costs, Accommodations: Dartmouth Alumni College tuition, which includes books, receptions, banquets, picnic, and cultural events, ranges from $355 for five days to $850 for twelve days; dormitory housing ranges from $115 to $600 and meal plan from $75 to $181. A $50 nonrefundable deposit must accompany application, with balance due on or before arrival. Land costs for Alumni Colleges Abroad range from approximately $3,500 to $4,100. Deposits and refund policies vary.

Facilities: Participants have full privileges in Baker and the satellite libraries, the Hopkins Center, and the Hood Museum. On-campus recreational activities include tennis and golf, swimming and boating in the nearby Connecticut River or New Hampshire lakes, and hiking in the White Mountains.

Contact: Dartmouth Alumni College, 308 Blunt Alumni Center, Hanover, NH 03755; (603) 646-2454.

DENVER MUSEUM OF NATURAL HISTORY (DMNH)
Denver, Colorado

One-day to three-week domestic and international tours year-round

The Denver Museum of Natural History travel program, begun in 1972, sponsors approximately 20 tours annually in the U.S. and abroad as well as day trips that include birdwalks at nearby state parks and behind-the-scenes visits to factories and public buildings. Number of participants ranges from 10 to 25, depending upon destination, and some trips offer academic credit. Worldwide cruises are offered in conjunction with the Discovery Cruise office of the America Museum of Natural History in New York.

Great Escapes, the domestic and international travel program for Museum members, offers a variety of trips that include the study of archaeology, anthropology, ethnography, and culture. Southwest Trading Post Tour, a popular trip designed for the serious collector, includes daily stops at trading posts and historic Indian sites as well as visits with local craftsmen to learn about their materials, methods, and traditions. The focus is on the trading post business, investing in Indian art, distinguishing between regional and tribal styles, and identifying quality. Geology and Ecology of the Grand Canyon, a 185-mile river rafting expedition offering 2 graduate units of credit from the Colorado School of Mines, studies the geology, ecology, archaeology, and history of the Grand Canyon and Colorado River.

International trips include Upper Amazon and Machu Picchu, a study of the wildlife, ecology, and native tribal cultures of Brazil, Ecuador, and Peru; Nomads of Central Asia, with a tour of the Central Asian collection at Leningrad's Hermitage Museum and visits to Leningrad, Moscow, and the Soviet Stepplande towns of Alma Ata, Tashkent, and Samarkand; and Belize, Cays and Barrier Reefs, featuring snorkeling and scuba diving with study of marine biology, Mayan archaeology, ethnology, and birdwatching.

Specialties: Tours that focus on the study of archaeology, anthropology, ethnography, natural history, and culture of the regions visited.

Faculty: Most tours are led by members of the DMNH curatorial staff, including Dr. Jane Day, Joyce Herold, Barbara Stone, Betsy Webb, Dr. Carron Meaney, David W. Bourcier, and Thielma Gamewell. Some tours are led by outside experts.

Costs, Accommodations: Day trips range from $17 to $40 for Museum members, $22 to $45 for nonmembers. Land costs, which can include accommodations, meals, and planned activities, range from $150 to $1,500 for domestic tours, $1,700 to $7,500 for international tours. A $50 to $400 deposit (nonrefundable unless space can be filled) must accompany reservation with balance due 30 to 60 days prior to departure. Museum membership, a requirement for participation in domestic and international tours, is $20 senior citizen, $25 senior couple, $30 individual, $40 family.

Location: In addition to the above, tours are scheduled to Hawaii, Chaco Canyon, the Salmon River, Costa Rica, Japan, Alaska, Scandinavia, Guatemala, Greece, Copper Canyon, and Tanzania, Zimbabwe, and Botswana.

Contact: Denver Museum of Natural History, Public Programs Dept., 2001 Colorado Blvd., Denver, CO 80205; ((303) 370-6307.

DILLINGTON COLLEGE FOR ADULT EDUCATION
Ilminster, Somerset, England

One to seven-day courses year-round; occasional tours abroad

Established in 1950, this residential college for adult education offers more than a hundred courses annually in a variety of subjects, including art, crafts, music, language, self development, literature, history, and culture. The courses are open to all, with enrollment ranging from eight in a participatory workshop to 60 in a lecture. Typical titles include Historic Parks and Gardens, exploring the origins and development of Somerset's parks; Archaeological Rambles in Somerset, featuring illustrated lectures and field trips to places of interest; and In the Steps of Thomas Hardy, with lectures and conducted tours to Hardy's Wessex and other locales in his novels. A 22-day study tour to Egypt focuses on its classical sites.

Specialties: A variety of topics, including literature, history, and culture.

Faculty: Individuals who are qualified and experienced in their subjects.

Costs, Accommodations: Fees, which cover tuition, accommodations, and full board, range from £12 to £17 for day courses and £65 to £200 for weekend to one-week courses. Students can enroll as nonresidents at a reduced fee. A nonrefundable £20 deposit reserves a space and balance is due one month prior to course. Cancellations at least two weeks prior are refunded half the fee.

Location: Dillington is about a mile north of Ilminster in Somerset, 10 miles from the Taunton railway station. Once the home of George III's prime minister, Lord North, this country house has extensive facilities, including a theatre, library, and exhibition gallery.

Contact: Dillington College, Ilminster, Somerset TA19 9DT, England; (44) 460 52427/53875.

DINOSAUR DISCOVERY EXPEDITIONS
Dinamation International Corporation
San Juan Capistrano, California

Six-day summer programs near Grand Junction, Colorado

Since 1989, Dinamation International Corporation has sponsored **Dinosaur Discovery Expeditions** that offer hands-on participation in dinosaur research at the fossil-rich Morrison Formation near Grand Junction, Colorado. Six-day expeditions, limited to 10 to 14 adults (and children ages 13 to 17 accompanied by an adult), are scheduled each Saturday to Thursday from May 1 through September 30. The program begins with instruction in laboratory and excavation techniques, enabling participants to work on individual projects. Ensuing days are devoted to exposing, excavating, and collecting dinosaur bones at the dig site; preparing and curating fossil materials in the lab; and making a plaster cast of a fossil to take home. Other activities include presentations on the geology and paleontology of the Grand Valley area, trips to important quarry sites, and evening social events. An optional two-day Colorado River-rafting excursion follows the expedition.

Specialties: Exploration and excavation of dinosaur fossils.

Faculty: Professional paleontologists.

Costs, Accommodations: Cost of $745 includes most meals, deluxe double occupancy hotel accommodations (single supplement $125) in Grand Junction, transportation to and from excavations, scheduled field trips, and social events. A nonrefundable $100 deposit must accompany reservation with balance due 60 days prior to arrival. Full refund of balance is granted cancellations more than 60 days prior, 50% refund is granted from 30 to 59 days prior; no refunds thereafter.

Location: Sites visited include the Colorado National Monument, Dinosaur Hill, and Riggs Hill, site of the discovery of the first known Brachiosaurus.

Contact: Dinamation International Corp., 27362 Calle Arroyo, San Juan Capistrano, CA 92675; (800) 547-0503 *or* (714) 493-7440.

DIRE WOLF NATURAL HISTORY TOURS
Ithaca, New York

Half-day and full-day tours in New York's Finger Lakes; overnight tours to the Adirondacks

Dire Wolf Natural History Tours offers interpretive tours that emphasize the unique geologic origins, diverse plant and wildlife, and American Indian and pioneer history of New York's Finger Lakes Region. The tours, which are designed for 1 to 14 persons, are offered as a half-day (four hours) of driving/walking or hiking and as a full-day program that combines both.

Specialties: Natural history tours involving site interpretation, hiking, nature photography, and fossil collecting.

Faculty: Ron Schassburger, a former zoo director who holds a Ph.D. in Neurobiology and Behavior, is co-founder and director of the Natural History Society of the Finger Lakes Region and teaches at Ithaca College. He is assisted by his canine companion Nikoni, an "expert in tracking and animal communication".

Costs: Cost of half-day tour ranges from $35 to $45; full-day tour is $75.

Location: Tours of the Ithaca area include such sites as Cascadilla Gorge and Cornell's Geology Museum and Rock Parks; Cornell Plantations and its native wildflower garden; Cornell Laboratory of Ornithology, the nation's first research facility for the study of living birds, and its 180-acre Sapsucker Woods Sanctuary; the "Lost Gorge" and marshes of Cayuta Lake; McLean Bogs, with its relics of the Pleistocene epoch; and various other natural areas, including fossil sites and former Native American sites.

Contact: Dire Wolf Natural History Tours, 124 Poole Rd., Ithaca, NY 14850; (607) 272-7409.

DUKE TRAVEL
Duke University
Durham, North Carolina
One to two-week domestic and international travel programs

Established in the early 1970's, the Duke University travel program now offers approximately a dozen tours annually, some of which are accompanied by Duke University faculty members. Typical itineraries include Antarctica, a two-week cruise accompanied by a geologist and naturalists; and Egypt, a fourteen-day excursion led by Duke's Chancellor.

Faculty: Duke University senior administrators and faculty members.

Costs: Land costs range from approximately $1,450 to $4,895. Payment and refund policies vary with travel booking agent.

Locations: In addition to the above, tour destinations include the Virgin Islands, India, South America, Austria, Russia, the Mediterranean, Barging in Burgundy, Southeast Asia, Scandinavia, Turkey and Greece, and Grand Canyon rafting.

Contact: Barbara DeLapp Booth, Duke Travel, 614 Chapel Dr., Durham, NC 27706; (919) 684-5114.

THE DYLAN THOMAS SCHOOL
The University College of Wales
Aberystwyth, Wales
Two-week summer school

Since 1988, the University College of Wales has offered the international Dylan Thomas School, a study of the poet's works in the geographic and cultural context of his home country, Wales. Limited to about 90 interested participants, the two-week course consists of a main series of lectures delivered by specialists in Thomas' poetry, prose, and Welsh background, supplemented by small group seminars, readings, special events and exhibitions, and guided visits to the places that nurtured his genius. Six academic credits are available.

Specialties: The works of Dylan Thomas.

Faculty: Leading experts on Dylan Thomas' work, including such scholars, critics, and writers as Ralph Maud, Paul Ferris, Walford Davies, John Wain, John Ackerman, Barbara Hardy, and Leslie Norris. Guest readings are given by Thomas' daughter, Aeronwy Thomas Ellis, and by invited contemporary poets.

Costs, Accommodations: The £550 fee covers tuition, lodging, all meals, and all activities and excursions. A £25 deposit must accompany application with balance due upon arrival. Housing is in university residence halls.

Location: Aberystwyth, located on the Cardigan Bay coast, is also the home of such other national institutions as the National Library, the College of Librarianship Wales, the Center for Advanced Welsh and Celtic Studies, and the Welsh Books Council.

Contact: Prof. Walford Davies, The University College of Wales, Aberystwyth SY23 2AZ, United Kingdom; (44) 970 617616.

EARTHWATCH
Watertown, Massachusetts
Ten-day to six-week projects in 27 states and 46 countries

This nonprofit institution, dedicated to increasing the public understanding of science and expanding the knowledge of earth and its inhabitants, sponsors scholarly field research by finding paying volunteers to help scientists on research expeditions around the world. Since its founding in 1971, more than 22,000 volunteers have assisted in more than 700 projects in 36 states and 85 countries. Currently, approximately 120 projects are scheduled annually, some requiring as few as three to four people, but most teams averaging 10 to 12 volunteers. Most expeditions range from two to three weeks and all are open to volunteers age 16 or older. No special skills or experience are required. *Earthwatch Magazine*, published bimonthly, summarizes current projects and each is described in-depth in a 25 to 75-page expedition briefing, which includes the history of the project, its research mission, background of the principal investigators and staff, field logistics, reference maps, in-country information, and bibliography.

The research projects encompass a broad range of interests, including art, archaeology, marine studies, and the life, social, and geosciences. For example, a year-round project at the Kewalo Basin Marine Mammal Laboratory in Honolulu, **Teaching Dolphins Language**, is devoted to determining the range and limits of dolphins' linguistic and conceptual ability. Volunteers move objects around the tank and record data during formal training sessions and socialize with the mammals during play periods. An expedition to determine the quality of life in Roman Carthage has uncovered more than 200 Roman, Byzantine, and Vandal graves, some covered in mosaics and enriched with gold coins dating from the fifth century. Volunteers excavate, sift dirt, and process artifacts. Those with skills in surveying, drawing, or photography assist in documenting progress.

Specialties: Research projects requiring volunteer assistance.

Faculty: Distinguished scientists conduct all expeditions. Their proposals are screened through a peer review process.

Costs, Accommodations: The tax-deductible contribution for a two-week expedition, which covers all expenses except transportation to and from the field, ranges from $800 to $2,000, with the average about $1,300. Some fellowships are available for teachers and students. Accommodations range from tent camping to rustic farmhouses to university dormitories. Volunteers must become members of Earthwatch. Annual dues of $25 include a subscription to *Earthwatch Magazine* and admission to member films, lectures, and other events that take place around the country. Expedition briefings are $25, credited to contribution. Volunteers should apply (by phone, mail, or fax) at least 90 days prior to expedition. Full contribution, payable by check or credit card, is required upon acceptance or 90 days prior, whichever comes first. Cancellations more than 90 days prior receive full refund; from 60 to 89 days prior $250 is forfeited; 45 to 59 days prior 50% is forfeited; no refund thereafter. A full or partial credit is granted those who transfer to another project.

Contact: Earthwatch, 680 Mt. Auburn St., Box 403-A, Watertown, MA 02172; (617) 926-8200, Fax (617) 926-8532.

EASTERN MICHIGAN UNIVERSITY TRAVEL PROGRAMS
Office of International Studies
Ypsilanti, Michigan

Twelve-day summer Galápagos Islands adventure; three-week summer Soviet Union and Eastern Europe tour

The Office of International Studies of Eastern Michigan University sponsors two annual international summer programs for college students and interested adults: a history tour of the Soviet Union and Eastern Europe and a biological tour of the Galápagos Islands. Both tours offer an optional three semester hours of undergraduate or graduate credit. European cultural history and humanities tours exclusively for college students are also offered.

Discover the Soviet Union and Eastern Europe, a mid-summer tour offered since 1985 and limited to 15 to 30 participants, focuses on history, culture, and politics, with emphasis on the changing face of communism. Participants attend informal lectures and have opportunities to meet Soviet teachers and/or students. The itinerary includes Moscow, Leningrad, Kiev, and Vilnius, site of the Lithuanian independence movement. Stops are also scheduled in Warsaw, Prague, and Brussels.

The **Galápagos Islands Adventure**, a July tour first offered in 1987 and limited to 12 to 20 participants, is an intensive biological tour of eleven key islands. Activities include snorkeling and hiking the volcanic terrain to get close to the unique species of wildlife.

Specialties: The history, politics, and culture of the Soviet countries; the biological environment of the Galápagos Islands.

Faculty: The tour of the Soviet Union is conducted by Dr. Walter Moss, Professor of Russian History at Eastern Michigan University and co-author of *The Twentieth Century: A Brief Global History*. The Galápagos Islands tour is conducted by Dr. Robert Neely, Professor of Biology at Eastern Michigan University.

Costs, Accommodations: All inclusive cost of the Soviet Union tour is $2,895, which includes airfare from/to New York. A $100 deposit must accompany reservation with $250 due by April 15 and the balance due by June 1. All inclusive cost of the Galápagos Islands tour is $2,995, which includes airfare from/to Miami. A $300 deposit must accompany application. Written cancellations received at least 60 days prior to trip forfeit $50.

Contact: Office of International Studies, 333 Goodison Hall, Eastern Michigan University, Ypsilanti, MI 48197; (800) 777-3541 *or* (313) 487-2424.

ECOTOUR EXPEDITIONS
Cambridge, Massachusetts
Ten-day to two-week tours of the Brazilian Amazon

Ecotours offers three tour itineraries to the remote forested areas of the Brazilian Amazon. Approximately a dozen trips are scheduled year-round, each limited to 10 to 15 participants who learn about the region's ecology and natural history.

The **Igapo, Flooded Forest and High Forest of the Rio Negro** consists of a seven-day boat trip on the Rio Negro, the second largest river in the world, and includes stops to hike in the forest, birdwatch, observe caiman by flashlight, fish for piranha, and visit river villages. **White Waters and Black** explores the confluence of the Solimoes, the Negro, and the Amazon Rivers with emphasis on the different types of plant and animal life these systems support. **Upper Reaches and the Thousand Streams of the Rio Negro**, an expedition along much of the length of the Negro River, focuses on local wildlife and features a three-day forest hike and a light plane tour of the nearby mountains and high plateaus.

Specialties: Ecology and natural history.

Faculty: Each tour is led by a scientific specialist and a regional guide.

Costs, Accommodations: Costs range from $1,750 to $2,650, including round-trip airfare from/to Miami, moderately priced double occupancy hotel accommodations (single supplement $450, first class lodging additional), all meals, and scheduled activities. A $300 deposit must accompany application with balance due 60 days prior to departure. Cancellations more than 60 days prior forfeit $100; thereafter penalty ranges from $300 (30 to 60 days prior) to 50% of trip cost (14 to 30 days prior); no refunds thereafter.

Contact: Ecotour Expeditions, P.O. Box 1066, Cambridge, MA 02238-1066; (617) 876-5817.

EDINBORO AT OXFORD EXPERIENCE
Edinboro University
Edinboro, Pennsylvania
Two week Oxford program in August

Edinboro University in Edinboro, Pennsylvania, sponsors an annual two-week educational program at Oxford's Exeter College that is structured to add intercultural awareness to traditional academic courses. The goal of the program, which is limited to 90 participants, is to relate course content to the people and culture from which it is derived. Students, who may audit or enroll for three semesters of undergraduate or graduate credit, select one of approximately a half dozen courses, including such titles as The Political Philosophies of England, British Literature and Life, Current Issues in Education — Ethics in Higher Education, and Art Travel/Study Workshop: A Survey of English Crafts and Craftsmen. Each course includes excursions to sites that enhance the course content and all participants visit places of historical interest in Oxford and other locales.

Specialties: Courses relating to England, its culture and people.

Faculty: Instructors at Exeter College include the university president, director of the university honors program, and faculty. Edinboro University staff members assist in coordinating the program.

Costs, Accommodations: The fee of approximately $775 includes room at Exeter College, breakfasts and dinners, courses, and planned excursions. Those who desire academic credit pay $91 per undergraduate credit, $121 per graduate credit. Air and ground transportation — New York to/from Oxford — is approximately $695. A $100 deposit must accompany registration, no later than May 1. The balance is payable by VISA or MasterCard.

Location: Oxford is one hour by train, 20 minutes more by bus, from London. In addition to the 35 residential colleges that comprise Oxford University, of which Exeter is the fourth oldest, the city offers museums, shops, classical music concerts, and theatre productions. Blenheim Palace, Stratford-Upon-Avon, Bath, Stonehenge, and Avenbury are situated nearby.

Contact: Edinboro University "Oxford Experience", Doucette Hall, Room 102, Edinboro, PA 16444; (814) 732-2884.

EDINBURGH UNIVERSITY SUMMER SCHOOLS
Edinburgh, Scotland

Four-day to three-week courses and study tours

The Centre for Continuing Education at the University of Edinburgh has offered summer vacation courses since 1960 and year-round study tours since 1970, both open to adults of all ages. Approximately 16 vacation courses are offered annually, most relating to Edinburgh International Festival events. The **Film Festival Course** features a week of film viewing, teaching, and discussion, followed by viewings and discussions of films being shown at the Festival. Other programs include **Festival Drama, Festival Music,** and **Festival Exhibitions,** which offer seminars, lectures and visits. Courses in **Scottish Gaelic Language and Literature** and **Scottish Culture** are also a part of the program. Approximately a dozen European study tours are scheduled annually to such locations as London, Rome and Florence, Paris, Hungary, and Barcelona.

Specialties: The Edinburgh International Festival and Scottish culture.

Faculty: Programs are conducted by Edinburgh University faculty and experienced teachers.

Costs, Accommodations: Course fees range from £70 to £250. A nonrefundable £30 deposit must accompany application with balance due at least one month prior to program. Study tours range from £200 to £800. Credit cards (VISA) accepted.

Contact: Centre for Continuing Education, University of Edinburgh, 11 Buccleuch Pl., Edinburgh, EH8 9LW, Scotland; (44) 31-677 1011, ext. 6686.

ELDERHOSTEL
Boston, Massachusetts

One-week programs in the U.S. and Canada; two to four-week programs abroad

Established in 1975 as a residential, college-based program for older adults, Elderhostel now enrolls close to 200,000 participants annually in a wide variety of science and liberal arts programs at more than 1,500 educational institutions in all 50 states, all 10 Canadian provinces, and more than 40 countries overseas. Participants are required to be at least 60 years of age (or at least 50 years of age if accompanied by a companion or spouse who is at least 60 years old). No credit is offered and no previous knowledge or study is required.

Most Elderhostel programs in the United States and Canada are one week in length, from Sunday afternoon to Saturday morning, and offer a choice of three courses that meet for 60 to 90 minutes each weekday. While participants are required to attend only one course, the schedule allows them to enroll in all three. A variety of extracurricular activities are offered, some as part of the host institution's regular cultural, educational, and recreational events, others organized specifically for Elderhostelers. **Intensive Studies Pro-**

grams provide an opportunity for more in-depth exploration of an academic subject than the regular Elderhostel format and may entail homework.

International programs, a combination of classroom learning and study tour, are developed cooperatively with a variety of organizations and host institutions throughout the world. Morning classes are devoted to courses on the history, culture, and geography of the region and afternoons are reserved for course-related excursions. Most programs are two to four weeks in length, combining week-long stays at different colleges and universities and a variety of course topics that provide a culturally diverse academic experience. Theme programs, on the other hand, focus on a specific subject. Each of the courses and excursions leads to an overall understanding of the subject theme and a specialized overview of the country's culture, geography, or history. The Experiment in International Living, founded in 1932, provides an opportunity to learn about people from another country by living with them. A one-week homestay with a host family is combined with two scheduled weeks of formal courses and related field trips. Homestay visits are available in Indonesia, Ecuador, India, France, and Mexico.

Specialties: A wide variety of academic subjects.

Faculty: Courses are taught by the faculty of the host institution.

Costs, Accommodations: Average one-week program cost, including registration, double occupancy dormitory lodging for six nights, all meals from Sunday dinner through Saturday breakfast, five days of classes, and extra-curricular activities, is $245 in the U.S., $270 in Canada. A limited amount of financial assistance is available for those who wish to attend a program close to home but cannot afford it. International program costs, including round-trip airfare and other transportation, full room and board (with exceptions), academic program, and planned excursions, average $2,000 for a two to three-week stay. A deposit of $40 for U.S./Canada programs, $100 for programs in Bermuda, Mexico, and Jamaica, and $250 for international programs must accompany application. Cancellation penalty ranges from $15 to $40 for U.S./Canada programs, from $50 to $100 for international programs (plus airline cancellation fees). A tax-deductible contribution to the Elderhostel Independence Fund, which provides financial support, is welcomed. Free course catalogs are published eight times a year.

Contact: Elderhostel, 80 Boylston St., Suite 400, Boston, MA 02116; (617) 426-7788.

ELON COLLEGE TOUR PROGRAMS
Elon, North Carolina

Two-week to one-month Soviet and East Asian Tours in spring-summer

Since 1979, Dr. David Crowe of the Department of History at Elon College has conducted study tours to Soviet and East Asian countries. The tours are limited to 25 to 27 participants of all ages, usually a mix of half students and half adults. One trip is scheduled during the late spring or early summer, either a tw- week tour of the USSR and Hungary or a one-month field trip to the USSR, Mongolia, China, and Hong Kong. The programs alternate depending upon interest and political and economic conditions.

The two-week trip features city sightseeing tours in Leningrad, Moscow, Odessa, and Budapest with visits to such attractions as the Hermitage, Russian Museum, Kirov, Kremlin, Moscow Art Theater, and the Budapest Royal Palace and National Museum. Highlights of the program may include a social evening with students, a visit to a cooperative, or a visit to an artist's studio. The four-week tour, which offers college credit, includes sightseeing in Leningrad and Moscow, Irkutsk, Ulan Bator, Beijing, Qufu, Jinan, Wuxi, Suzhou, Shanghai, Guangzhou, and Hong Kong. In addition to visiting monuments, museums, and historical sites, participants climb the sacred Mt. Taishan, take a day-long Grand Canal Cruise from Wuxi to Suzhou, and visit a collective farm.

Specialties: Soviet and East Asian countries, including Hungary, Mongolia, China, Hong Kong, and the Soviet Union.

Faculty: Dr. David Crow is a Professor of Russian/Soviet and East Asian history at Elon College and Chairperson of the Department of History. He has contributed to six books and published or delivered more than 90 articles, reviews, and papers on the various aspects of Russian, Soviet, East European, and Asian history and literature. Dr. Crowe has visited the USSR 11 times and travels frequently to East Asia.

Costs, Accommodations: The $2,975 ($4,799) cost of the two-week (one-month) trip includes round trip airfare from/to New York, ground transportation, double occupancy first class hotel accommodations, most meals, and admissions to most attractions. A $100 ($300) deposit, refundable until two months prior to departure, secures a reservation. The balance of payment is due in two installments. Refund is prorated for cancellations within two months of travel. Handicapped persons can usually be accommodated.

Contact: Dr. David Crowe, Elon College, Campus Box 2147, Elon, NC 27244; (919) 584-2387 (office), (919) 584-4419 (home).

ENGLISH LITERATURE SUMMER SCHOOLS
Sheffield, England

Two-week summer courses in South Yorkshire, England

Established in 1978, English Literature Summer Schools offers three two-week courses in June, July, and September that study some of England's great writers and explore the Northern countryside that inspired them. The program consists of small group discussions that focus on the works of the Brontës, Jane Austen, Wordsworth, Coleridge, D.H. Lawrence, and Shakespeare, combined with excursions to many of the writers' homes and a scheduled performance at Stratford. Participants stay with families and participate in such community social activities as visits to pubs, garden parties and folk dances, and theatres and museums.

Specialties: English literature.

Faculty: Includes lecturers from the English Literature Department at Sheffield University.

Costs, Accommodations: Total cost, which includes single room and board, all visits, and theater tickets, is $950. A nonrefundable $50 deposit must accompany registration with balance due approximately seven weeks prior to program. Full refund less deposit is granted cancellations more than six weeks prior; thereafter cancellation charge ranges from 30% (29 to 42 days prior) to 60% (1 to 14 days prior). Students are lodged in local private homes; hotel accommodations are available for a supplementary charge.

Location: The course center, a Victorian villa, is situated in a parkland setting near the Derbyshire Peak District. Course excursions are scheduled to Grasmere, Stratford, Eastwood and Newstead Abbey, Haworth and Heptonstall, and Chatsworth and Hathersage.

Contact: Wilson & Lake International, 330 York St., Ashland, OR 97520; (800) 545-5228, (503) 488-3350, Fax (503) 488-7759 *or* English Literature Summer Schools, 10 Victoria Rd., Sheffield S1O 2DL, England ; (44) 742-660766.

ESSEX INSTITUTE
Museum and Historic Houses
Salem, Massachusetts

One weekend domestic trip per year

The Essex Institute sponsors one trip each year to an historic location in the United States. A typical three-day program, Spring Sojourn to Charleston, includes such activities as a presentation on the city's 18th century interiors and decorative arts, participation in Historic Charleston Foundation's Festival of Homes Tour, and tours of private homes and historic sites.

The Institute, dedicated to the preservation and promotion of New England history, operates a museum and the James Duncan Phillips Library, manages several local historic edifices, offers educational programs, and publishes books, pamphlets, exhibition catalogs, and the quarterly journal, *Historical Collections.*

Specialties: Historic sites.

Costs, Accommodations: Cost of the Charleston trip, including airfare, double occupancy hotel lodging (single supplement available), most meals, and a $100 tax-deductible donation, is $1,095.

Contact: Essex Institute, 132 Essex St., Salem, MA 01970; (508) 744-3390.

EYE OF THE WHALE MARINE/WILDERNESS ADVENTURES
Kapa'au, Hawaii

Five to ten-day trips year-round

Established in 1988, Eye of the Whale offers three different itineraries that combine nature study and adventure with recreation and relaxation. Through a combination of sailing, snorkeling, and hiking, participants are introduced to the natural history of Hawaii, with emphasis on the origin and identification of tropical flora, the development and exploration of coral reef ecosystems, volcanology, and the biology and observation of marine animals. Hands-on participation is encouraged in taking photographs and recording vocalizations of whales and porpoises as well as hoisting the sails and taking the helm while sailing. The three itineraries are the 10-day **Hawaiian Hiking Odyssey**, limited to 10 persons and scheduled approximately ten times annually; the seven-day **Earth Fire & Sea**, limited to six persons and scheduled about a dozen times a year; and the five-day **Whale Tales**, limited to six persons and offered about a half dozen times from January through March, in which participants collect baseline data, photo-identify humpback whales, and record their mating songs as part of ongoing research for the nonprofit North Gulf Oceanic Society.

Specialties: Natural history of the Hawaiian Islands.

Faculty: Biologist Beth Goodoni has taught field classes in marine mammal biology and coral reef ecology and has conducted research on humpback and killer whales and bottlenose dolphins. Mark Goodoni, a U.S. Coast Guard-licensed captain, earned a BS in Marine Resource Development and is an alumnus of the Sea Education Society.

Costs, Accommodations: Costs range from $950 to $1,295, which includes double occupancy lodging, most meals, ground transportation, inter-island airfare, and activities. A $150 nonrefundable deposit secures a reservation with balance due 60 days prior to departure. Balance less deposit is refunded cancellations at least 45 days prior or if space can be filled.

Location: The islands of Kauai, Molokai, and Hawaii.

Contact: Eye of the Whale, P.O. Box 1269, Kapa'au, HI 96755; (800) 657-7730 *or* (808) 889-0227.

FAIRFIELD UNIVERSITY STUDY TOURS IN ITALY
Fairfield, Connecticut

Ten-day and one-month programs in spring and summer

Each year since 1980, Fairfield University has offered two annual study tours of Italy: a ten-day **Art Discovery Tour** limited to 30 to 35 participants and a month-long **Summer Campus in Florence** limited to 40. The programs, which are organized and directed by Fairfield University faculty members Philip and Yael Eliasoph as a joint program of the Fine Arts Department and the School of Continuing Education, are open to undergraduates and part-time degree students desiring academic credit as well as adults seeking personal enrichment.

The **Art Discovery Tour**, scheduled in March, includes visits to such cities as Rome, Florence, Venice, Orvieto, Perugia, San Gimignano, Assisi, and Siena. The tour features first-class hotels and restaurants and emphasizes an artistic itinerary with selected excursions to museums, monuments, and other places of cultural and historical interest. A slide lecture-meeting with the faculty, held on-campus during the month prior to departure, is designed to prepare tour members for viewing the art they will see. Students wishing to receive three credits of academic credit in art history develop an independent project to be submitted upon return.

The **Summer Campus in Florence**, which is held in July at the Lorenzo de' Medici Institute and offers structured graduate and undergraduate coursework or general auditing, presents a variety of courses in studio arts, art history, Italian opera, cooking, and language at all levels. Typical courses include Italian Opera: History and Appreciation, Renaissance Art History in Italy, and Archaeology: History and Methods. Each course, based on the "Florentine Workshop" tradition, includes nine hours of formal lessons each week (36 contact hours total, equivalent to three-credit hours), and a portion of Art History class time includes field trips to such city museums as the Uffizi, Bargello, and Pitti Palace. Studio Arts participants are issued a key to allow access for work in the studios at any time. There are no prerequisites — instruction is structured to each student's level of achievement — and students may enroll in up to three courses for a total of nine credit hours. Attendance is mandatory and those enrolled for academic credit receive a grade based on a written paper, written exams, and/or oral exams. A group orientation session is held on-campus ten days prior to departure and for two days upon arrival at the Institute, followed by a day-long field trip to Assisi and Perugia. Weekends are free for for leisure activities and day trips to nearby cities and customized travel arrangements can be arranged for the end portion of the tour. The program concludes with a farewell banquet and graduation ceremonies.

Specialties: Studio arts (drawing, painting, sculpture, photography, serigraphy/textiles, jewelry), art history, archaeology, Italian opera, language, and cooking.

Faculty: Dr. Philip Eliasoph, Professor of Art History in the Fine Arts Department and author of encyclopaedia articles about Florence and its masters, serves as art guide. Professor Yael Eliasoph, who teaches Italian language and literature in the Modern Languages Department, serves as linguist and interpreter. Academically qualified local guides accompany some excursions. Courses at the Lorenzo de'Medici Institute are taught by the school's faculty.

Costs, Accommodations: The $2,900 ($3,160 for three academic credits) cost of the Art Discovery Tour includes round-trip motorcoach from/to Fairfield University and airfare from/to New York, deluxe and first-class hotel accommodations, all meals, ground transportation, and all scheduled activities; single supplement is $390. A $900 deposit must accompany application with balance due 60 days prior. Initial deposit is fully refundable for cancellations more than three months prior. Cost of the one-month summer campus in Florence, which includes round-trip airfare from/to New York, tuition, ground transportation, and weekday luncheons, ranges from $3,650 to $4,700 depending on level of boarding accommodations and whether enrolled in credit or noncredit program. A $1,000 deposit must accompany application with balance due one month prior. Full refund is granted cancellations more than two months prior; thereafter penalty ranges from $1,250 to $1,750 with entire cost forfeited for cancellations on day of departure or during program. Accommodations for students on a limited budget are assigned in small "pensioni" — apartments and rooms in Florentine hotels; a better level is available in Second Category Superior hotels with air-conditioned rooms and private baths.

Contact: Dr. Philip Eliasoph, Professor of Fine Arts, Canisius Hall 210, Fairfield University, Fairfield, CT 06430; (203) 254-4220, ext. 2912 *or* Mrs. Betty Walker, Travel Coordinator Ass't., School of Continuing Education.

FAR HORIZONS CULTURAL DISCOVERY TRIPS
San Anselmo, California
Nine to eighteen-day trips in the U.S. and abroad

Founded by archaeologist Mary Dell Lucas, Far Horizons offers archaeology and cultural trips to a variety of out-of-the-way locations. Each trip is limited to no more than 15 participants and features dining on native foods, opportunities to meet local people and visit their homes, and on-site lectures and discussions. Typical itineraries include a stay on a reef-protected private island in Belize; a cruise along the Turquoise Coast of Turkey aboard a sailing yacht; participation with costumed natives in their ritual festivities in Guatamala, Belize, the American Southwest, Easter Island, and Mexico; and a float by rubber raft down Central America's largest river through uncut rainforests. More rugged adventures include a muleback trip to the ancient Maya capital of El Mirador or by logging truck to Calakmul.

Specialties: Archaeology and cultural tours.

Faculty: Tour leaders include archaeologists, anthropologists, and other specialists who have lived in the area visited.

Costs, Accommodations: Costs range from $1,750 to $3,800, which includes double occupancy lodging in first class or best available hotels, most meals, and ground transportation. Accommodations may be restored historical buildings, castles, inns, and guest houses, each with private facilities and selected to enhance the cultural aspect of the trip. A $400 deposit secures reservation with balance due 60 days prior to departure. Cancellations at least 60 days prior receive full refund less $60; no refunds thereafter.

Location: Tour destinations include the Yucatan Peninsula, Belize, Guatemala, the British and Welsh countryside, the Four Corners area of southwestern U.S., Turkey, Easter Island, and northern Chile.

Contact: Far Horizons, P.O. Box 1529, 16 Fern Lane, San Anselmo, CA 94960; (415) 457-4575, Fax (415) 457-4608.

FARM TOURS, ETC.
Tulare, California
15-day tour of California farms

Since 1987, Ron Perry has offered two to eight tours annually, each limited to 6 to 15 individuals with an interest in agriculture. These combination farm study-sightseeing tours visit the major farming regions of California, Chile, Spain, and New Zealand.

Specialties: Study of farm crops.

Faculty: Ron Perry is a grape and walnut farmer in the San Joaquin Valley.

Costs, Accommodations: Costs, which include ground transportation, lodging, and most entrance fees, range from $50 to $100 per night, depending upon accommodations. A $100 nonrefundable deposit must accompany registration with balance due two weeks prior to tour.

Contact: Ron Perry, Farm Tours, Etc., 1150 N. Gem St., Tulare, CA 93274; (209) 688-2479.

FAULKNER AND YOKNAPATAWPHA CONFERENCE
Center for the Study of Southern Culture
The University of Mississippi
University, Mississippi
Six-day summer conference

Begun in 1974, this annual end-of-July conference features a variety of lectures, readings by a southern literary figure, small-group discussions, and special events. Each year, the conference focuses on a specific theme relating to William Faulkner, such as Faulkner and Religion or Faulkner and the Short Story. Special events include tours of North Mississippi; a picnic at Faulkner's home, Rowan Oak; discussions by Faulkner friends and family; a slide lecture, *Knowing William Faulkner*, delivered by J.M. Faulkner and Jo Marshall; a session on *William Faulkner of Oxford*, conducted by M.C. Faulkner; readings of *Voices from Yoknapatawpha*; and presentation of the Eudora Welty Awards to young Mississippi writers. Faulkner manuscripts, photographs, and memorabilia are on display at the John Davis Williams Library and Faulkner films are shown during the week.

Specialties: William Faulkner and his work.

Faculty: Noted literary scholars and critics.

Costs, Accommodations: Conference fee of $200 ($150 for students, $175 for Friends of the Center for the Study of Southern Culture) includes all conference events, opening buffet supper, picnic, and bus tour of Faulkner Country. Attendance is limited and applications, submitted with a $50 deposit, are accepted on a first-come, first-served basis. Written cancellations received more than 12 days prior to conference receive full refund less

$10. Daily rates at the on-campus Alumni House, a motel-type facility, begin at $30.74, single, $38.16 double occupancy. Dormitory, sorority, and motel accommodations may also be arranged.

Location: University is 80 miles from Memphis. Transportation to and from Memphis International Airport can be arranged for $25 oneway or $45 roundtrip.

Contact: Faulkner and Yoknapatawpha, Center for the Study of Southern Culture, The University of Mississippi, University, MS 38677; (601) 232-5993.

FEDERATION OF ONTARIO NATURALISTS (FON)
Port Elgin, Ontario, Canada
One-day to one-week programs in Ontario

The Federation of Ontario Naturalists membership trip program provides opportunities for novice and veteran naturalists to learn more about the natural environment. The program offers more than 150 day and weekend nature trips year-round, three week-long study workshops and adult natural history camps and three youth natural history camps during the summer months, and an annual conference.

Trips, which are usually limited to 15 participants (except camps), can focus on many aspects of nature or on a single subject. Popular subjects include flora and fauna, particularly the birds of the region, including eagles, owls, hawks, Carolinian warblers, Grebes, raptors, herons, egrets, grouse, warblers, Whimbrels, and waterfowl. Some trips are devoted to teaching a specific skill, such as wilderness living, kayaking, or birdwatching. The study workshops, adult natural history camps, and youth camps feature a week of activities that are designed to expand knowledge of the natural world and the native flora and fauna. Activities include instructional sessions, evening slide presentations, and group get-togethers. The annual three-day conference features guided tours, concurrent lecture sessions, and a choice of several one-day field trips. Extended one-week field trips are scheduled at the conclusion of the conference.

Specialties: Natural history and wildlife of Ontario.

Faculty: All trips are conducted by volunteer naturalists who are members of FON.

Costs, Accommodations: Cost of day trips ranges from C$21 to C$75; weekend trips range from C$150 to C$225; one-week workshops and camps range from C$495 to C$585. Accommodations are included in cost. A deposit of the lesser of C$50 or full cost of trip (C$100 for one-week programs) must accompany application with balance due 30 days prior to trip. For trips, full refunds are granted written cancellations received at least three weeks prior. For workshops and camps, a full refund less C$25 fee is granted written cancellations received at least four weeks prior; full refund less deposit is granted cancellations more than ten days prior; no refunds thereafter. Registration for the annual conference is approximately C$50. Lodging, meals, and field trips are additional. FON annual membership dues are C$28 individual, C$35 family, C$17 student, and C$18 for senior couple.

Contact: FON Membership Trips, P.O. Box 1647, Port Elgin, ON N0H 2C0, Canada; (519) 832-5928.

FIELD STUDIES IN NATURAL HISTORY
Office of Continuing Education
San Jose State University (SJSU)
San Jose, California
Two to five-day spring and summer programs

Field Studies in Natural History, a nonprofit organization associated with San Jose State University, sponsors approximately four to five programs each year during the spring and summer. One or two units of degree credit, general education credit, or teacher inservice training are available.

Typical programs include Jedediah Smith State and Redwoods National Parks, a week-long summer session that focuses on the natural history of California's northern coastal region, including the 2,000-year-old giant redwoods and their surrounding environment; Plumas-Eureka State Park, an exploration of the area's unique glacial evidence, historic gold mining tunnels, and natural history; Death Valley, an annual trek (the week prior to Easter) that studies the desert's geology, botany, zoology, ecology, and mining, supplemented by evening discussions, films, and star gazing; and the Grand Canyon, a 16-day, two-part raft trip down the Colorado River that explores the Canyon's natural history. Summer trips also offer a concurrent supervised junior program in natural history for children ages 6 to 16. A limited number of scholarships are available for each program.

Specialties: Natural history.

Faculty: Instructors with specialites in the fields of geology, zoology, botany, ecology, and biology.

Costs, Accommodations: Course fees, which must accompany registration, range from $100 to $190; fees for Grand Canyon are approximately $1,600. Accommodations are available at nearby motels and local park campgrounds.

Contact: Field Studies in Natural History, Office of Continuing Education, San Jose State University, One Washington Sq., San Jose, CA 95192-0135; (408) 924-2680.

FIELD STUDIES COUNCIL (FSC)
Great Britain
Three to seven-day courses year-round

Established more than 40 years ago, the educational charity Field Studies Council, whose ethic is "Environmental Understanding for All", offers more than 300 courses annually at nine residential Field Centres in Great Britain as well as more than 30 annual Expeditions Overseas. Most courses are one week in length, running from Friday to Friday, although some Centres schedule their courses different days and durations. All courses are open to anyone over the age of 16 and most are suited to beginners, with a few geared to a more advanced level. Some Centres also offer family courses.

Course topics cover a wide range of environmental interests, including natural history, ecology and conservation, birds and other animals, flowers and other plants, geology, landscape, and climate. Courses concerned with scenery and landscape may present an overview of the effects of earth movements, erosion, and deposition on a geological time scale, or focus on the specific features of rocks, minerals, and fossils. Courses in natural history subjects may use several habitats and deal with a diversity of plants and animals or concentrate on a particular group or species. Human history and prehistory provide themes for courses dealing with the environment studied through examination of towns and villages, the architecture of houses and churches, and the archaeological features of the past. Practical courses in photography, crafts, painting, and drawing are also offered.

Faculty: Each Centre is headed by a Warden and Director of Studies qualified in an appropriate academic subject and having experience in field investigation and teaching. The Warden and other members of the trained permanent staff of the Centre run many of the courses while others are taught by tutors who are selected for their expertise and teaching ability.

Costs, Accommodations: Field Centre course fees range from £50 to £210, which includes tuition, board and double occupancy lodging (single rooms are available at some Centres for a surcharge of £10 to £25); use of the library, laboratory, and other facilities; and transporation during the course (except for boat trips). Nonresidents are welcome (and pay a reduced fee) at some Centres. A nonrefundable deposit of £30 (£20 for a weekend) plus single supplement must accompany booking form with balance due prior to arrival. Those who cancel within 30 days of arrival are responsible for payment of the balance. Members of FSC can deduct £3 from the course fee. Annual dues are £5 for an individual, £6 for a family. For an additional £7 per year, members receive a subscription to the five-part *Field Studies* journal of the Field Studies Council, which contains scientific papers relating to the environmental subjects studied at the Field Centres.

Location, Facilities: A description of each Field Centre's location follows this listing. All Centres have laboratory facilities, field study equipment, and libraries with an extensive selection of books relating to the course subjects.

Field Studies Council (FSC)
DALE FORT FIELD CENTRE
Haverfordwest, Dyfed, Wales

The Dale Fort Field Centre offers approximately 30 weekend and one-week courses from late March to early October, most featuring boat trips to the offshore islands. The Pembrokeshire Coast and Offshore Islands is an introduction to the ecology of the islands of Skomer, Skokholm, Grassholm, and Ramsey, with emphasis on breeding seabirds, maritime flowers, marine biology, and geology. Other courses include The Bristol Channel and Islands, Birds, and Boating.

Location: This converted military fortification is situated on the tip of a narrow peninsula jutting into Milford Haven. The cliffs are broken by sandy bays and rocky coves of varying degrees of exposure to the Atlantic, offering opportunities for shore and marine biology.

Contact: D.C. Emerson, Warden and Director of Studies, Dale Fort Field Centre, Haverfordwest, Dyfed SA62 3RD, Wales; (44) 64065 205.

Field Studies Council (FSC)
EXPEDITIONS OVERSEAS
Five-day to three-week trips year-round

Since 1978, FSC has conducted overseas trips that emphasize the unique natural features of the areas visited, including the study of birds, flowers, butterflies, and landscapes, as well as painting and photography. Currently more than 30 travel programs are scheduled annually, each limited to 10 to 14 participants who are usually accompanied by two leaders. Programs include An African Kingdom: A Journey Through Swaziland, Paradise of Jahangir: Natural History in Kashmir, Iceland: Land of Ice and Fire, and Volcanos of Southern Italy, an exploration of Vesuvius, Etna, Vulcano, and Stromboli to observe lava flows, bombs, hot springs, and fumaroles.

Faculty: Tour leaders are mostly experienced members of the FSC academic staff who are experts in appropriate subjects.

Costs, Accommodations: Costs range from £250 to £2200, which includes travel from/to Great Britain, lodging, comprehensive insurance, and ground transportation. A nonrefundable £50 to £100 deposit must accompany booking with balance due 10 weeks prior to departure. No refunds thereafter.

Location: Travel destinations include Canada, Kenya, Jamaica, Andalucia, Greece, Italy, Turkey, France, Morocco, Ireland, Kashmir, Sicily, and Everglades National Park.

Contact: Anne Stephens, Expeditions Overseas, Field Studies Council, Montford Bridge, Shrewsbury SY4 1HW, England; (44) 743 850164.

Field Studies Council (FSC)
FLATFORD MILL FIELD CENTRE
Colchester, Essex, England

Flatford Mill Field Centre offers more than 100 three to seven-day courses year-round on a variety of subjects. Some courses focus on a specific topic, such as A Weekend on Bats, an introduction to the identification and natural history of flying mammals, combining illustrated talks with observation at twilight. Other titles include Wildlife on an Estuary, Suffolk's Spring Flowers, and Woodland Management for Conservation.

Location: The Centre is located on the Suffolk side of the River Stour, in the farmlands of Constable's country. Above the 18th century Mill, the river, ponds and dykes offer opportunities for aquatic biology.

Contact: Edward Jackson, Warden & Director of Studies, Flatford Mill Field Centre, East Bergholt, Colchester, Essex CO7 6UL, England; (44) 206 298283.

Field Studies Council (FSC)
JUNIPER HALL FIELD CENTRE
Dorking, Surrey, England

The Juniper Hall Field Centre offers more than 50 courses from April to November, including such topics as Badgers and Smaller Mammals, Making Sense of the Weather, Lichens Near London, and Life in Ponds and Streams. June Chatfield's Mollusc Course is an introduction to snails and slugs in the area around Box Hill.

Location: Situated in Southern England on National Trust land around Box Hill, Juniper Hall is accessible to the wild areas of the North Downs as well as the forest and heath country of the Western Weald. A variety of inland habitats are located nearby.

Contact: John Bebbington, Warden & Director of Studies, , Juniper Hall Field Centre, Dorking, Surrey, RH5 6DA, England; (44) 306 883849.

Field Studies Council (FSC)
MALHAM TARN FIELD CENTRE
Settle, North Yorkshire, England

Malham Tarn Field Centre offers approximately 25 courses, with many devoted to the plants, animals, and geology of the region. More advanced courses include Small Mammal Ecology Weekend, which features instruction in the live trapping techniques, animal handling, and data interpretation required for mammal survey work, and Fens and Bogs: The Ecology of Peatlands, an examination of the environmental factors that differentiate the various types of peatland.

Location: The Centre is situated above the shore of the 153-acre Tarn, on a 1,300-foot plateau of carboniferous limestone. An area of geological interest, the Malham Moor contains a variety of vegetations and animal habitats, ranging from peat systems to limestone grassland, from shallow calcareous waters to acid peat pools.

Contact: Kingsley Iball, Warden & Director of Studies, Malham Tarn Field Centre, Settle, North Yorkshire BD24 9PU, England; (44) 7293 331.

Field Studies Council (FSC)
NETTLECOMBE COURT
The Leonard Wills Field Centre
Taunton, Somerset, England

The Leonard Wills Field Centre offers more than 30 courses annually, year-round. Weekend courses run from Thursday or Friday to Sunday while one-week courses usually begin and end on Wednesday. Typical course offerings include A Nettlecombe Fungus Foray, Natural History from the Coastal Footpath, Winter Botany, and Discovering Mammals, a guide to the wild mammals of Exmoor and its surroundings, including bats, badgers, mice, voles, otter, and red deer.

Location: Nettlecombe Court, a part-Elizabethan mansion, is in a west Somerset valley between the Brendon Hills and the Bristol Channel, 15 miles northwest of Taunton (the nearest railway station), seven miles southeast of Minehead, and four miles south of the coast. Situated on the boundary between upland and lowland Britain, the Centre offers opportunities for geographical fieldwork with a range of terrestrial and freshwater habitats supplemented by the shores of the Bristol Channel.

Contact: Dr. J.H. Crothers, Warden & Director of Studies, Field Studies Council at Nettlecombe Court, Williton, Taunton, Somerset TA4 4HT, England; (44) 984 40320.

Field Studies Council (FSC)
ORIELTON FIELD CENTRE
Pembroke, Dyfed, Wales

The Orielton Field Centre offers approximately 15 courses from April to September that explore the environs of Pembrokeshire. Titles include Pembrokeshire Coast Path Rambles, Insights into Nature — An Introduction to the Natural History of Pembrokeshire, and Exploring the Pembrokeshire National Park, an examination of the area's rocks, beaches, birds, bats, cliffs, castles, cromlechs, and wild flowers.

Location: The Centre is set in a wooded 54-acre estate in a corner of the Angle peninsula, two miles south of Pembroke. The salt marsh and mud flats of Milford Haven are located to the north and the limestone cliffs of the Atlantic shore are to the south.

Contact: R.G. Crump, Warden and Director of Studies, Orielton Field Centre, Pembroke, Dyfed SA71 5EZ, Wales; (44) 64-681 225.

Field Studies Council (FSC)
PRESTON MONTFORD FIELD CENTRE
Montford Bridge, Shrewsbury, England

The Preston Montford Field Centre offers more than 70 courses from March until mid-October. Courses of local interest include Stone Buildings of Shropshire, a study of the various types of rocks of the area and how they've been used by masons and builders from Roman to modern times; Rocks, Minerals, and Mines, an opportunity to explore one of the most complete geological sequences in Britain; and Discovering Mediaeval Buildings in the Marches, which includes illustrated talks and visits to the area between England and Wales and some of its finest remains.

Location: The Centre is in pasture and parkland overlooking the River Severn in the North Shropshire lowland, and area rich in geographical, historical, and archaeological features.

Contact: J.A. Bayley, Warden and Director of Studies, Preston Montford Field Centre, Montford Bridge, Shrewsbury SY4 1DX, England; (44) 743 850380.

Field Studies Council (FSC)
RHYD-Y-CREUAU
The Drapers' Field Centre
Betws-y-coed, Gwynedd, Wales

Rhyd-Y-Creuau offers approximately 25 three to seven-day courses year-round on a variety of subjects, particularly the geology of the region. The Geology and Scenery of the Borderland examines the geology of Shropshire with investigation of extinct volcanos, fossil coastlines, ancient deserts, and past glaciers. Other courses include Rocks and Minerals of North Wales and Mountain Weather, a week of learning about the weather with experts from the Meteorological Office.

Location: The Centre, which is accessible to the north Welsh coast, is located in the lower Conwy valley a mile northeast of Betws-y-coed. The valley separates the Denbigh moors, on Silurian rocks, to the east from the igneous and pre-Silurian rocks of Snowdonia to the west. Situated nearby are acid sessile oak woodland, plantations of various ages, moorland and rocky heath, mountain and improved lowland pastures, and soft water streams.

Contact: A.J. Scharer, Warden and Director of Studies, Rhyd-Y-Creuau, The Drapers' Field Centre, Betws-y-coed, Gwynedd LL24 OHB, Wales; (44) 69-02 494.

Field Studies Council (FSC)
SLAPTON LEY FIELD CENTRE
Slapton, Kingsbridge, Devon, England

The Slapton Ley Field Centre offers approximately 10 courses during the summer months, from June through August. Topics, which focus on the Devon area, include Wild Flowers of South Devon, Natural History Photography in Devon, and Mosses: Their Identification and Ecology.

Location: The Centre is situated in a small Devon village next to a valley that drains into a freshwater lake, Slapton Ley, which is separated from the sea by Slapton Sands. The Centre's 460-acre Nature Reserve includes two large deciduous woods.

Contact: K. Chell, Warden and Director of Studies, Slapton Ley Field Centre, Slapton, Kingsbridge, Devon TQ7 2QP, England; (44) 548 580466.

FOUNDATION FOR FIELD RESEARCH
Alpine, California

Two-day to two-month projects throughout the world

Founded in 1982 to coordinate research expeditions that require volunteer assistance, this nonprofit organization meets the needs of scientists by finding individuals who are interested in contributing, both physically and financially, to research projects. Volunteers are provided for more than 40 expeditions annually, ranging from long term, large scale endeavors, for which the Foundation's support is just a part, to smaller projects that derive all their support from the Foundation. The number of volunteers on a team ranges from five to twenty, with an average of ten. Ages range from 14 to 86 and no previous experience is required, although those who have specific skills, such as writing, drawing, photography, or scuba diving, have an opportunity to use them. Volunteers are sent a 50 to 75-page Preparatory Booklet that fully describes the research subject and ongoing instruction is provided in the field. Disciplines include anthropology, archaeology, botany, entomology, ethnography, herpetology, historic architecture, geology, mammalogy, marine biology, ornithology, paleontology, and primatology.

A typical major expedition in Grenada consists of five projects, allowing volunteers to alternate their time between various disciplines: **Prehistoric People of Pearls,** an archaeological excavation at the Pearls site to research Caribbean pre-history; **Endangered Sea Turtles,** an expedition to study mature female Leatherbacks as they return to their birthplace to produce offspring; **Endangered Mammals and Birds,** an excavation for fossils of extinct animals; **Endangered Tropical Plant Life,** an effort to document and inventory all species of plant life on the island; and **Endangered Folklore of Grenada,** a project to record oral traditions on tape and paper.

Specialties: Research projects requiring volunteer assistance.

Faculty: Accomplished scientists conduct all expeditions. Their proposals are screened through a peer review process. A Foundation field manager accompanies each expedition to handle cooking and cleanup and other logistical details.

Costs, Accommodations: Each volunteer contributes a share of costs — from $150 to $1,900 — to cover the expedition expenses. A $200 deposit secures a reservation and balance is due 100 days prior to expedition. Credit card (VISA, MasterCard, American Express, Diners, Carte Blanche) registrations accepted. No refunds are granted but cancellations more than 30 days prior can transfer 100% of the contribution to another expedition, 80% within 30 days. One unit of college credit, costing $30, is available for some expeditions through San Diego State University College of Extended Studies. Tax deductibility of costs may also be available. The cost of each Preparatory Booklet is $18, which is credited to the cost of the expedition. A yearly subscription to the 52-page quarterly *Explorer News*, which contains descriptions of upcoming expeditions, is $8.

Contact: Foundation for Field Research, P.O. Box 2010, Alpine, CA 92001-0020; (619) 445-9264.

THE FOUR CORNERS SCHOOL OF OUTDOOR EDUCATION
Monticello, Utah

Three-day to two-week programs from February to November

The nonprofit Four Corners School (FCS) offers more than 40 programs annually in archaeology, geology, ethnography, history, biology/zoology, and photography/writing relating to the 2,500 square mile region known as the Colorado Plateau. Programs are rated as to level of difficulty on a scale of one to ten with the higher levels requiring off-trail hiking with heavy full pack, ten or more miles daily, or difficult whitewater or cold weather. Most participants range in age from 35 to 65 with a minimum age requirement of 14 without adult supervision. Graduate or undergraduate credit is available for all programs, teacher recertification credits are available for some programs, and approximately one-quarter of the programs are tax-deductible research expeditions. FCS programs are co-sponsored by more than 20 educational institutions, including Earthwatch, Elderhostel, Sierra Club, Adirondack Mountain Club, International Research Expeditions, Rice University, and the Denver and Utah Museums of Natural History. Custom itineraries are available.

Archaeology programs include Pottery Styles of the Four Corners Area with hands-on lessons in primitive pottery-making and examination and identification of pottery in museums and the field; The Chaco Canyon Phenomena, an in-depth look at the Anasazi culture with evening seminars and discussions on the prehistory of the Southwest; and Grand Canyon Archaeology, a research expedition to map, photograph, and describe prehistoric sites along inner canyon trails for the purpose of cultural resource preservation. Geology and biology/zoology programs include Biogeography of Lake Powell, a houseboat trip to archaeological sites along the lake with day hikes to see Anasazi rock art and hands-on workshops in Native American plant uses; and In Pursuit of the Peregrine, a research expedition to survey the canyon country for nesting falcons. Ethnography and history programs include immersions in the Hopi and Navajo cultures and Canyonlands Pioneers, a backpack journey with a descendant of one of the original Hole-in-the-Rock Expedition families, featuring exploration of seldom-visited parts of the Needles District of Canyonlands National Park and campfire stories about regional history and pioneer lore. Photo/Writing Workshops involve participants in making visual and written images that reflect their personal impressions of the environment. Instruction encompasses the elements of active seeing, visual design, technical considerations, and literary imagery.

Specialties: Archaeology, geology, ethnography, history, biology/zoology, and photography/writing relating to the Colorado Plateau.

Faculty: The consulting staff of approximately 30 college professors and experts in their field, members of which accompany every program, include biologists, archaeologists, geologists, historians, and photographers. Many have published textbooks and reference materials on their subjects.

Costs, Accommodations: Costs, which include tuition, meals, and lodging, range from $275 to $1,395, with most programs in the $300 to $800 range. Lodging ranges from motels to basecamps (rustic bunkhouse or tents). A $100 nonrefundable deposit must accompany application with balance due 30 days prior to program. VISA and MasterCard accepted. Cancellation fee ranges from full balance (more than 59 days prior) to 50% of total tuition (less than 30 days prior). Academic credit is available from Mankato State University, Prescott College, or Central Wyoming College. Participants who request college credit cannot deduct the costs of research expeditions.

Location: Most programs originate in Monticello, which is accessible by Delta Airlines and Alpine Air commuter service from 25 major cities through Salt Lake City. Some programs originate in Cortez, CO, and Albuquerque.

Contact: Four Corners School, East Route, Monticello, UT 84535; (800) 525-4456 *or* (801) 587-2859.

FRESCO TRAVELS THROUGH TIME
London, England
One to three-week tours abroad

Established in 1983, Fresco specializes in tours with an historic emphasis. Approximately eight to ten itineraries are offered annually, each scheduled once during the months from April through October. Most are limited to 25 participants.

A trip to western France focuses on the caves of the Vezere, Dordogne, and Lot valleys and the stone monuments of the Breton coast. The island of Sicily is the destination for a tour that concentrates on the well-preserved remains of ancient Greek colonies at such sites as Syracuse, Segesta, Selinunte, and Agrigento. The Cyprus tour explores the combination of archaeology, history, and landscape as reflected by the Greeks, Romans, Byzantines, French, Venetians, and Turks.

Specialties: International tours with a history/archaeology focus.

Faculty: Fresco is managed by Jim Black of the Institute of Archaeology, London, and advised by John Manley, Clwyd County Archaeologist. All tours are led by selected experts in archaeology/history.

Costs, Accommodations: Costs, which include round-trip airfare from/to London, double occupancy hotel accommodations (single supplement available), at least two meals daily, and all planned activities, range from £650 to £1,995. A £75 nonrefundable deposit must accompany booking with balance due at least 10 weeks prior to departure. Cancellation penalty ranges from 30% of total tour price (35 to 59 days prior) to 60% of total (15 to 34 days prior); no refund thereafter.

Location: Other itineraries include Turkey, Nile, Castile and Estremadura, North Yemen, Peru, and Namibia.

Contact: Fresco Ltd., 36 Great Russell St., London WC1B 3PP, England; (44) 71 323 4690.

FRIENDS OF THE KENNEDY CENTER TRAVEL PROGRAM
Washington, D.C.

Weekend to three-week trips in the U.S. and abroad

The Friends of the John F. Kennedy Center for the Performing Arts offer approximately a dozen travel programs annually, about half being weekend theatre trips to New York City. Typical domestic and international tours include a New York-to-Los Angeles cruise featuring on-board music personalities; a trip to Charleston's Spoleto Fesitval with behind the scenes visits; and a cruise from Lisbon to Copenhagen, with a private tour of the Van Gogh retrospective exhibition in Amsterdam.

Specialties: Tours with a performing arts focus.

Costs, Accommodations: Theatre trips range from $480 to $680, which includes transportation from/to Washington, D.C., tickets, double occupancy accommodations, and scheduled events. Land costs for four to five-day domestic trips range from $1,135 to $2,350 and overseas trips range from $2,630 to $9,630, depending on destination and accommodations. Payment and refund policies vary. Friends membership dues begin at $25.

Contact: Friends of the Kennedy Center, The John F. Kennedy Center for the Performing Arts, Washington, D.C. 20566-0003; (202) 416-8300.

FUDAN MUSEUM FOUNDATION
Ambler, Pennsylvania

Three to six week summer programs in China

Since 1983, Fudan Museum Foundation has sponsored three to six-week Summer Programs at Shanghai's Fudan University for high school seniors, undergraduate and graduate students, high school and college faculty, and interested adults. The three-week program, scheduled from late July to mid-August and limited to 15 participants, is a seminar course: **Chinese Life and Art** (in English). The six-week program, from early July to mid-August and also limited to 15 participants, offers a choice of **Chinese Art and Culture** (in English) or **Chinese Language** (beginning to advanced). Three academic credits are offered for each course. The program features visits in and around Shanghai, weekend tours, and a tour of East China, including Beijing, Ming Tombs, Great Wall, Louyang, Xian, and Nanking. The Foundation also sponsors a special four-week program, scheduled from mid-July to mid-August for teachers and interested adults, that includes one week of study in Shanghai and a 12-day tour of East China. The programs are accessible to handicapped persons.

Specialties: Chinese art and culture.

Faculty: Alfonz Lengyel, Ph.D., serves as Advisory Professor at Fudan University Institute of Museology and helped build the first Institute for Museology in China at Fudan University. He is Consulting Professor of Archaeology at Xian Jiaotong University in Xian and President of Fudan Museum Foundation.

Costs, Accommodations: Costs range from $2,900 (three weeks) to $3,500 (six weeks) and include round-trip airfare from/to New York, tuition, double occupancy lodging in student dormitory, three meals daily, and scheduled trips and activities. A $200 nonrefundable deposit must accompany application by mid-April with balance due April 30. Cancellations at least one month prior to departure receive a refund of half the balance. Scholarships are available.

Contact; Dr. Alfonz Lengyel, Fudan Museum Foundation, 1522 Schoolhouse Rd., Ambler, PA 19002; (215) 699-6448.

GALLATIN ABROAD IN ITALY
New York University (NYU)-Gallatin Division
New York, New York
Three-week June seminar

Since 1987, NYU's Gallatin Division has offered a four-credit summer humanities seminar in Florence, limited to 25 students and adults, that is devoted to study of the art and literature of the Italian Renaissance. Readings, which are drawn from literature, art, and cultural history, include such works as Dante's *Divine Comedy*, Boccaccio's *Decameron*, and Antel's *Florentine Painting and Its Social Background*. One required class, scheduled in New York prior to departure, is designed to present an overview of the art to be seen in Florence and information on each student's personalized art itinerary.

Specialties: Art and literature of the Italian Renaissance.

Faculty: NYU professors Bella Mirabella (Literature) and Bertram Katz (History of Art).

Costs, Accommodations: The $2,100 fee includes lodging, breakfast, and four academic credits. Application and a $150 deposit must be submitted at least 16 weeks prior to program, $475 is due 14 weeks prior, and balance is due 10 weeks prior. Full refund, less $75 fee, is granted cancellations more than 14 weeks prior; a $200 fee is assessed between 10 and 14 weeks prior; no refunds thereafter. Students are lodged in a simple, well-located hotel in the heart of the city.

Contact: Dr. Bella Mirabella *or* Prof. Bert S. Katz, New York University-Gallatin Division, 715 Broadway, 6th Floor, New York, NY 10003; (212) 998-7370.

GEO EXPEDITIONS
Sonora, California
Ten-day to three-week tours to Africa, Latin America, Asia, and the Pacific

Established in 1982, Geo Expeditions offers approximately 25 itineraries that visit a variety of destinations known for their wildlife, culture, and/or natural history. Most tours are limited to 15 participants. Tours stressing an appreciation of the global ecosystem include the Route of Alexander Von Humboldt, which follows the path of the famous German geographer and scientist into Ecuador's highlands; Indonesia Wildlife, which focuses on the diverse and unique animal and plant life found in this country's extensive archipelago; and Costa Rica Natural History, an exploration of such diverse geography as tropical rainforests, high elevation dwarf forests, active volcanoes, and coral reefs.

Specialties: Tours that focus on wildlife, culture, and natural history.

Faculty: Trip leaders, who are often citizens of their respective countries, are experienced naturalists, conservationists, and anthropologists.

Costs, Accommodations: Base trip fees, which include first-class or best available hotels and lodges (when appropriate), all meals except where stipulated, and local surface transport, range from approximately $1,300 to $4,000; single supplement is available. A 10% to 15% surcharge is levied in the event of less than minimum enrollment. Travel and lodging range from motor car touring and comfortable lodge accommodations to trekking and overnight stays in primitive villages. A $200 deposit must accompany application with balance due 90 days prior to departure. Cancellations more than 90 days prior forfeit $75; between 60 and 90 days prior penalty is 30% of land cost; thereafter nonrecoverable costs are added.

Location: In addition to the above, destinations include East Africa, the Galapagos Islands & Peru, Patagonia, Malaysia, Thailand, Hawaii, Papua New Guinea, Australia, and New Zealand.

Contact: Geo Expeditions, P.O. Box 3656, Sonora, CA 95370; (800) 351-5041 *or* (209) 532-0152.

THE GEORGE WASHINGTON UNIVERSITY
SUMMER FIELD PROGRAM IN MEXICO
Washington, D.C.

Three-week June program in even-numbered years

Since 1968, the Anthropology Department and the American Studies Program of George Washington University have sponsored a summer study program in Mexico that examines ancient and modern Mexican culture from an interdisciplinary perspective. The program, which is limited to 7 to 12 participants, explores the relationships among art, architecture, ecology, and socio-political systems. Lectures and discussions are held at archaeological and historical sites and students have the opportunity to observe the data used by scientists and researchers in the theoretical reconstructions of Meso-American culture and history. Those desiring three or six hours of academic credit are required to focus on a topic of individual interest and complete a daily journal.

Specialties: Ancient and modern Mexican culture.

Faculty: Course Directors Robert L. Humphrey, Professor of Anthropology and co-author of *Ancient Washington: American Indian Cultures of the Potomac Valley*, and Bernard Mergen, Professor of American Civilization and senior editor of *American Studies International*.

Costs, Accommodations: Cost, which includes round-trip airfare from/to Washington, D.C., double occupancy hotel lodging, all meals, and local transportation, is $2,620 for three credit hours, $3,670 for six credit hours. A nonrefundable $200 deposit is required eight weeks prior to departure with balance due approximately three weeks later.

Location: The itinerary includes the museums of Campeche, La Venta Park, and Merida; archaeological sites of Dzibilchaltun, Mayapan, Acanceh, Labna, Kabah, Sayil, Xlapak, and Loltun; the underwater park at Xel-Ha; the colonial town of Izamal; Mayan ruins and pyramids; the archaeological park at Chichen Itza; the caves of Balancanche; the Mayan city of Uxmal; the Lacondon forest; and the city of Veracruz.

Contact: Dept. of Summer Sessions, The George Washington University, 2121 I St., N.W., 5th Floor, Washington, DC 20052; (202) 994-6360.

GEORGETOWN UNIVERSITY
SCHOOL FOR SUMMER AND CONTINUING EDUCATION
Washington, D.C.

Two to four-week summer programs abroad

The Georgetown University summer travel program, established in 1974, offers seven courses in Europe and South America, three of which are devoted to the study of specific aspects of the country's literature and heritage. Each course is limited to 20 to 25 participants and offers three or six academic credits.

Life and Thought in Ancient Greece, a 17-day three-credit study-travel course offered since 1983 in cooperation with The Society for the Preservation of the Greek Heritage, involves visits to famous historical and archaeological sites combined with the study of related Classical texts, including *The Homeric Hymns,* Aeschylus' *Oresteia,* Herodotus' *Histories,* and early Platonic dialogues. **Dublin, Ireland,** a 15-day three-credit course offered since 1988, explores the influence of Irish history and politics on Irish writers and how these poets and novelists have shaped our understanding of the country's culture. The program includes walking tours, museum visits, trips to the Abbey and Gate Theaters and experimental theatre programs, and readings and lectures by contemporary Irish writers. **Shakespeare: Text and Performance,** a 24-day six-credit course first offered in 1990, considers the plays currently in repertoire at the Royal Shakespeare Company through lectures, discussions, and theatre visits. To enhance understanding, students explore the texts through action and performance and examine the works of Shakespeare contemporaries Ben Jonson and John Donne.

The summer schedule also includes five to six-week programs in Germany, Italy, France, and Ecuador, each limited to 50 to 60 students, that combine intensive language study with cultural enrichment.

Specialties: Ancient Greek culture, Irish poets and writers, the plays of Shakespeare, foreign language and culture.

Faculty: Georgetown University faculty includes Dr. Alfonso Gomez-Lobo, Professor of Philosophy (Ancient Greece); Dr. John B. Breslin, Lecturer in English and Director of Georgetown University Press (Dublin, Ireland); and Professor Michael Scott, Head of the School of Arts at Leicester Polytechnic, and Dermot Cavanagh, Lecturer in English at Exeter University (Shakespeare).

Costs, Accommodations: Tuition for Ancient Greece is $2,886, which includes airfare, local travel, all hotels, two meals daily, and museum fees. Cost of the Ireland trip is $1,150, which includes room, some meals, and local transportation. The Shakespeare course costs $2,185, which includes room, partial board, and tickets and transportation to performances.

Location: The Ancient Greece course visits such locales as Athens, Delphi, Corinth, Mycenae, and Ephesus (Turkey). The Ireland program is held on the campus of Dublin's 400-year-old Trinity College and includes a visit to the Yeats country around Sligo and the Gaelic-speaking area of Connemara. The Shakespeare course is held at Leicester Polytechnic in Leicester, a medium-sized city approximately 90 minutes north of London. It has one of the largest markets in Europe, two major theaters, and sports facilities. Participants also attend performances in London and Stratford.

Contact: School for Summer and Continuing Education, Georgetown University, Washington, DC 20057; (202) 687-5942.

THE GLACIER INSTITUTE
Glacier National Park, Montana
One to five-day summer classes

This nonprofit corporation, established in 1983, sponsors natural science, art, and photography field courses that are taught on-site within the Glacier National Park ecosystem. Typical two to five-day classes include Bears and People, which features visits to bear habitats and a series of lectures and discussions that cover such topics as people living with bears and how bears "make a living"; Looking Up in Glacier, a study of clouds, fronts, weather patterns, storms, and mountain meteorology; People of the Mountain World, which focuses on the skills (tracking and stalking animals), history, and crafts of the Blackfeet Indians; Rivers of Ice, an investigation of the process of ice formation, the variety of landforms created by glaciers, and the possible causes of glacial periods; and Tracking the Earth as a Manuscript, an intensive field study on observing and interpreting animal signs.

A series of one-day explorations are devoted to such topics as bird watching, storytelling, maps and compass, tracking wildlife, and discovering wildflowers. Most classes include credit from Flathead Valley Community College.

Specialties: Natural history indigenous to the Glacier National Park.

Faculty: Includes Dr. Lex Blood, a geologist and veteran instructor at Flathead Community College; Dr. O. Fred Donaldson, who has taught at the University of Washington and the Yellowstone Institute; Von Walden, a graduate student in geophysics at the University of Washington; Kathy Ahlenslager, associate curator of the University of Montana's herbarium; plant ecologist Dr. June Freedman; Dr. Charles Jonkel, an expert on bears and professor of research at the University of Montana; and wildlife biologist David Shea.

Costs, Accommodations: Course fees, which include instruction, transportation, and college credit, are payable with application and range from $90 to $200; one-day explorations cost $20 for individuals, $30 for two family members, and $8 for each additional member. An 80% refund is granted cancellations at least two weeks prior to workshop, 50% refund two days to two weeks prior, no refunds thereafter. Lodging options include cabins at the Institute facility, nearby campgrounds, and motels in the West Glacier area. Participants may cook in the basic kitchen at the Institute or purchase meals at nearby cafes and restaurants.

Location, Facilities: Glacier National Park, located on the Canadian border in northwestern Montana, offers a rich variety of wildlife and diverse glaciated landscapes ranging from alpine cirques to broad forested valleys.

Contact: The Glacier Institute, P.O. Box 1457A, Kalispell, MT 59903; (406) 752-5222 or (406) 888-5215 (June 15-Aug. 15).

GREAT JOURNEYS
Jameson Travel, Inc.
Ipswich, Massachusetts
Five to nineteen-day tours in the U.S. and abroad

Established in 1978, Great Journeys sponsors a variety of cultural and historical tours, including a series of **Campaigns of the Civil War.** Some programs are planned to take advantage of seasonal events, such as the **Scottish Festivals in the Highlands,** while others emphasize a specific locale or period in history. These are not study tours and readings are not required, however bibliographies are available.

Approximately eight historical itineraries are offered abroad, each designed in conjunction with the historian who leads it and operated in partnership with the History Book Club of Stamford, Connecticut. Programs, which range from 15 to 19 days and are generally limited to 32 participants, include The Legacy of British India, Imperial Egypt & the Nile Cruise, Salisbury Plain & Megalithic Brittany, Imperial Russia: Georgia & the Caucasus, The Age of the Tudors & Sites of the 100 Years' War, Roman Asia: The Turkish Coast & Islands, and Pilgrimage to Santiago.

Campaigns of the Civil War, five historian-escorted tours designed for Civil War enthusiasts, include walks through the battlefields, discussions of tactics and maneuvers, and interpretations of the military events. Tours, which range from five to nine days, include War in the Trans-Mississippi, Gettysburg, and Grant and Lee — The Road to Appomattox.

Great Journeys also offers a variety of cultural tours in England, Scotland, France and the U.S. International programs include Wales & the Welsh Marches, Undiscovered Villages of France, London Theatre Week, and Scottish Highlands & Festivals; domestic programs include Antebellum South, Santa Fe & the American Southwest, and The Hudson River Valley & New England Tour.

Specialties: Historical, military, and cultural tours in the U.S. and abroad.

Faculty: Historical and military tours are accompanied by authorities in their fields, including Dr. Priscilla Roosevelt of Washington's Catholic University, John Gillingham of the London School of Economics, British archaeologist Dr. Aubrey Burl, James Powers of Holy Cross College, Dr. Michael Grant, formerly of Edinburgh University, and Civil War historians Ed Bearss and John Hennessy. Cultural tours are led by knowledgable guides.

Costs, Accommodations: Costs range from $3,500 to $4,500 for historical tours, $500 to $1,100 for military tours, and $1,600 to $3,300 for cultural tours. International tours include round-trip airfare from/to the U.S., double occupancy accommodations (single supplement available), most meals, ground transportation, and all scheduled activities. Lodging is provided in comfortable hotels and inns that reflect the local culture. Deposit ($300 to $500 for international tours, $100 for domestic tours) must accompany reservation with balance due 60 days prior to departure. Cancellation fee ranges from $25 (at least 60 days prior) to 25% of tour cost plus nonrecoverable expenses (within seven days).

Contact: Great Journeys, Jameson Travel, Inc., P.O. Box 669, Ipswich, MA
01938; (800) 225-2553 *or* (508) 356-1272 (in Mass.).

HF HOLIDAYS LIMITED
Great Britain
Weekend and one-week holidays year-round

Established more than 75 years ago, the nonprofit HF offers a wide variety
of special interest holidays, such as natural history, birdwatching, literature,
British heritage, garden visits, music weeks, dancing, sports, and bridge, as
well as arts and crafts for adults of all levels. Both the natural history and
birdwatching holidays include explorations to a variety of Britain's countryside locations. The literature programs combine visits to the locales that
inspired England's great authors with discussions about the writers and their
works. British Heritage consists of visits to historic and culturally significant
sites. Evening activities include slide shows, lectures, and excursions.

Specialties: A variety of topics, including natural history, literature, and
British heritage.

Faculty: Instructors and professionals in their fields.

Costs, Accommodations: Cost, which includes double occupancy lodging
and full board, ranges from £99 for a weekend holiday to £245 for a week
(seven nights). Single supplement is available. A £5 reduction is granted
paid-in-full reservations prior to the end of February. Participants usually
stay in HF-owned country houses with lounges, game rooms and, in some
cases, tennis courts, libraries, and heated swimming pools.

Location: More than 20 resort locales in Great Britain, including Loch Leven
and Loch Awe in the Scottish Highlands, Conwy in North Wales, Derwent-
twater and Conistonwater in the Lake District, Bourton-on-the-Water in the
Cotswolds, and Lyme Regis and Swanage in Dorset.

Contact: HF Holidays Limited, 142-144 Great North Way, London NW4
1EG, England; Administration (44) 81 203 3381, Reservations (44) 81 203
0433, Fax (44) 81 203 1114.

HERITAGE GENEALOGICAL TOURS
Pennsylvania German Research Society (PGR)
Sugarloaf, Pennsylvania
13 and 19-day tours of Germany, Austria, and Switzerland

The Pennsylvania German Research Society offers two tours a year, in the
spring and fall, for those who want to research their heritage and family
history in the homeland of their ancestors. Each tour emphasizes the culture
and philosophies of the Germanic countries and includes individual research
recommendations and assistance, designated archive stops, sightseeing with
discussions of local history, and regional entertainment. College credit is

available through Nicholls State University.

Specialties: Genealogical research in the Germanic countries.

Faculty: Each tour is accompanied by a professional genealogist.

Costs, Accommodations: Land costs, which include double occupancy hotel lodging (single supplement available) and some meals, range from $1,793 to $2,319. A nonrefundable $300 deposit must accompany application with balance due 90 days prior to departure. Cancellations within 90 days forfeit deposit plus nonrecoverable costs. Annual PGR membership dues are $16. Members receive a quarterly bulletin, access to the research library, a computerized Germanic surname exchange, and ancestral searches.

Location: Tour stops include Heidelberg, Munich, Kaiserslautern, Oberammergau, Vienna, and Lucerne.

Contact: The Heritage Tours, Pennsylvania German Research Society, RR 1 Box 478, Sugarloaf, PA 18249; (717) 788-5133.

HIGH MUSEUM OF ART TRAVEL PROGRAMS
Atlanta, Georgia
One-day to two-week domestic and international trips

Since 1982, Atlanta's High Museum has offered art-oriented trips for its members. Approximately a dozen trips are scheduled annually, each limited to 25 to 50 participants and planned by the travel committee of the Members Guild. Day trips to nearby locales and three and four-day weekend tours, scheduled to such cities as Asheville, Baltimore, Boston, Phoenix, and Washington, D.C., usually focus on current museum exhibitions and often include visits to private collections and artists' studios. Trips abroad may include such destinations as East and West Berlin, with visits to private collections; Belgium and Holland, featuring the Van Gogh retrospective commemorating the centennial of his death; and Egypt, with a Nile cruise from Cairo to Aswan and visits to the ancient monuments.

Specialties: Trips emphasizing art.

Faculty: Tours are led by guest lecturers.

Costs: Day trips range from $45 to $55. Costs, which include round-trip airfare, accommodations, and meals, range from $1,000 to $1,500 for three and four-day weekend trips and from $2,350 to $4,400 for travel abroad. Deposit, which must accompany reservation, ranges from full payment for day trips to $500 for two-week tours. Museum membership ($40 individual, $50 family) is required for participation in travel programs. Additional membership benefits include free museum admission, priority entrance to special exhibitions, the Members Calendar, invitations to previews and parties, and priority appointments for the monthly Curators Clinic.

Contact: Members Guild Office, High Museum of Art, 1280 Peachtree St., N.E., Atlanta, GA 30309; (404) 898-1152.

HUCKLEBERRY FINN UNIVERSITY
Detours
Rock Island, Illinois

Two to five-day Mississippi River expeditions from June-September

Since 1988, Detours adventure travel company has offered Huckleberry Finn University expeditions that explore the characters, the history and literature, and the art and architecture of the 700-mile stretch of the Mississippi River Valley from St. Paul to St. Louis. More than 30 houseboat trips are scheduled during the summer, each including overnight stays in historic inns, on-shore visits to museums and historic sites, and informal sessions in melodrama, 19th century politics, songwriting, poetry, and birdwatching.

Specialties: The history, lore, and culture of the Mississippi Valley.

Faculty: College professors and other specialists.

Costs, Accommodations: Costs are approximately $150 per day, which includes lodging (country inns, bed & breakfasts), river travel, ground transportation, two meals, and planned activities. A 50% deposit must accompany registration with balance due 10 days prior to trip. Credit cards (VISA, MasterCard, American Express) are accepted. Full refund is granted cancellations more than ten days prior; thereafter a 25% fee is assessed.

Location: Stretches of the Mississippi River between St. Paul and St. Louis.

Contact: Detours, 1705 Second Ave., Suite 422, Rock Island, IL 61201; (800) 369-3061 *or* (309) 788-8687.

THE HUMANITIES INSTITUTE
Belmont, Massachusetts

Five-day to three-week domestic and international programs

Established in 1976 by Dr. William R. Mueller, former Chairman of the English Department at Goucher College, the Humanities Institute sponsors 15 to 20 Travel and Learn programs annually that offer academic/cultural content in art, education, language, literature, or history. Designed primarily for adults desiring personal enrichment, many of the programs include 12 to 15 hours of classroom work and grant three optional undergraduate or graduate credits from the University of North Carolina (Greensboro) or Lesley College in Cambridge, Massachusetts. Others have a cultural, historical, or literary focus and are offered on a noncredit basis in cooperation with the School of Continuing Studies at the University of Toronto. All attendees are expected to complete class reading assignments while those receiving credit must fulfill additional written requirements. The programs also include evening lectures, wine and cheese parties, and afternoon and weekend field trips.

Travel and Learn in Cambridge, England, an annual 19-day summer program planned to coincide with the Cambridge Arts Festival, offers a choice of five concurrent morning courses, including such titles as Dramatic

Forms and Literary Techniques in Shakespeare, British Fiction of the Early Modern Period, and Drama Skills Workshop, in which students study and act out scenes from the dramas of Euripedes, Shakespeare, Ibsen, Chekov, Pinter, Brecht, and others. Each course is limited to 25 students, who can join an optional four-day excursion to Bath and/or a day tour and theater performance at Stratford-Upon-Avon. **Travel and Learn in Greece**, an 18-day summer program offered since 1987, traces the oral and literary traditions in Greek literature. Excursions include Gortys, Matala, Sparta, Olympia, Athens, Cape Sounion, and Delphi. Spring programs include The Cultural Influences on Life in the Antebellum South (Mississippi and Louisiana) and Egypt Beyond the Pyramids and fall/winter programs feature Renaissance Art and Architecture (Italy), Australian Contrasts, and Leafing Through New England History. Noncredit programs include **Travel and Learn in Israel**, in which participants learn the basics of archaeological fieldwork, assist in excavating at the Phoenecian site of Achziv, and attend lectures.

Specialties: Travel programs with academic/cultural emphasis on art, education, language, literature, or history.

Faculty: Humanities Institute Director Martha B. Mueller, Ph.D., daughter of the founder, graduated Phi Beta Kappa from Brown University and earned her doctorate in political science from Brandeis University. All programs are conducted by professors or tour leaders who are from the area of the tour and have demonstrated teaching ability.

Costs, Accommodations: Most programs range in cost from $2,200 to $4,400, which includes round-trip airfare, double occupancy accommodations (single supplement available), some meals, tuition, and some excursions. Credit cost is $175 for three semester-hours. A $250 deposit must accompany registration with balance payable in two installments, four and three months prior. Cancellations six months prior receive full refund; cancellation penalty ranges from $150 (four months prior) to $650 (two months prior); no refund thereafter.

Location: In addition to the above, includes Canada, Austria, Czechoslovakia, France, Hungary, Japan, Scotland, and the Soviet Union.

Contact: Dr. Martha Mueller, The Humanities Institute, P.O. Box 18-SH, Belmont, MA 02178; (800) 327-1657 *or* (617) 484-3191.

INDIANA UNIVERSITY MINI UNIVERSITY
Bloomington, Indiana

Five days in June

Since 1971, the Indiana University Alumni Association and School of Continuing Studies-Bloomington has sponsored Mini University, a five-day family vacation program that hosts up to 500 participants who can in enroll in any number of more than 100 discussion courses in the arts, humanities, business, domestic and international issues, human growth and development, science, and health, fitness, and leisure. Classes are scheduled mornings and afternoons from Monday until Friday morning with evenings reserved for such activities as picnics, tours, sports, receptions, theatre performances, and rap sessions. The children's program, for ages 5 to 16, offers instruction in gymnastics and sports skills by the School of Health, Physical Education, and Recreation staff, and 2 to 5-year-olds are cared for by a state-licensed nursery.

Typical course titles include The World of Shakespeare's Theatre, Managerial Ethics and Social Responsibility, The Ethics of the News Media, Teaching Teenagers About AIDS, Interpersonal Diplomacy: How to Get Along in Difficult Situations, The Archaeology of Indiana, Recent American Novels: A Sense of Place, Israel and the Palestinians, An Update on South African Politics, The Real and Illusionary Roles of Vitamins and Minerals in Health and Disease, and The Coevolution of Life Forms and Our Global Environment.

Specialties: A variety of topics, including art, business, domestic and foreign issues, human growth and development, humanities, science, and health.

Faculty: All courses are taught by Indiana University faculty members.

Costs, Accommodations: The registration fee, which covers the course program, is $80 per adult, $60 per child. Dormitory housing begins at $150 single, $250 double occupancy.

Contact: Mini University, Indiana University Alumni Association, Indiana Memorial Union M-17, Bloomington, IN 47405; (812) 855-1711.

INNERASIA EXPEDITIONS
San Francisco, California

Two to five-week trips to Asia, Alaska, Japan, and South America

Established in 1981, this travel organization specializes in exotic destinations in Asia and the Pacific, with emphasis on culture/education, wildlife/natural history, and/or walking/trekking. Some trips are organized as customized academic itineraries for special groups, such as the Society for Asian Art and Stanford University, but are open to anyone who shares the interests of the group.

Specialties: Art, culture, natural history.

Faculty: Programs are led by faculty of the sponsoring organization.

Costs, Accommodations: Land costs average $2,500 to $3,000, which includes deluxe double occupancy accommodations, some meals, and transportation during the trip. A $300 deposit must accompany application with 50% of land cost due 90 days prior to departure and balance plus airfare due 60 days prior. Cancellation penalty ranges from $100 (more than 60 days prior) to 75% of land cost (less than 15 days prior). Credit cards (VISA, MasterCard, American Express) accepted.

Contact: InnerAsia Expeditions, Inc., 2627 Lombard St., San Francisco, CA 94123; (800) 777-8183 *or* (415) 922-0448.

THE INSTITUTE FOR BRITISH AND IRISH STUDIES (IBIS)
Almont, Colorado and Dublin, Ireland

Two to ten-week summer term; three-month terms during academic year (October-June)

Founded in 1980 by a group of academics, each of whom had graduated or was associated with one of the sponsoring universities, the Institute for British and Irish Studies aims to provide undergraduates, graduates, and mature students with the opportunity to study with British and Irish professors in an historic environment. The Summer Programme at Oxford, Cambridge, and Dublin affords students the opportunity to register any week for any number of weeks, with a minimum of two and maximum of ten. In addition to an application form and fee, prospective students are required to submit three recommendations, writing sample, and a written statement of purpose. Undergraduates must also provide a transcript and graded writing sample. Personal and telephone interviews are available. Those desiring academic credit must complete weekly assignments and pass the final exam and may apply through their own college.

The basic tool for instruction is the tutorial — a weekly meeting between a tutor and one or two students in which assigned reading and written work is discussed. The goal of the program is scholarship, derived from an attitude of cooperation between pupil and tutor. Students may register for credit or enrichment, however most take one or two tutorial courses for credit, with each course requiring 20 to 25 hours weekly for reading, essay preparation, and tutorial meetings. Introductory level tutorials may be supplemented by lecture classes that provide general background information. Lecture enrollment ranges from 10 to 15 students in the summer and 10 to 40 during the academic year. More than 800 tutorials are offered in anthropology/sociology, architecture, art history, biology, chemistry, classics, criminology, economics, education, English, history, languages, law, literature, mathematics, music, philosophy, physics, political science, psychology, religion, and women's studies. The tutorials offer complete flexibility and are tailored precisely to each student's background, motivation, and ability. Students may study virtually any subject they desire. Professional development tutorials, for doctors, lawyers, dentists, architects, executives, teachers, and clergy, enable professionals to work with their British or Irish counterparts in nearly any subject.

Visiting students are integrated into the student body and are expected to participate in the wide variety of activities that are offered. In addition, summer weekends feature excursions to surrounding areas and evening performances. A pre-study one or two-week travel program, designed for students who would like to visit cultural and historic sites that are inaccessible via public transportation, is scheduled prior to the summer session.

Specialties: More than 800 topics as well as custom-designed courses.

Faculty: Professors of the sponsoring universities.

Costs, Accommodations: Cost of the Summer Programme ranges from approximately $2,000 for two weeks to $7,000 for ten weeks, which includes tutorials, college services, private room and board, receptions, weekend excursions, and tickets for cultural events. Cost of the three-month term is $6,670. A $45 nonrefundable fee must accompany application with a $700 deposit required within one month of acceptance. Cancellation penalty ranges from 30% of deposit (six to eight weeks prior to program) to 90% (two to four weeks prior); no refund thereafter.

Location: Oxford (Magdalen, Manchester, New College, Plater, St. Anne's, St. Stephen's House, University, Westminster, and Wolfson); Cambridge (particularly strong in the field of English literature); Trinity College in Dublin; and University of London (Birkbeck College, The Hansard Society).

Contact: IBIS, USA Information Office, Camford House, Almont CO 81210; (303) 248-0477, Fax (303) 641-2853 *or* IBIS, Front Suite, First Floor, Dublin 2, Ireland; (353) 21-618490, Fax (353) 21-618493.

INTERHOSTEL
University of New Hampshire (UNH)
Durham, New Hampshire

Two to three-week international programs year-round

Established in 1980 by University of New Hampshire Continuing Education and Summer Session, INTERHOSTEL offers approximately 35 programs each year for intellectually alert and physically active adults over 50 years of age (or at least 40 and accompanied by someone who is over 50). Developed to provide international learning opportunities, promote cross-cultural understanding, and give participants a greater appreciation for other lands and peoples, each program is designed with the cooperation of an overseas university or other educational institution. Presentations are led by resident experts and cover a broad range of topics, including the region's history, politics, natural environment, economics, literature, arts, and music. Excursions to sites of historical or cultural significance enhance classroom learning and planned activities allow participants to meet with local residents. Most programs are approximately two weeks in length (three weeks to more remote locations) and average 30 participants (40 maximum).

The program locales include major cities and cultural centers. A two-week program, East Meets West, features five days of excursions in West Berlin, with field trips to the Berlin Wall, Platz der Akademie, and the Bodemuseum and lectures at the Free University of Berlin, the host institution, that cover such subjects as the city's political past, present, and future. The group then travels to Leipzig for five days, where scheduled activities include tours that are guided by Karl Marx University representatives and a visit to Dresden; the final three days are spent in Hamburg, where local experts lecture on the city's culture, history, and economy and conduct tours of places of interest. Bangkok and Phuket, Thailand, a two-week program hosted by Bangkok University, consists of lectures on Thai history, customs, religion, politics, and classical music and dance combined with tours of museums, temples, and other important sites. The final portion of the tour is held at Phuket Island, where students attend lectures on island history, industry, ecology, marine life, and Thai festivals and holidays, and participate in the traditional moonlight festival called Loy Krathong.

Specialties: International educational and cultural programs for mature adults.

Faculty: All programs are conducted by an educational institution in the host country. Lectures and seminars are conducted by faculty members and/or resident experts. A UNH representative accompanies each group and acts as a liaison-in-residence between INTERHOSTEL and the host institution.

Costs, Accommodations: Ground costs range from $1,100 to $1,850 and include double occupancy accommodations (single supplement may be available), all meals, ground transportation, educational program, and scheduled activities. Participants are required to book air transportation on group-designated flights through the INTERHOSTEL-contracted travel agent. Lodgings are provided in multi-unit residence halls with shared baths or modest hotels that may or may not have private baths and most meals are served at the host institution's facilities. A nonrefundable $200 deposit, payable by check, VISA, American Express, or MasterCard, reserves a space with balance due approximately two months prior to departure. A 50% refund of balance is granted cancellations at least 45 days prior; no refund thereafter.

Location: In addition to the above, program locations include Australia, New Zealand, Mexico, China, Costa Rica, Kenya, Puerto Rico, Soviet Union, Thailand, and more than a dozen European countries.

Contact: INTERHOSTEL, 6 Garrison Ave., Durham, NH 03824; (800) 733-9753.

INTERNATIONAL ACADEMIC PROJECTS SUMMER SCHOOLS
The Institute of Archaeology, University of London
London, England

Five-day courses in the United Kingdom and other locations

International Academic Projects, an educational charity that provides education and training primarily in the areas of conservation, archaeology, and museum studies, was formed in 1989 to run courses at the Institute of Archaeology of the University of London, elsewhere in the United Kingdom, and other locations. The Summer Schools, established in 1983, offer more than 40 intensive courses annually, many in conjunction with such institutions as English Heritage, Museums and Galleries Commission, and the Smithsonian Institution. Enrollment is limited to 4 to 25 participants, depending on course, who receive up to seven hours of instruction daily. Visits to museums in and around London are also part of the program.

Courses suited to the novice include **Archaeological Excavation Techniques**, which covers the recording of plans and sections, wet and dry sieving, sampling and finds processing, and an introduction to archaeological surveying, photography, and conservation. **Archaeology of North West England** uses a combination of lectures and site tours to trace the development of this region from the days of its garrisoning by the Romans in the 1st century A.D. **Discovery and Exploration of Ancient Egypt**, of interest to those with some knowledge of Egyptian history, covers aspects of the development of field archaeology in the Nile delta and valley and desert regions of Egypt and analyzes the current state of the discipline. Hands-on experience is provided with sessions in the Petrie Museum teaching collection and handling of Egyptian ceramics.

Specialties: Conservation, archaeology, and museum studies.

Faculty: Summer Schools coordinator James Black was Lecturer in the Department of Conservation at the University of London and trained in Italy as a wall paintings restorer. Faculty includes conservators, college professors, art historians, and other specialists.

Costs, Accommodations: Tuition ranges from $350 to $995, which includes materials, use of equipment, and course handbook. Full payment must accompany registration. Bed and breakfast lodging is $210 per week. A $15 nonrefundable booking fee and 10% deposit secures a booking. Credit cards (MasterCard, Access, VISA) accepted. Cancellations prior to June 1 receive a full refund less $25 fee and lodging deposit. Scholarships may be available.

Contact: James Black, Coordinator, Summer Schools, 31-34 Gordon Square, London WC1H 0PY, England; (44) 71 387 9651.

INTERNATIONAL RAIN FOREST WORKSHOP
International Expeditions, Inc.
Birmingham, Alabama
Eight-day March program in Peru

The 1st Annual International Rain Forest Workshop, designed to stimulate appreciation and understanding of the rain forest and its contribution to global ecology, is scheduled for March, 1991, in Peru's Amazon jungles. Hands-on workshops devoted to topics that range from rain forest dynamics to man and conservation also focus on cooperation between nations and institutions in the utilization of resources and the promoting of ecotourism. Another aim of the program is to generate funds for the Amazon Center for Environmental Education and Research to be built on a 4,200-acre preserve of primary forest on the Sucusari River near Iquitos. Developed by International Expeditions, Inc., the event is co-sponsored by the Iquitos, Peru-based Exploraciones Amazonicas, and the Lima-based Peruvian Foundation for the Conservation of Nature. International Expeditions also offers a variety of world-wide travel programs that promote the philosophy of environmental awareness and conservation through tourism.

Specialties: Rain forest ecology and conservation.

Faculty: Approximately 15 distinguished natural scientists from the U.S. and Peru.

Costs, Accommodations: Workshop fee, all-inclusive from Miami, is $1,298.

Contact: International Expeditions, Inc., 1776 Independence Ct., Birmingham, AL 35216; (800) 633-4734 *or* (205) 870-5550.

INTERNATIONAL RESEARCH EXPEDITIONS (IRE)
Menlo Park, California
One to three-week expeditions throughout the world

Established in 1985, the nonprofit International Research Expeditions offers approximately 30 expeditions annually that bring field research scientists together with five to ten volunteers of all ages who provide assistance with their projects. Research topics include anthropology, archaeology, botany, ecology, entomology, marine biology, ornithology, primatology, and zoology. No special expertise is required but some skills are helpful for certain projects.

Africa in the New World, an investigation of the native food, clothing, traditions of folk medicine, marriage, kinship, and courtship of Barbados residents of African descent, involves volunteers in log keeping, photography, and the taking of life histories. An investigation of the alarm calls of the Red-backed Hawk of the Juan Fernandez Islands, Chile, requires volunteers to trap birds for measurement and banding studies and assist in nest site, prey, habitat, and distribution observations. A series of excavations in the Four Corners region of the U.S. Southwest includes documentation of Anasazi ruins on Lake Powell, behind-the-scenes museum work at the Bureau of Land Management's Anasazi Heritage Center, and a systematic survey of southeast Utah canyons, which requires location, documentation, mapping, and photographing of sites.

Specialties: Research expeditions in anthropology, archaeology, botany, ecology, entomology, marine biology, ornithology, primatology, zoology.

Faculty: Scientists involved in research in the field.

Costs, Accommodations: Tax deductible contribution ranges from $425 to $1,790, which includes ground transportation, meals, accommodations that range from tent camps to first class hotels, and orientation materials. A $200 deposit must accompany application with balance due 90 days prior to expedition. Credit cards (VISA, MasterCard, American Express) accepted. Deposit is refundable within 15 days of receiving a detailed project description. Project descriptions are $10 each for non-volunteers. Membership in IRE is $25, which entitles contributors to receive quarterly publications on discoveries in the field and updates on ongoing and future expeditions.

Location: Locations in Africa, Asia, the Caribbean, Europe, North, Central, and South America, Australia, and islands in the South Pacific.

Contact: International Research Expeditions, 140 University Dr., Menlo Park, CA 94025; (415) 323-4228.

INTERNATIONAL SUMMER SCHOOL IN IRISH STUDIES
University College, Cork (UCC)
Ireland

Four-week July on-campus program

Since 1979, University College, Cork has offered a summer school program in Irish studies that consists of lectures, films, day-long field trips, and visits to sites of cultural and historical importance. The four-week integrated course, which is open to scholars, students, and all interested individuals, focuses on understanding Irish identity and culture through its history and literature, including music, archaeology, folklore, geography, art, education, and sociology. A twelve-hour introductory course in Irish is available and tutors are appointed to assist students with research topics and individual pursuits. Students desiring academic credit (three in history, three in literature) are assigned papers and/or examinations at the end of the course. UCC, established in 1845 and now a Constituent College of the National University of Ireland, also offers a variety of undergraduate, postgraduate, and research programs.

Specialties: Irish studies, with focus on history and literature.

Faculty: Senior Professors and Lecturers from the UCC Faculty of Arts, including Academic Director John Murphy, UCC Senator Professor and author of *Ireland in the Twentieth Century*; Course Director Dr. Máirtin O Fathaigh; and invited guest speakers.

Cost, Accomodations: Cost, which includes tuition, bed and breakfast in nearby guest houses, and travel and meals on field trips, is IR£850. An IR£100 deposit is due one month prior and is not refundable thereafter. A limited number of scholarships are offered.

Location: Cork, the second largest city of the Republic of Ireland, is situated on the southern coast, 160 miles south of Dublin, 250 miles south of Belfast, and 75 miles from Shannon International Airport. UCC is within easy walking distance of the city center. The city and county have a rich archaeological cultural heritage and the Irish language is spoken as a vernacular in several nearby communities.

Contact: Dr. Máirton O Fathaigh, Director, Summer School in Irish Studies, Dept. of Education, University College, Cork, Ireland; (44) 353-21-276871, Fax (44) 353-21-275948.

INTERNATIONAL ZOOLOGICAL EXPEDITIONS, INC. (IZE)
Sherborn, Massachusetts

One to three-week Belize expeditions from December-August

International Zoological Expeditions, Inc., established in 1970, conducts more than 20 Belize expeditions annually for groups ranging from 1 to 150 participants. Programs, many of which are co-sponsored by schools and colleges, may be general in nature or focus on a specific aspect of the region, such as its birds, wildlife, coral reefs, or rainforests. Credit is available for teachers and students.

During the annual eight-day **August Herpetology Expedition,** offered since 1981, participants spend days and nights in the rain forest keying and photographing herps for a journal to be published with the cumulative findings. Two days at the cayes are devoted to visiting isolated populations of boa constrictors and ground iguanas. Other programs include a general wildlife expedition that explores the interior's primary rain forests and marine ecosystems of the Western Hemisphere's longest barrier reef; a birding expedition to the Crooked Tree Wildlife Sanctuary and Jaguar Preserve; a special expedition focusing on the area's primitive and remote peoples, rainforests, and Kekchi and Maya indian villages; a mini-course in tropical marine biology; a Venezuelan tropical natural history trip; and an excursion that includes one week in Costa Rica's national parks.

Specialties: Wildlife and ecology of Belize.

Faculty: Tour leaders, all experienced in the study and research of the tropical biology and ecology of Belize, include Dr. Jim Parker, Dr. Phil Savoie, and IZE Director Fred Dodd.

Costs, Accommodations: Approximate land costs, which include meals, ground transportation, and lodging, range from $349 to $1,999. All flights must be arranged through IZE.

Location: Roughly the size of Massachusetts, Belize borders Mexico on the Yucatan Peninsula. Its diverse natural habitat includes lowland savannahs, tropical rain forests, more than 250 cayes and inland waterways, mangrove swamps, sea bird rookeries, and an extensive barrier reef.

Contact: International Zoological Expeditions, Inc., 210 Washington St., Sherborn, MA 01770; (508) 655-1461.

INTERSEA RESEARCH, INC.
Friday Harbor, Washington
Ten-day expeditions in Southeast Alaska and the South Pacific

Established in 1979, Intersea Research Inc. conducts eight oceanographic research expeditions a year that focus on the endangered humpback whale. Each voyage is limited to 14 participants who examine in depth the whale's relationship to the environment and other species, including prey, other marine animals, and humans. Participants have the opportunity to actively assist the ship's scientist in such optional daily activities as collecting data and samples, locating and identifying marine mammals and birds and examining their ecological requirements, and documenting and correlating whale feeding behaviors using the ship's computers. During encounters with whales, participants may also assist in the photographic documentation of individuals and subsequently process film for catalogue identification and population estimation. Evenings are typically devoted to lectures and slide show/ discussions that cover the marine mammals, birdlife, and natural history of the area, as well as the history of ships. Frequent island stops are scheduled.

Specialties: Natural history research expeditions that focus on the humpback whale.

Faculty: Core staff includes Founding Director and President Russell Nilson, an experienced ship's captain and former Executive Director of Ocean Research Under Sail (ORUS); Vice President and Program Director Cynthia D'Vincent, a specialist in the study of whales, contract field biologist for the National Marine Fisheries Service since 1974, and author of *Voyaging with the Whales*; and Research Director Garv Hoefler, who has led natural history expeditions for 15 years.

Costs, Accommodations: Voyage cost is $2,490. A $600 deposit must accompany application with balance due the earlier of March 1 or four months prior to departure. Cancellations prior to March 1 receive an 80% refund; between 45 and 90 days prior, refund is 50%; no refunds thereafter.

Location: June to September expeditions are conducted aboard a 126-foot luxury diesel yacht in the whale feeding area of Southeast Alaska. Voyages are planned throughout the islands of the South Pacific to study the Southern Hemisphere humpback whales.

Contact: Intersea Research, Inc., P.O. Box 1667, Friday Harbor, WA 98250; (206) 378-5980.

THE JOHNS HOPKINS UNIVERSITY ALUMNI COLLEGES
Baltimore, Maryland

One-week summer programs

The Johns Hopkins University Alumni College offers approximately two week-long summer programs, each year on different topics. All programs feature in-depth daily lectures, discussions, and field trips to related sites.

Representative titles include America's Southwest: The Land and the Culture, which is based in Santa Fe and includes lectures and discussions of the area's geologic history and evolution, native art, and the three indigenous cultures — Anglo, Hispanic, and Indian — as well as field excursions to Taos and Tierra Amarilla, museum tours, and operatic performances; and The Civil War, which is held at a West Virginia resort/conference center and explores such topics as military strategies and campaigns, social and political issues, prominent leaders and personalities of both sides, music of the era, and the question of historical preservation of battlefields. Field trips to Harper's Ferry, Antietam, and Gettysburg are also scheduled.

Specialties: A variety of topics.

Faculty: Three to five professors from Johns Hopkins and other universities conduct each program.

Costs, Accommodations: Costs, which include lodging, most meals, books, and planned excursions, range from $845 to $995; single supplement is available. A $50 deposit must accompany reservation; due date of final payment varies. No refunds are granted cancellations after final payment date unless space can be filled. Credit cards (VISA, MasterCard) accepted.

Contact: The Johns Hopkins University Alumni Colleges, Steinwald Alumni House, 3211 N. Charles St., Baltimore, MD 21218; (301) 338-7963.

JOURNEYS
Seattle, Washington
Eleven to nineteen-day international trips

Established in 1978, Journeys offers trips to Central and South America that focus on natural history, ecology, birds, archaeology, and photographic opportunities of the regions visited. Group size is limited to 10 to 14 participants and itineraries include the Ruta Maya Odyssey, focusing on Mexico's archaeological sites; Patagonian Wildlands Safari, emphasizing the region's wildlife; and Costa Rica Tropical Odyssey, which features visits to the Carara Biological Reserve and the Marenco Biological Station.

Specialties: Natural history, birds, archaeology, photography.

Faculty: Includes ornithologist Hector Ceballos-Lascurain, co-author of *Birds of Mexico City*, and naturalist-ornithologist Ricardo Clark, author of *The Birds of Tierra del Fuego.*

Costs, Accommodations: Land costs range from $1,600 to $2,000, which includes double occupancy accommodations, most meals, and ground and air transportation during the trip. A minimum $300 deposit must accompany reservation with balance due 60 days prior to departure. Cancellation penalty ranges from $100 (more than 60 days prior) to 70% of land cost (from three to nine days prior).

Contact: Journeys, 3516 NE 155th St., Suite K, Seattle, WA 98155; (800) 345-4453 *or* (206) 365-0686.

JOURNEYS EAST
San Francisco, California
16-day Japan tours in spring and fall

Established in 1984 by Davis Everett and Debra Loomis, Journeys East offers four tour itineraries that explore various aspects of Japanese culture and cuisine. Each tour is scheduled three or four times annually and limited to 10 to 16 participants of all ages. **Mountains, Temples, and Hamlets** blends outdoor and cultural adventure; **From Farmhouse to Teahouse** focuses on folk architecture and regional cuisine; **Brushes with the Past and Present,** a highlights trip, includes meetings with artists and performers with emphasis on the evolution of traditional disciplines into modern gardens, textiles, fashions, and theater; and **Inner Japan: From Sumo to Zen** features visits to temples and shrines and discussions of past and present philosophies with Buddhist monks and Shinto priests.

Specialties: The culture and cuisine of Japan.

Faculty: Tours are led by Debra Loomis, formerly an actress, toy designer, and attorney, and her husband, Davis Everett, who was an anthropology major at Harvard and has been a National Geographic Wilderness Coordinator and Alaskan river and mountain guide. Both have traveled extensively in Japan.

Costs, Accommodations: Land costs, which include double occupancy lodging (single supplement available), most meals, ground transportation, and scheduled activities, range from $2,685 to $2,985. Accommodations include inns, mountain lodges, and Japanese-style hotels. Round-trip airfare from/to the U.S. ranges from $990 to $1,385. A $200 deposit secures reservation with a second payment of $400 due four months prior to departure and the final payment due 60 days prior. Cancellation fee ranges from $50 (more than five months prior) to 75% of land cost within 13 days; no refund after start of trip.

Contact: Journeys East, 2443 Fillmore St., #289B, San Francisco, CA 94115; (415) 647-9565.

JOURNEYS INTO AMERICAN INDIAN TERRITORY
Westhampton Beach, New York
One-week programs in Oklahoma

Since 1988, anthropologist Robert Vetter has offered one-week Journeys that offer 10 to 30 participants the opportunity to experience Indian life and traditions. Each Journey emphasizes a different aspect of Indian culture, including religion and spirituality, art and crafts, social relations, and music and dance. Participants travel throughout Oklahoma, home to 66 American Native tribes, and visit Indian families in their homes, learn Native American cuisine, tour burial mounds and other sacred and historic sites, participate in ceremonies and rituals, and learn about politics, values, and spirituality.

Specialties: Life and culture of American Indian people.

Faculty: Robert Vetter studied anthropology at the University of Oklahoma. Robert Field is a full-blooded Pawnee Indian and Adjunct Professor of Anthropology at the University of Oklahoma.

Costs, Accommodations: Program cost is $545, which includes van transportation and lodging in a teepee that participants learn how to set up.

Contact: Robert Vetter, Journeys Into American Indian Territory, P.O. Box 929, Westhampton Beach, NY 11978; (516) 878-8655.

KNUSTON HALL
Wellingborough, Northamptonshire, England
One-day to one-week courses year-round

Established in 1951 as an adult residential college, Knuston Hall offers more than 80 courses in a variety of topics, including literature, history, and arts and crafts. Typical courses include Ancient Egypt: The First Thousand

Years, The Home Front: Britain at War 1939-1945, and Travelers in Egypt: Then and Now.

Specialties: A variety of topics, including literature and history.

Faculty: All courses are taught by individuals who are knowledgeable in their fields.

Costs, Accommodations: Costs range from £12.50 for a day course to £171 for a one-week course, which includes meals and double occupancy lodging. Course fee must accompany application unless it is more than £60, in which case 50% is due with application and the balance two weeks prior to course. Access and VISA credit cards are accepted.

Location: Knuston Hall is situated in central Northamptonshire. The nearest railway station is Wellingborough on the London to Sheffield Line.

Contact: The Principal, Knuston Hall, Irchester, Wellingborough, Northamptonshire, NN9 7EU, England; (44) 933 312104.

LAMAR UNIVERSITY SUMMER TRAVEL PROGRAMS
Beaumont, Texas

Three-week international trips

Since 1975, Lamar University has sponsored summer programs that provide college credit and instruction combined with travel. A travel study trip to Rome, conducted by the Art Department, offers courses devoted to The Art of Ancient Rome, Studies in Italian Culture, and The Art of the Renaissance and Baroque Styles in Rome. Other activities include visits to historic and well-known sites, museums, the buildings and sculpture of the Baroque masters, and day trips and excursions to Capri and Tivoli. An orientation session and on-campus classes are scheduled prior to departure.

Specialties: Art and humanities.

Faculty: Includes Lamar University faculty member Lynne Lokensgard, Associate Professor of Art History, who specializes in Italian Renaissance and 19th century French art.

Costs, Accommodations: Program cost of $2,979 includes six college credits, round-trip airfare from/to Houston, hotel, meals, ground transportation, and guided tours. Participants may enroll for an additional three credit hours at a cost of $84. A nonrefundable $125 deposit must accompany application with balance due six weeks prior to departure.

Location: Trip locations include Italy, England, Germany, France, and Mexico.

Contact: Lamar University Summer Study Program, Division of Public Services & Continuing Education, P.O. Box 10008, Beaumont, TX 77710; (409) 880-8431.

LEARN AT LEISURE
University of Nottingham Department of Adult Education
Nottingham, England
Weekend to one-week courses in the United Kingdom

The University of Nottingham Extra-mural Department, which has offered travel-learn programs for more than 30 years, has, since 1985, marketed them under the name Learn at Leisure Educational Holidays. More than 100 courses are scheduled each year on a variety of topics, including history, nature, literature, music, archaeology, marine biology, geology, art, architecture, and arts and crafts. Courses are open to all, with enrollment limited to 15 to 25 participants.

Specialties: A variety of topics, including history, nature, literature, music, archaeology, marine biology, geology, art, and architecture.

Faculty: All tutors are academically qualified and specialists in the topic area.

Costs, Accommodations: Costs range from approximately £90 to £200, which includes bed and breakfast accommodations and scheduled activities.

Contact: Learn at Leisure (Educational Holidays), University of Nottingham, 14 Shakespeare St., Nottingham NG1 4FJ, England; (44) 602 483838, Fax (44) 602 472977.

LEARNING WEEKENDS
University of New Hampshire (UNH)
Durham, New Hampshire
Weekend programs from May-October

Learning Weekends, the University of New Hampshire's study and travel program created in 1990, offers adults the opportunity to visit and learn about famous locales in the New England area. The five scheduled weekends include day trips, lectures, and discussions that focus on the region's history, culture, and environment.

Programs include A Shaker Experience, a tour of the Canterbury Shaker Village with workshops/discussions on Shaker history, religion, furniture making, cooking, music, and dance; Land, Sea, and Literature: The Vision of Robert Frost and Celia Thaxter, an exploration of the landscapes that served as inspirations to these writers; Exploring the New Hampshire Coast, an investigation of current marine research, practices, and discoveries with visits to marine research laboratories and educational facilities along the North Atlantic, the Great Bay, and the area's tidal wetlands; and Leaf Peeping: The Wonder of Autumn, a conservation-oriented study of the forest and such problems as acid rain, climatic warming, and natural pests.

Specialties: The history, culture, and environment of famous New England locales.

Faculty: Members of the UNH faculty and local experts.

Costs, Accommodations: Costs, which include double occupancy lodging, meals, and ground transportation, range from $245 (single occupancy $300) to $395. Participants are lodged in the New England Center, a modern residential conference facility located on campus. Payment in full must accompany registration and credit cards (VISA, MasterCard) are accepted. Refund, less $50 fee, is granted written cancellations received prior to the program's registration deadline (usually two to three weeks before program); thereafter, a 50% refund is granted more than five days before; no refund within five days.

Contact: University of New Hampshire Continuing Education, 24 Rosemary Ln., Durham, NH 03824; (603) 862-1088.

LEELANAU OUTDOOR CLASSROOMS
The Leelanau Center for Education
Glen Arbor, Michigan
One-week summer workshops

Established in 1982, The Leelanau Center for Education sponsors outdoor natural history workshops, summer art workshops, and a writers conference. Approximately a half-dozen Natural History Workshops are offered in the summer, including such titles as The Nature Hiker, a series of daily hikes that concentrates on such remote habitats as dunes, meadows, bogs, forested areas, and swamps and emphasizes edible wild plants and mushrooms; Family Ecology, activities designed for the environmentally concerned family; The Natural History of Mushrooms, which focuses on the common characteristics of mushroom families and identification of the edible and poisonous species; Tunes in the Dunes, a course in field identification of various species of crickets, grasshoppers, and katydids by sight and song; and Stress Sensing, a special enrollment course with an instructor whose research activities include the early detection of stress in forest vegetation, design and completion of land cover use inventories, and environmental monitoring with low cost remote sensing systems.

Specialties: Natural history.

Faculty: Has included Ellen Elliott Weatherbee, head of the adult education program and wild plants consultant for the University of Michigan's Matthaei Botanical Gardens; Dr. Charles Olson, Jr., Professor of Natural Resources at the University of Michigan; Harvey Ballard, Preserve Design Ecologist for The Nature Conservancy; and Walter Sturgeon, consultant for the Audubon Society *Field Guide to North American Mushrooms* and contributing editor of *Mushroom.*

Costs, Accommodations: The $180 enrollment fee includes lunches and local transportation and room and board ranges from $175 to $290. A $100 deposit must accompany application. Full refund, less $15 fee, is granted cancellations more than 30 days prior to course; cancellations within 30 days forfeit deposit. Accommodations consist of on-campus single or double dormitories and rustic cabins sleeping six. Meals are served cafeteria style.

Location: The Center is located on 83 acres of forest within Sleeping Bear Dunes National Lakeshore, 30 miles west of Traverse City. Facilities include a library, tennis courts, a private beach on Lake Michigan, and canoes.

Contact: The Leelanau Center for Education, One Old Homestead Rd., Glen Arbor, MI 49636; (616) 334-3072.

LEISURE LEARNING WEEKENDS
Embassy Hotels
Burton-on-Trent, Staffordshire, England
Weekend programs from May-November in Great Britain

From late spring through fall, Embassy Hotels offers approximately 50 Leisure Learning Weekends at its more than 20 hotels throughout England. Each weekend begins at 7 pm Friday and ends Sunday afternoon and is devoted to study of a specific subject, such as art appreciation, literature, music and theatre, cities and towns, famous people, or historic houses. The programs consist of informal talks, films, and slide presentations, highlighted by visits to course-related sites.

Specialties: The cultural heritage of Great Britain.

Faculty: Course leaders, all specialists in their fields, include art historian Clare Ford-Wille and Robin Allan, actor and international lecturer.

Costs, Accommodations: Costs, which include tuition, meals, single or double occupancy accommodations, field trips, admissions fees, and VAT, range from £103 to £155. A £15 nonrefundable deposit must accompany booking. Cancellations more than one month prior to weekend may transfer deposit to another program.

Location: Embassy Hotels throughout Great Britain.

Contact: Leisure Learning Weekends, Embassy Hotels, Ltd., 107 Station St., Burton-Upon-Trent, Staffordshire DE14 1BZ; (44) 283 66587.

LIFE ENHANCEMENT TOURS
Hillsdale, New York

Six to twelve-day tours of Switzerland and Great Britain

Life Enhancement Tours sponsors travel programs that focus on the homes and locales of famous literary figures, particularly diarists. Group size is limited to approximately 25 participants.

The trip to England, Wales, and Scotland features a tour of the Letts diary and appointment book factory and visits to the homes and sites associated with Sir Walter Scott, Mary Queen of Scots, child diarist Marjorie Fleming, Queen Victoria, Robert Burns, Beatrix Potter, John Ruskin, William Wordsworth, Lady Anne Clifford and Lady Sackville, Sir Harold Nicolson, Henry James, Rudyard Kipling, Virginia Woolf, Vanessa Bell and Duncan Grant, Thomas Hardy, T.E. Lawrence, Jane Austen, Barbara Pym, Francis

Kilvert, William Shakespeare, and Sir Winston Churchill. The Switzerland tour features James Joyce, Max Frisch, Paul Klee, Richard Wagner and Cosima List, Lord Byron, and others.

Specialties: Homes and locales associated with noted diarists and literary figures.

Faculty: Tour leader Jane Begos teaches a course in women's diary literature at Ulster County Community College. She is the editor of *Women's Diaries* and is contributing editor for *Diarist's Journal*.

Costs, Accommodations: Land cost, which includes all breakfasts and some dinners, double occupancy lodging (single supplement available), ground transportation, and all planned activities, is $2,495 and optional extension is $995. A $250 deposit must accompany registration with balance due 45 days prior to departure. Cancellation penalty is $50.

Contact: Life Enhancement Tours, Inc., 47 Forest Dr., Hillsdale, NJ 07642; (800) 548-8254.

LOS ANGELES COMMUNITY COLLEGE DISTRICT (LACCD) INTERNATIONAL EDUCATIONAL PROGRAM
Los Angeles, California
Eight-day to five-week summer and spring-break study trips abroad

Established in 1977, the Los Angeles Community College District International Education Program offers college credit study tours for individuals of all ages. Fifteen programs are scheduled during spring break and summer, including such titles as Arts of Spain: The Artistic Traditions of Spain, focusing on both ancient and contemporary Spanish art and culture; Spring Theatre in London, an investigation of world theatre; Marine Biology of the Gulf of California, snorkeling off the island system in Bahia de los Angeles, Mexico, with the study of plant communities, invertebrates, fish, whales, dolphins, and sea lions; and Natural History of Costa Rica, including La Selva Biological Station. The District also sponsors language and language/culture programs abroad.

Specialties: A variety of topics, including theatre, natural history, art, culture, and foreign languages.

Faculty: Instructors are selected from the nine Los Angeles Community Colleges.

Costs, Accommodations: Costs range from $900 to $2,850, which includes round-trip airfare, ground transportation, lodging, some meals, and entrance fees. A $150 to $200 deposit must accompany application with half the balance due 90 days prior to departure and remaining balance due 60 days prior. Cancellation penalty ranges from $75 (at least 90 days prior) to $400 (7 to 29 days prior). A registration fee of from $5 to $25 is due with registration and California nonresident tuition is approximately $112 per semester unit.

Contact: International Education Program, LACCD Institute for International Programs, 855 N. Vermont Ave., Los Angeles, CA 90029; (213) 666-4255.

LOS ANGELES WORLD AFFAIRS COUNCIL
Los Angeles, California
Nine-day to three-week domestic and international tours

Established in 1953, the nonprofit Los Angeles World Affairs Council offers its members approximately a half dozen tours annually that feature private diplomatic briefings at U.S. embassies and foreign ministries. Group size is usually limited to 15 to 24 participants. The annual Week in the Capital tour of Washington, D.C., includes briefings and private receptions with experts and ambassadors of various countries and visits to the Departments of State and Defense, the White House, and Congress.

Specialties: Tours that feature briefings with government officials.

Faculty: Participants have opportunities to hear briefings by government officials on the current political, economic, and social issues confronting the regions visited.

Costs, Accommodations: Land costs range from $2,322 to $4,875, which includes a $250 tax-deductible contribution to the Los Angeles World Affairs Council, first class double occupancy accommodations (single supplement available), most meals, ground transportation, and scheduled activities. A $500 deposit must accompany reservation with balance due 45 days prior to departure. Cancellation penalty ranges from $100 (more than 60 days prior) to $200 plus nonrecoverable costs (less than 35 days prior). Annual membership dues begin at $50 for an individual, $75 for a couple, which includes a subscription to the monthly *World Affairs Journal*.

Location: International tour destinations may include Africa, Bali, China, Romania, the Soviet Union, and South America.

Contact: Ms. Louise Gessford, Director, Diplomatic Tours, Los Angeles World Affairs Council, 900 Wilshire Blvd., Suite 230, Los Angeles, CA 90017; (213) 628-2333 *or* Diplomatic Tour Dept., Travel International (213) 652-4675.

THE LOWE ART MUSEUM
The University of Miami
Coral Gables, Florida
Weekend and longer trips in the U.S. and abroad

The Lowe Art Museum sponsors trips for members and Friends that feature guided museum tours and visits to private collections and artists' studios. Groups are usually limited to 25 to 30 participants, who are accompanied by a member of the Museum's curatorial staff. Four to five-day weekend trips visit such art centers as New York City, Chicago, Dallas, and Washington, D.C. Destinations abroad may include Paris, the Greek Isles, and other cultural sites. Membership dues begin at $30 individual, $40 family. Friends dues begin at $200.

Contact: The Lowe Art Museum, 1301 Stanford Drive, Coral Gables, FL 33124-6310; (305) 284-3536.

MIT QUARTER CENTURY CLUB ALUMNI TRAVEL PROGRAM
Massachusetts Institute of Technology
Cambridge, Massachusetts

One to five-week international tours

Since 1970, MIT has offered travel programs for alumni and interested adults and currently sponsors approximately 25 tours annually to destinations worldwide. Typical itineraries include Antarctica, Canadian Rockies, Amazon River/Grenadines, South Pacific, Western Mediterranean, Britain, the Seine River, Holland and Belgium, Scandinavia, the Soviet Union, Japan, and Egypt/Jordan/Red Sea.

Specialties: Tours to popular locations throughout the world.

Faculty: Tours are accompanied by college professors or other field experts who provide cultural, historical, and scientific enrichment.

Costs: Land costs range from approximately $2,000 to $7,300. Deposit requirements and refund policies vary.

Contact: Massachusetts Institute of Technology Quarter Century Club, Room 20A-023, MIT, Cambridge, MA 02139; (617) 253-7914.

MARYLAND ZOOLOGICAL SOCIETY
Baltimore, Maryland

Day, weekend, and two to three-week domestic and international trips

The Maryland Zoological Society's travel program, established in 1980, offers day and weekend trips to zoological attractions in the U.S. and approximately three international trips annually to such locations as the Amazon region, the Galápagos Islands, and the Soviet Union. Group size is limited to 15 to 20 to participants, who are accompanied by a member of the Society's curatorial staff. The cost of international tours ranges from $1,200 to $7,000.

Contact: Curator of Education, Maryland Zoological Society, Druid Hill Park, Baltimore, MD 21217; (301) 467-4387.

MASSACHUSETTS AUDUBON SOCIETY
Wellfleet Bay Wildlife Sanctuary
South Wellfleet, Massachusetts

One-week summer courses

Since 1984, the Wellfleet Bay Wildlife Sanctuary has sponsored the Cape Cod Natural History Field School's one-week courses in natural history, writing, photography, and art that focus on the interpretation, exploration, and protection of Cape Cod and its environs. Enrollment is limited to 10 to 15 adults and emphasis is on outdoor experience complemented by indoor discussions and slide talks.

Typical courses include Diamondback Terrapin and Box Turtle Field Study, which highlights the ongoing scientific research on these species and consists of data collection, radio telemetry, sonic receiving, field observation, and mark and recapture studies; Coastal Ecology, a hands-on exploration of the coast's marine-life and the environment — saltmarshes, barrier beaches, tidal flats, and tidal creeks — they inhabit; Coastal Ornithology, an examination of the natural history, migration patterns, and breeding biology of Cape Cod's bird-life plus field visits, birding cruises, and an evening heron watch; and Cape Cod Natural History, a study of the area's birds, coastal plant communities, marine and terrestrial mammals, saltmarsh ecology, and reptiles and amphibians.

Massachusetts Audubon Society, one of the oldest conservation groups in the world and the largest in New England, is a voluntary association open to all who value preservation of the environment. Programs sponsored by the Society encompass the areas of conservation, education, and research. Wellfleet Bay Wildlife Sanctuary, one of 17 staffed sanctuaries, also presents a variety of programs dedicated to the interpretation, exploration, and protection of Cape Cod and its environs.

Specialties: Natural history of Cape Cod and its environs.

Faculty: Experts in the field of natural history.

Costs, Accommodations: Course fees range from $220 to $400 for Society members and $250 to $410 for non-members (includes one-year membership). Housing cost is $105 per week. A nonrefundable $50 deposit must accompany application with balance due 30 days prior to course. No refunds less than 30 days prior. Accommodations are shared rooms; private rooms for couples are available on a first-come, first-served basis. First and last evening dinners are included and participants are responsible for remaining meals.

Location: Wellfleet Bay Wildlife Sanctuary preserves over 700 acres of pine woods, moorland, fresh water ponds, tidal creeks, and saltmarsh. Lodging is in a secluded house with small kitchen overlooking Nauset Marsh in the Cape Cod National Seashore with a view past a barrier beach to the Atlantic Ocean.

Contact: Massachusetts Audubon Society, Wellfleet Bay Wildlife Sanctuary, P.O. Box 236, South Wellfleet, MA 02663; (508) 349-2615.

METROPOLITAN MUSEUM OF ART
Travel With the Met
New York, New York
Nine to eighteen-day international tours

New York's Metropolitan Museum of Art offers approximately a half dozen trips a year, most of them featuring cruises and visits to international destinations noted for their art, architecture, and culture. All trips include lectures and special activities. Red Sea Passage, a 12-day cruise offered nine times since 1978, includes Cairo, Dendera, Thebes, Luxor, Abu Simbel, Aqaba, and an optional five-day Sinai soujourn. The 18-day Ancient and Imperial Russia trip, limited to 24 participants, includes visits to Kiev, Tbilisi, Erevan, Moscow, Suzdal, Leningrad, and Novgorod.

Specialties: Tours with an art and culture focus.

Faculty: Trips are accompanied by a Metropolitan Museum lecturer and/or specialist in the regions visited.

Costs, Accommodations: Costs range from $5,225 to $9,080, which includes round-trip airfare from/to New York, first class shared accommodations (single supplement available), most meals, ground transportation, scheduled activities, and a tax-deductible gift to the Museum. Most tours require a 25% deposit with reservation and balance is due eight weeks prior to departure. Cancellations at least 10 weeks prior receive full refund less $100; recoverable costs are refunded thereafter.

Location: In addition to the above, locations may include Greece, Rome, Great Britain, and the Black Sea.

Contact: Raymond & Whitcomb Co., 400 Madison Ave., New York, NY 10017; (212) 759-3960.

METROPOLITAN OPERA GUILD (MOG)
MEMBERS TRAVEL PROGRAM
New York, New York
Weekend tours in New York City; one to three-week tours abroad

Established in 1984, the Members Travel Program offers members of the nonprofit Metropolitan Opera Guild approximately 25 guided opera and music tours annually throughout the world, including about a half dozen weekend tours to New York City. All tours feature specially selected operatic and other musical performances, behind-the-scenes activities, the opportunity to meet with members of the cultural community in the cities visited, deluxe accommodations, and dining at fine restaurants.

New York City weekend tours, limited to 45 participants, include a welcoming reception, most meals, sightseeing, Metropolitan Opera performances, a Broadway play, and a concert. International tours, limited to 25, feature several opera and musical performances as well as visits to historical and cultural attractions.

Specialties: Opera and music tours.

Faculty: Tour leaders are selected for their knowledge of music, art, history, and language.

Costs, Accommodations: New York City tours range from $1,469 to $1,695, which includes deluxe double occupancy accommodations (single supplement available) at the Pierre Hotel, tickets to all planned events, and most meals. Land costs for international tours range from $3,500 to $5,800, which includes deluxe double occupancy hotel accommodations (single supplement available), continental breakfasts and most meals, tickets to performances, and sightseeing attractions. A deposit of $500 (international) or $250 (New York) must accompany reservation with balance due 60 days prior to departure. Cancellation penalty ranges from $50 (more than 41 days prior) to 70% of land costs (less than 7 days prior). A voluntary contribution of $100 is requested for education purposes. Annual membership dues, which include a subscription to *Opera News* magazine, begin at $50.

Location: International tour locations include the Soviet Union, Eastern Europe, France, Germany, Austria, and the Iberian Peninsula.

Contact: Members Travel Program, Metropolitan Opera Guild, 1865 Broadway, New York, NY 10023; (212) 582-7500.

MEXI-MAYAN ACADEMIC TRAVEL, INC. (MMAT)
Chicago, Illinois

One to two-week tours to Mexico, Guatamala, South America, India, and Indonesia

Established in 1971 as a nonprofit educational organization, Mexi-Mayan Academic Travel plans trips to destinations of significant archaeological and cultural interest. Approximately six to twelve tours are offered annually, each limited to 12 to 15 participants. Itineraries include Guatamala Safari, an expedition into the heart of Peten; Sacred Places, Ritual Spaces, a study of the pyramids and temples of the Valley of Mexico; Dia de Los Muertos (Day of the Dead), scheduled during this annual Mexican celebration, which is similar to our Halloween; and Indonesia: Temples and Dancers.

Specialties: Archaeology and culture.

Faculty: Tour leaders include MMAT founders and directors Robert Stelton, archaeologist and former Fulbright Scholar, and Deb Stelton, artist and art historian; archaeologist Mark Aldenderfer of Northwestern University; and Ed Kurjack and Larry Conrad of Western Illinois University.

Costs, Accommodations: Costs range from approximately $1,000 to $2,200, which includes airfare from/to the U.S., ground transportation, accommodations, most meals, and planned activities. A $500 deposit must accompany registration. Refunds are granted less nonrecoverable costs and a service charge.

Contact: Robert Stelton, Mexi-Mayan Academic Travel, Inc., 2216 W. 112th St., Chicago, IL 60643; (312) 233-1711, Fax (313) 239-1208.

MILITARY HISTORY TOURS
Military History Quarterly (MHQ)/Great Journeys

MHQ: The Quarterly Journal of Military History, in conjunction with Great Journeys (page 78), a travel company that specializes in historical tours, offers its readers tours that focus on military history. The first tour/cruise, in October, 1990, is **Ancient Warriors and Battlefields of Asia Minor and the Greek Islands**, visiting Turkey and Greece. The program is limited to 30 participants and combines lectures, commentary, and informal discussions with visits to the sites of historic battles and campaigns from early antiquity to the 20th-century. The first half of the tour is held in Istanbul, Ankara, and Antalya, after which participants board a chartered vessel for a voyage to ancient strongholds and battlefields located in the Greek islands and along the Turkish coast. Highlights include visits to the ancient capital of the Hittite Empire, important sites of the Peloponnesian War and Crusades of the Middle Ages, Constantinople, and Gallipoli.

Specialties: Military history.

Faculty: This tour is hosted by Dr. Arther Ferrill, a professor at the University of Washington-Seattle, contributing editor to *MHQ*, and author of *Origins of War: From the Stone Age to Alexander the Great* and *Fall of the Roman Empire: The Military Explanation.*

Costs, Accommodations: Cost per person, which includes airfare, lodging, and all meals, ranges from $3,895 to $4,095; single supplement is $600. A $500 deposit must accompany application with balance due 60 days prior to departure. Cancellation fee ranges from $25 (more than 60 days prior) to 25% of tour costs plus nonrecoverable expenses (less than seven days prior). Accommodations are in deluxe main or upper deck cabins aboard a 395-ton, 30-passenger motor-vessel with a crew of 26.

Location: Turkey, Greece, and other sites of major military campaigns

Contact: Jameson Travel, Inc., P.O. Box 669, Ipswich, MA 01938; (800) 225-2553 *or* (508) 356-1272.

MODERN ENGLISH LITERATURE & CULTURE COURSES
International Language Centres (ILC)
Cambridge, England
Three and four-week July-August courses in Cambridge

Since 1964, ILC has offered Modern English Literature Courses, a blend of literature, arts, and culture courses for students, teachers, and individuals with an interest in these subjects. The courses consist of morning lectures and seminars on specific topics relating to literature, art, architecture, and such aspects of English life as government, education, media, and music. Participants receive a reading list before the program. Occasional afternoon visits and Saturday trips are scheduled to places associated with the authors and books studied, and evening activities include folk singing, the English Teaching Theatre, and visits to local museums.

Specialties: English literature, arts, and culture.

Faculty: Senior university tutors and distinguished guest speakers.

Costs, Accommodations: Course fee, which includes accommodations, breakfast, temporary membership in the Cambridge University Graduate Centre, and VAT, is £150 per week. A £50 deposit must accompany registration with balance due 21 days prior to course. Major credit cards are accepted. Cancellations within 21 days of the program forfeit the greater of the deposit or 10% of the total fee. Accommodations are with host families or in university guest houses.

Location: Courses are held in Peterhouse, founded in 1284 and the oldest University College in Cambridge. Recreational and cultural facilities include a sports center, swimming pool, tennis courts, museums, art galleries, and places of historical interest.

Contact: Wilson & Lake International, 330 York St., Ashland, OR 97520; (800) 545-5228, (503) 488-3350, Fax (503) 488-7759 *or* International Language Centres, International House, White Rock, Hastings, East Sussex TN34 1JY, England; (44) 424-720100.

JACQUELINE MOSS MUSEUM TOURS
Stamford, Connecticut

Sixteen to twenty-six-day international trips

Since 1977, Jacqueline Moss has conducted cultural tours with an emphasis on art, archaeology, architecture, crafts, and dance. Typical trips include an art, architecture, and archaeological tour of Egypt and Jordan, art and architecture tours of France and the Eastern Bloc, and a Southeast Asia tour focusing on the art, architecture, crafts, and dance of Thailand, Burma, Singapore, and Indonesia. Groups are limited to 25 participants.

Specialties: Art, archaeology, architecture, crafts, dance.

Faculty: Art historian, lecturer, and writer Jacqueline Moss accompanies all tours. Guides include scholars who lecture to the group during museum visits and sightseeing excursions and conduct informal dialogue.

Costs, Accommodations: Costs range from $2,000 to more than $3,500 and include round-trip airfare from/to the U.S., ground transportation, accommodations, many meals, and scheduled activities. A $200 to $350 deposit must accompany reservation with balance due 60 days prior to departure. Cancellations at least 60 days prior receive full refund less $50; within 60 days minimum penalty is $200.

Contact: Jacqueline Moss Museum Tours, 131 Davenport Ridge Lane, Stamford, CT 06903; (203) 322-8709.

MOZART'S EUROPE
Now Voyager International Tours
New York, New York

Twelve to eighteen-day European tours from May-October

Since 1986, Dr. Norman Eagle has conducted walking/bus tours to Europe, each limited to 29 participants with 2 tour guides, that visit important sites relating to the life of Mozart. Emphasis is on recapitulating some of the composer's many excursions around the Continent, with stops at the sites or buildings where he lived, performed, visited, or lodged.

Four tour variations are scheduled from May to October: **Mozart's Europe with the Dresden Music Festival**, with **Vienna In-Depth**, with the **Rovereto Festival** (Italy), and **Mozart in Italia**. Highlights include private concerts and musical demonstrations in Mozart family homes, attendance at eight to eleven opera/concert performances, discussions with local music historians, a performance of Mozart improvisations by an organist who has completed and published them, and accommodations and refreshments where Mozart lodged and dined.

Specialties: Tours focusing on the life and music of Mozart.

Faculty: The tour itineraries are researched and conducted by Dr. and Mrs. Norman Eagle. Dr. Eagle is author of the *Mozart Site-Guide*, which is provided to each participant.

Costs, Accommodations: Land costs (based on an exchange rate of $1 = 1.9 W. German Marks), which include first class double occupancy lodging (single supplement available), some meals, tickets to performances, and scheduled excursions, range from $2,900 to $3,550. A $200 deposit must accompany application with balance due 65 days prior to departure. Cancellation fee ranges from $50 (more than 65 days prior) to $500 plus nonrecoverable costs (from 1 to 44 days prior).

Location: Countries visited on some or all of the tours include Austria, Czechoslovakia, Germany, Hungary, and Italy.

Contact: Now Voyager International Tours, P.O. Box 642, New York, NY 10034; (212) 567-1924.

MUSEUM OF AMERICAN FOLK ART EXPLORERS' CLUB
New York, New York

One to five-day tours in the New York City vicinity and to other U.S. cities

Established in 1987 for members of the Museum of American Folk Art and their guests, the Folk Art Explorers' Club first offered day trips in the New York metropolitan area and has since expanded to include extended tours to such art centers as Santa Fe/Taos, San Francisco, and New Orleans. Approximately a half dozen day, weekend, and five-day trips are scheduled annually, each limited to 10 to 40 participants, who visit museums, private folk art collections, studios of artists and craftspersons, and sites of cultural and historical interest. New destinations are selected each year. Efforts are made to allow maximum accessibility to handicapped persons.

The weekend **New York City Tour**, designed for out-of-towners, features guided tours of the Museum's exhibitions, visits to private collections and the home of the Museum Director, and a Broadway show. A five-day San Francisco Quilt Tour includes visits to private and museum quilt collections and a full-day design workshop.

Specialties: Tours focusing on American folk art.

Faculty: Staff of the Membership Department of the Museum of American Folk Art.

Costs, Accommodations: Day trips average $40 to $60; longer trips vary. Land cost of the five-day Santa Fe trip, which includes double occupancy first class hotel accommodations, ground transportation, admissions, and most lunches and dinners, is $595 for members, $625 for guests. Longer trips require a registration deposit with balance due one month prior to departure. Credit cards (VISA, MasterCard, American Express) accepted. Individual membership dues are $35 per year. Some day trips are free to Sustaining Members ($250 per year or more).

Contact: Museum of American Folk Art, Explorers' Club, 61 W. 62nd St., New York, NY 10023; (212) 977-7170 (Beth Bergin or Chris Cappiello).

THE MUSEUM OF MODERN ART (MOMA)
New York, New York
One-day to one-week tours in the U.S. and abroad

The Museum of Modern Art offers seminars and day trips for both members and nonmembers and one to seven-day programs and tours for members only. Typical programs open to all include a study tour of midtown Manhattan architecture, a guided tour of the Newark Museum, and a private viewing of the art collection of the Equitable Life Assurance Society. Programs for Contributing Members feature guided museum tours and visits to private collections and artists' studios with opportunities to learn about and discuss their work.

Specialties: Tours and trips focusing on 20th century art and architecture.

Faculty: Programs are conducted by members of the Museum's curatorial staff, artists, and other art scholars.

Costs, Accommodations: Programs for all range from $52 to $60 (members $40 to $55). Tours for Contributing Members (annual donation $200 or more) begin at $90 for day tours, $500 for weekend and longer tours, including meals and first class accommodations. Full payment must accompany application and no refunds are granted unless space can be filled.

Location: In addition to New York City and its environs, trips are scheduled to art centers in the U.S. and abroad.

Contact: Dept. of Membership, The Museum of Modern Art, 11 W. 53rd St., New York, NY 10019; (212) 708-9696.

LA NAPOULE ART FOUNDATION
SPRING WORKSHOP IN LANDSCAPE DESIGN
La Napoule, France

Twelve-day April program

La Napoule Art Foundation offers an introductory level **Spring Workshop** that is designed to provide the novice in landscape design with a foundation in the field from which to refine specific skills. The program emphasizes basic design principles, drafting techniques, and concepts from the history and philosophy of garden design and includes faculty critiques of students' design projects and field trips to prominent gardens in the Provence region and along the Cote d'Azur. Since 1984, the Foundation has also sponsored a three-week summer advanced level landscape design workshop for professionals and advanced students.

Specialties: Landscape design.

Faculty: John Brookes, former director of the Inchbald School of Landscape Design, recipient of four Gold Medals from The Royal Horticulture Society and the BPI Garden Writer's Award, and author of *The Gardens of Paradise* and *The Country Garden*; and guest lecturers.

Costs, Accommodations: The nonrefundable workshop fee of approximately $2,000 includes accommodations, continental breakfast, and most other meals. Application, which must include a letter of intent and $25 fee, should be submitted at least three months prior to program. A $375 deposit is required upon acceptance with balance due 60 days prior. Participants are lodged at the Chateau La Napoule or the adjacent Villa Marguerite.

Location: The Chateau, a memorial to the expatriate American artist and sculptor Henry Clews, who entrusted it to La Napoule Art Foundation, is situated in four acres of formal gardens on the Mediterranean just west of Cannes. First built by the Romans more than 2,000 years ago, it was recreated and restored by Clews and his wife, Marie, in the tradition and spirit of the 13th century and now serves as a center for promoting the exchange of American and European art and culture.

Contact: La Napoule Art Foundation, 217 E. 85th St., Suite 411 E, New York, NY 10028; (212) 628-2996.

NATIONAL AQUARIUM IN BALTIMORE
Baltimore, Maryland

One-day to three-week domestic and international trips

The National Aquarium in Baltimore sponsors a variety of educational programs and travel opportunities that are open to both members and non-members. One-day and weekend trips include A Day at Cape Henlopen State Park, a collecting and exploring trip timed to coincide with the horseshoe crab egg-laying season; a Garden Excursion that features exclusive tours of Dumbarton Oaks and Tudor Place; and Spring at Cape May, which includes a tour of the Wetlands Institute and visit to the Stone Harbor heronry.

Representative out-of-state and international trips include Learning With Dolphins, a week at Florida's Dolphin Research Center that consists of informal seminars on behavior, communication, reef ecology, training and husbandry, and opportunities to swim with the dolphins and assist in their training and feeding; New England Whale Watching, which features two half-day watches, an experienced naturalist to interpret the action at the feeding grounds, and a lecture by staff of the Cetacean Research Unit; Travel to Argentina, a marine mammal study expedition along the country's western coastline highlighted by visits to research sites and in-depth discussions with local scientists; and The Puffins of Westmannjer, a trip to Iceland in which 16 participants join four staff researchers in their study and observation of the puffins during the nesting season.

Specialties: Natural history and aquatic animals.

Faculty: National Aquarium staff and local specialists.

Costs: Day trips range from $27 to $68 ($22 to $60 for members). Costs of longer trips, which usually include airfare, lodging, and meals, range from approximately $375 to $4,000. Member discounts are offered for some trips. Annual membership dues begin at $29.

Contact: Member Programs, National Aquarium in Baltimore, 501 E. Pratt St., Baltimore, MD 21202; (301) 576-3870.

THE NATIONAL MUSEUM OF WOMEN IN THE ARTS (NMWA)
Department of Education
Washington, D.C.

One to two-week domestic and international travel programs

The National Museum of Women in the Arts' travel program, established in 1988, offers one domestic and two foreign tours a year. Number of participants varies, depending upon tour, and although Museum membership is a requirement, some tour participants become members later. The tour itineraries are designed to focus on the lives and works of women of accomplishment, particularly women artists whose work is in the Museum's collection. Museum visits, lectures, meetings with notable women, and visits to private collections are part of each program. Pre-departure programs include lectures about the artists and topics covered in the trip.

A one-week Christmas holiday tour to the U.S. Southwest features a visit with a 75-year-old Santa Clara Indian who demonstrates the making and firing of black-on-black pottery, a craft she learned from her mother. Other highlights include a visit with Eya Fechin, the daughter of Russian artist, painter, sculptor, and woodcarver Nicholai Fechin, and private tours of the Millicent Rogers Museum and the estate of Mabel Dodge Luhan, who was responsible for attracting many women artists, including Georgia O'Keeffe, to New Mexico. A Vienna study tour includes visits to the 16th century chateau and art collection of Countess Harrach, the studio of Austrian fashion designer Lore Heuermann, and meetings with Austrian artist Maria Lassnig and Jenny Strasser, widow of Austrian politician and activist Peter Strasser.

A tour extension to Budapest features a visit to the home of early 20th century composer Béla Bartók with a performance of his works by a woman pianist.

Specialties: Art tours focusing on the lives and work of distinguished women.

Faculty: The tours are conducted by scholars and specialists in the art and culture of the area visited.

Costs, Accommodations: Tour costs range from $1,200 to $5,000, which includes double occupancy deluxe accommodations (single supplement available), ground transportation, some meals, planned activities, a $150 to $500 NMWA contribution, and pre-trip bulletins and reading list. Deposit and refund policies vary.

Contact: Dr. Mary Louise Wood, Education Dept., The National Museum of Women in the Arts, 1250 New York Ave., N.W., Washington, DC 20005-3920; (202) 783-5000.

NATIONAL TRUST FOR HISTORIC PRESERVATION
Washington, D.C.
Five-day to three-week domestic and international tours

The National Trust for Historic Preservation began offering study tours for its members in 1970 and currently offers 20 programs annually throughout the year. Groups range in size from 12 to as many as 120 for cruises. The tours focus on architecture and historic preservation but include a variety of activities and time for individual pursuits. Each program features presentations by study leaders, private receptions, and opportunities to meet local individuals involved with historic preservation.

A popular domestic tour, **Architecture and Landscape of the American Southwest** includes visits to pueblos, adobe churches, Indian ruins, and museums, and tours of private homes and haciendas that house important collections and are of architectural interest. **Historic Preservation in England**, a two-week Oxford program offered in odd-numbered years since 1983, is designed for 30 National Trust members by the Department for External Studies of Oxford University. The first week consists of daily lectures on English architecture, landscape design, and preservation, complemented by course related field trips. Participants select one of three courses offered during the second week on such topics as The Survival of Britain's Country Houses, Cathedrals and Parish Churches of England, and The Making of the English Landscape. Each course is limited to 10 participants, who attend two-and-a-half days of discussion and spend two days visiting related sites. Weekend excursions and a theater evening are also planned.

Specialties: Architecture and historic preservation.

Faculty: Faculty/tour leaders include museum directors and curators, university professors, and specialists in the regions visited.

Costs, Accommodations: All-inclusive domestic (international) tour land costs range from approximately $1,000 ($2,800) to $3,000 ($7,000) or more for longer trips and cruises. A tax-deductible donation to the National Trust is additional. Deposit and refund policies vary. National Trust annual membership dues begin at $15 single, $20 for a family. Benefits include a subscription to the monthly *Preservation News* and the bimonthly *Historic Preservation* magazine and free admission to National Trust properties.

Location: In addition to the above, destinations may include Hawaii, the Hudson River, New Orleans, Savannah, Charleston, Washington, D.C., Italy, the British Isles, France, Japan, Morocco, the Near East, Scandinavia, the Soviet Union, and South America.

Contact: Special Programs, National Trust for Historic Preservation, 1785 Massachusetts Ave., N.W., Washington, D.C. 20036; (202) 673-4138.

NATURAL HISTORY MUSEUM OF LOS ANGELES COUNTY TRAVEL PROGRAM
Los Angeles, California
Five-day to one-month domestic and international tours year-round

The Natural History Museum's Travel Program, begun in the mid-1960's, currently offers more than 15 trips a year for its members, focusing on wildlife, native cultures, archaeology, and other aspects of natural history. Group size is usually limited to 15 to 30 participants.

A typical domestic tour is the Santa Fe Indian Market and Ethnographic Study Tour, which features guided visits to museums, archaeological sites, national monuments, and pueblos, with opportunities to celebrate feast days with Indian families in their homes. Representative international tours include Treasures of Precolumbian Mexico, an exploration of the complex societies that inhabited the central and highland areas of Mexico; and Tunisia, which includes a visit with the Tunisian Minister of State, a lecture on the Judaic-Berber culture, and dinners with Tunisian families.

Specialties: Tours that focus on wildlife, native cultures, archaeology, and other aspects of natural history.

Faculty: Tours are accompanied by study leaders who are members of the Museum's curatorial staff.

Costs, Accommodations: All-inclusive costs of domestic tours range from $1,000 to $1,700; international tour costs range from $3,000 for a two-week trip to Peru to $13,000 for a one month cruise to Antarctica. Deposit and refund policies vary. Annual museum membership dues are $35 for a family. Benefits, in addition to trips, include free museum admission, a subscription to *Terra* magazine, workshop and gift shop discounts, and invitations to special events.

Location: In addition to the above, tour locations may include Antarctica, Australia, Baja, East Africa, Egypt, Indonesia, South America, Thailand.

Contact: Karen Hovanitz, Museum Travel Program Coordinator, Natural History Museum of Los Angeles County, 900 Exposition Blvd., Los Angeles, CA 90007; (213) 744-3350.

NATURE EXPEDITIONS INTERNATIONAL (NEI)
Eugene, Oregon
Nine to thirty-day worldwide trips

Established in 1973, Nature Expeditions International offers 20 to 30 itineraries with 60 to 100 wildlife and cultural expeditions annually, each limited to 6 to 18 participants ranging in age from 25 to 75. Each expedition is graded according to physical activity, from leisurely nature and cultural walks to 10-mile treks on rugged terrain at high altitudes, and includes study of the wildlife, flora, environment, history, culture, and peoples of the area. Informal lectures are offered in the evenings.

Itineraries include the Galápagos **Islands Expedition**, a comprehensive study of the islands led by an NEI biologist and local naturalist; the **Alaska Wildlife Expedition**, featuring visits to Glacier Bay, Kenai Fiords, and five days of study in Denali National Park; the **East Africa Wildlife Safari** and search for the rare mountain gorilla; and the **New Zealand Walking Expedition**, with opportunities to study the region's geology, plants, and animals.

Specialties: Wildlife and cultural expeditions.

Faculty: NEI President and co-founder David Roderick is an accomplished photographer and pianist who earned graduate degrees in geology, chemistry, and science education and taught oceanography and chemistry for 16 years. Trip leaders are specialists in anthropology, natural history, or biology. In addition to having lived or traveled extensively in the host country, each leader is required to have an M.A., Ph.D., or equivalent professional training, and teaching experience on the college level.

Costs, Accommodations: Land costs range from $1,400 to $4,600, which includes double occupancy accommodations (single supplement available), all meals, ground transportation, and entrance fees. Accommodations are graded according to comfort level, from first class hotel lodging to tent camps, mountain huts, and rustic lodges. A $300 deposit must accompany reservation with balance due 60 days prior to departure. Cancellations at least 60 days prior receive full refund less $50 fee. Thereafter, fee ranges from $300 (31 to 59 days prior) to $600 (15 to 30 days prior); no refund thereafter. A 10% land cost surcharge is added for enrollments of less than 11 participants.

Location: Itineraries include North America (Alaska, Hawaii, Southwest U.S.), South America (Peru, Bolivia, Ecuador, Galápagos Islands), Mexico and the West Indies, Africa (Kenya, Tanzania), Asia (Bhutan, Burma, Thailand, Nepal, India, Japan), and Oceania (Australia, Easter Island, New Zealand, Papua New Guinea, Polynesia).

Contact: Nature Expeditions International, 474 Willamette St., P.O. Box 11496, Eugene, OR 97440; (800) 869-0639 *or* (503) 484-6529.

THE NELSON-ATKINS MUSEUM OF ART TRAVEL PROGRAM
Kansas City, Missouri

One-day to two-week domestic and foreign travel programs

Each year, The Nelson-Atkins Museum of Art offers approximately eight to ten travel programs for its two membership groups, the Friends of Art and the Society of Fellows. **Programs for Friends,** begun in 1960 and limited to 40 participants, usually start with pre-departure lectures and discussions and include such weekend itineraries as Monet in the 90's: The Series Paintings, an excursion to the Boston Museum of Fine Arts and Museums and Galleries of New York with a tour of a special exhibit at the Metropolitan Museum of Art. **Programs for Fellows,** first offered in 1970 and limited to 25 participants, feature private collections, homes, and receptions. Representative itineraries include Turkey: Crossroads of Civilization, highlighted by guided tours of a variety of museums and visits to sites of historical and cultural importance; and The Cote D'Azur and Paris.

Specialties: Trips and tours with an art focus.

Faculty: Friends tours are lead by travel coordinator Margaret Doan, an art historian and college teacher; Fellows tours are led by the museum director, curators, and the executive secretary of Fellows.

Costs, Accommodations: Costs of weekend trips, including airfare, some meals, double occupancy hotel accommodations (single supplement available), entrance fees, and a contribution to the museum, range from $788 to $975 and up to $4,900 for two-week foreign itineraries. A $50 to $200 deposit is required. Annual Friends membership begins at $40 for an individual, $55 for a family. Annual membership in the Society of Fellows begins at $750.

Contact: The Nelson-Atkins Museum of Art, 4525 Oak St., Kansas City, MO 64111-1873; (816) 561-4000.

THE NEW MUSEUM OF CONTEMPORARY ART
New York, New York

Weekend to two-week spring and fall trips in the U.S., Canada, and abroad

Since 1982, The New Museum has conducted two or three tours annually to important exhibition openings and international art shows such as Documenta, the Venice Biennale, and the Carnegie International. All trips focus on contemporary art and feature visits to artists' studios and private collections, special museum and gallery tours, and exhibition openings.

Typical programs include a weekend trip to Minneapolis to attend the opening of Art Into Life: Russian Constructivism, 1914-1932, part of the Goodwill Arts Festival; a five-day Los Angeles trip featuring visits to the studios of Laddie John Dill, Chuck Arnoldi, John Baldessari, and Lita Albuquerque; a ten-day Venice trip with viewings of the Peggy Guggenheim, Villa di Celle, and Panza de Buimo collections; and a two-week trip to Moscow, Leningrad, Tbilisi, and Prague.

Specialties: Trips with a contemporary art focus.

Faculty: New Museum curators accompany each tour.

Costs: All-inclusive costs range from $1,000 to $5,000, which includes a $500 contribution to The New Museum. A nonrefundable $500 deposit must accompany reservation with balance due six weeks prior to departure. Credit cards (VISA, MasterCard) accepted. Membership dues (not required for travel programs) begin at $45 per couple.

Contact: The New Museum of Contemporary Art, 583 Broadway, New York, NY 10012; (212) 219-1222.

THE NEW YORK BOTANICAL GARDEN (NYBG)
Bronx, New York
One to sixteen-day programs in the U.S., Europe, and Central and South America

For more than 20 years, The New York Botanical Garden has offered domestic and foreign garden trips and tours designed for those interested in horticulture, garden design, and the natural world. Day hikes and trips to nearby public and private gardens, as well as other places of horticultural, ecological, or plant-related interest, are scheduled 10 to 12 times a year and limited to 13 participants. Study and research tours to sites of NYBG research in Central and South America, limited to 8 to 17 participants, are scheduled about four times a year. Luxury garden tours and cruises, offered once or twice a year, usually visit European gardens.

A popular international tour, **Amazon Adventure,** explores the Rio Negro and its tributaries and areas of the Amazon that are the focus of botanical and ecological research conducted by members of the Garden's Science staff. Galápagos — The Enchanted Isles offers a comprehensive view of the 13 main islands, an excursion to Quito, the Otovalo market, and Cotopoxi National Park.

The **French Guiana Research Expedition** offers eight selected volunteers the opportunity to study the plants and ecology of the region's tropical forest. Participants are trained in such field techniques as collection of plant specimens, observation of pollinators and dispersal agents, and various ecological studies. Informal discussions supplement the field work and an extensive reading list is provided. The **Belize Research Expedition,** a combination research expedition and tour, involves participants in a major effort by the Garden and the National Cancer Institute to discover plants that are effective in the treatment of cancer and AIDS. Team members collect and process plant material to be analyzed for potential anti-carcinogenic compounds. A tour of nearby archaeological sites and snorkeling at Ambergris Cay follows the expedition.

Specialities: Tours and research expeditions relating to horticulture, botany, ecology, and the natural world.

Faculty: Day hikes and trips are led by experienced and qualified naturalists and horticulturists, as well as garden owners and special guides. Foreign tours and research expeditions are led by specialists and scientists with expertise in the flora of the region visited.

Costs, Accommodations: Day trips range from $32 to $56 ($29 to $52 for members). All-inclusive costs for foreign trips and expeditions range from $1,500 to $3,500. Luxury tour prices vary. Full payment, which is fully refundable for cancellations at least seven working days prior to trip, must accompany registration for day trips. Deposit and refund policies vary for longer trips. Credit card (VISA, MasterCard) registrations accepted. NYBG membership dues are $35 for individuals and seniors, $45 for a family.

Location: The New York Botanical Garden is situated at Bedford Park Boulevard and Southern (Kazimiroff) Boulevard.

Contact: Travel Program, Education Dept., The New York Botanical Garden, Bronx, NY 10458-5126; (212) 220-8982.

NEW YORK UNIVERSITY (NYU)
School of Continuing Education
New York, New York

Two-week summer program in Cambridge; ten to sixteen-day international travel programs

The International and Special Programs division of New York University's School of Continuing Education offers two types of adult educational travel programs: a two-week noncredit summer study program at Emmanuel College in Cambridge, England, and tours of about two week's duration abroad.

The Cambridge program, first offered in 1989 and limited to 45 participants, offers an opportunity for in-depth study of a specific English historical period or theme, which changes each year. The schedule includes two 90-minute morning lectures each weekday, twice weekly 90-minute small group seminars, theme-related field trips and excursions, and informal meetings with faculty.

Ten to twelve other tours are offered annually, each with a specific focus, such as art, archaeology, history, culture, or food, and include visits to out-of-the-way places. Typical tours, which accommodate from 15 to around 28 participants, include Turkey: Past and Present, with exploration of the remains of Graeco-Roman cities and visits to Istanbul and the Aegean coast; Egypt: A Journey Through Time, including a Nile cruise and archaeological sites; and Edinburgh Festival: A Musical Journey, featuring rehearsals, performances, interpretations, and informal meetings with musicians. Pre-trip briefings and suggested readings are provided.

Specialties: Study in Cambridge, England, and other international tours with a specific educational focus.

Faculty: The Cambridge Study Program is taught by British faculty selected by the University of Cambridge Board of Extra-mural Studies. A New York University faculty member accompanies and arranges field trips and excursions. Tour leaders, who are selected for their enthusiasm and expertise, are often NYU faculty members and natives of the countries visited.

Costs, Accommodations: The cost of the Cambridge Study Program is $3,090, which includes tuition, round-trip airfare from/to New York, ground transportation, accommodations in single rooms, most meals, and all planned activities. A $400 deposit must accompany reservation with balance due three months prior to departure. Cancellations more than three months prior receive full refund less $100; thereafter deposit and nonrecoverable costs are forfeited. Tour costs to other destinations average $3,200 to $4,000 for a two-week trip abroad, which includes round-trip airfare, ground transportation, double occupancy accommodations (single supplement available) in deluxe or first class hotels, most meals, and planned activities. Deposit and refund policies vary.

Location: In addition to the above, tour destinations include Egypt, France, Holland and Belgium, India, Italy (one trip to the Veneto, another to Sicily), Spain, Tunisia, and Morocco.

Contact: Dr. Vera Jelinek, Director of International Programs, New York University School of Continuing Education, 331 Shimkin Hall, New York, NY 10003-9903; (212) 998-7133.

NEW YORK ZOOLOGICAL SOCIETY
Bronx, New York

One-day and weekend domestic trips; international trips of varying length

The New York Zoological Society sponsors tours for the general membership and specific project trips for support groups within the Society. Typical one-day and weekend programs include Jamaica Bay Bird Walk, a visit to this 9,000-acre wildlife refuge, noted for its bird migrations; Whale Watching — Plymouth, which features lectures, a slide show, shore birding, and excursions to Stellwagen Bank in search of humpbacks, finbacks, minkes, and right whales; and Hudson Sail, a trip along the lower Hudson River aboard a sloop.

The Society's field science research division, Wildlife Conservation International (WCI), supports conservation projects worldwide, involving local residents in promoting ecology-sensitive tourism. Members of the support group are offered the opportunity to travel to these areas to observe first-hand the results of these efforts. A trip to Rwanda focuses on the mountain gorilla, once close to extinction and now being protected by the people of Rwanda. A Kenya trip highlights WCI's project to save elephants and black rhinos.

Specialties: Natural history and ecology-related wildlife projects.

Faculty: Society and WCI staff members, including Dr. Amy Vedder, initiator of the Rwanda conservation/tourism program.

Costs, Accommodations: Costs of short-term trips, usually including transportation and lodging, range from $20 to $350. International trips begin at $2,500. Deposit and refund policies vary.

Location: In addition to the above, planned destinations include Alaska, Baja, Belize, Costa Rica, Ecuador and the Galapagos Islands, and Patagonia.

Contact: New York Zoological Society, P.O. Box 108, Bronx, NY 10460; (212) 220-5085. Members Afield International, 217 E. 85th St., #200, New York, NY 10028; (212) 879-2588.

92nd STREET YM-YWHA
New York, New York
One to fifteen-day domestic and international tours

The 92nd Street Y's tour program, established in 1978, now offers approximately eight walking and bus tours each week and five international travel programs per season. Bus tours, which run from one to three days, are scheduled to a variety of out-of-town museums, historical homes, and cultural events. Typical itineraries include one-day trips to the Boston Museum of Fine Arts, Historic Homes and Art in Hartford, the New Paltz Craft Fair, and Marine Life in Mystic Seaport, and such weekend programs as Art and History in Southampton and Montauk, Cape Cod and Martha's Vineyard, and Berkshires Art and Music.

The one to two-week journeys abroad, usually preceded by a pre-tour orientation talk, stress such themes as art and architecture, music and dance, literature and poetry, crafts, and film. Representative programs include Holland, Paris, and Southern France, which traces the life of Vincent Van Gogh from Amsterdam to Provence; Literary Ireland, following in the footsteps of the greatest Irish authors; and to Oaxaca, Mexico, to celebrate The Day of The Dead.

Specialties: Tours that emphasize topics in the arts and humanities.

Faculty: A variety of specialists in their fields, including professors, authors, and historians.

Costs, Accommodations: Out-of-town bus tour costs range from $40 to $375 (weekend tours include lodging and may include some meals). International program costs, which include airfare, some meals, first class or deluxe hotel accommodations, and local transportation, range from $1,100 to $4,300. Deposit requirements and refund policies vary.

Location: All bus tours leave from and return to the 92nd Street Y, which is located on Manhattan's Upper East Side.

Contact: Tours & Talks, 92nd Street Y, 1395 Lexington Ave., New York, NY, 10128; (212) 415-5600.

NORLANDS LIVING HISTORY CENTER
Livermore Falls, Maine
Three-and-a-half to five-day programs

Norlands Living History Center, the re-creation of a 19th century homestead, offers three-and-a-half-day **Adult Live-in Weekends** and two five-day **Institutes** that involve participants in playing the roles of 19th century townspeople. College and recertification credits are available.

The **Adult Live-in Weekends**, offered eight times from February to November and limited to 14 participants, age eight and over, provide an in-depth total experience in rural Maine life of the 1870s. For three days and three nights, participants assume the names and roles of people who actually lived and died in Livermore. Daily activities include farm chores, spinning, quilt making, cooking, and attending church. Depending on the season, activities may also include plowing and harrowing, haying, harvesting, ice cutting, and cutting wood.

The two experience-centered Institutes — each offered once during the summer and limited to 18 adult participants — are **Why They Came; Why They Left**, an on-location study of the evolution and decline of a 19th century New England Crossroads community from 1800 to 1870, and **19th Century Education in Rural New England**, in which each participant becomes a schoolmaster or schoolma'am who taught in a country school. The Institutes are held from 8 am to 4:30 pm, Monday through Friday, and two evenings from 6 to 8:30 pm. Participants use the schoolhouse and primary research sources in the Norlands Library. Those desiring recertification or college credit are required to complete a research paper or unit of study.

Specialties: Re-enactment of life in a 19th century rural community.

Faculty: Norlands Living History Center founder and director is Mrs. Alfred Q. (Billie) Gammon.

Costs, Accommodations: All-inclusive cost of the Live-Ins is $195 for adults, $125 for teenagers, $97.50 for children. Cost of the Institutes ranges from $171 to $195, which includes college or recertification credit. Lodging is available at nearby motels. A $25 registration fee must accompany reservation.

Location: The 450-acre Norlands Living History Center is situated off of Route 4 a few miles east of Livermore. Norlands was originally the estate of Israel Washburn, whose sons served as congressmen, governors, Secretary of State, founder of Gold Medal Flour, and founder of Pillsbury.

Contact: Billie Gammon, Washburn-Norlands, RFD 2, Box 3395, Livermore Falls, ME 04254; (207) 897-2236.

ROGER NORRINGTON'S MUSIC WEEKENDS
London, England

Three-day programs in the United States and London

Conductor Roger Norrington's **Music Weekends**, scheduled once or twice a year, offer an in-depth study of the life and music of a renowned composer, with emphasis on the derivation and development of an important work. Designed to provide the listener with an understanding of the influences and cultural forces of the period during which the composer lived, the Weekends consist of concerts, lectures and discussions, recitals, open rehearsals, and participatory events that culminate in a performance of the featured work.

A Weekend devoted to Beethoven, focusing on the Ninth (Chorale) Symphony, begins with a concert of pieces by composers who influenced or were influenced by Beethoven. Lectures and discussions cover such topics as Beethoven's reasons for writing the Ninth, events surrounding its first performance, and interpretations of its meaning. Demonstrations of dances of the period, playing of the Choral Fantasy (precursor to the Ninth), and a rehearsal of the Ninth with the audience as chorus are also featured. The weekend concludes with a performance of the symphony. Other composers featured during Music Weekends include Haydn, Mozart, and Berlioz.

Specialties: Music weekends focusing on the life, times, and work of a noted composer.

Faculty; Roger Norrington is founder-director of the London Classical Players.

Costs: Music Weekends range from $90 to $110. Meals, available on-site, and accommodations are additional.

Location: Locations, which vary depending on the sponsoring organization, include the Royal Festival Hall in London, the Performing Arts Center of the State University of New York (SUNY) at Purchase, and Davies Symphony Hall in San Francisco.

Contact: Historic Arts, 15 Percy St., London W1P 9FD, England ; (44) 71 323 2140, Fax (44) 71 323 2139.

NORTH MUSEUM
Franklin & Marshall College
Lancaster, Pennsylvania

One-day to two-week domestic and international tours

The North Museum's travel program, established in 1974, offers 45 to 50 tours annually, of which 35 to 40 are day trips to nearby locales and about a dozen are longer trips to U.S. and foreign destinations. Most trips are limited to 40 participants, who are museum members, college alumni, or friends of the museum or college. A typical domestic trip, Boston and Monet, includes a morning at the Boston Museum of Fine Arts and tours of sites relating to such writers as Henry Thoreau, Louisa May Alcott, Ralph Waldo Emerson, and Nathaniel Hawthorne. A typical international trip, The Soviet Union: A Study in Contrasts, visits historical landmarks and such museums as the State Armory Museum, The Outoor Cultural Museum, and the Hermitage.

Specialties: Art-related and natural history-related travel.

Faculty: Tour leaders are museum staff members and individuals who are knowledgeable about the area visited.

Costs, Accommodations: Costs for domestic and international tours range from approximately $400 to $3,000, which includes meals, lodging, and transportation. On day trips a 75% refund is granted cancellations at least one week prior. Deposit and refund policies vary on longer trips. Handicapped persons can be accommodated. Some trips require museum membership, which begins at $20.

Location: In addition to the above, locations may include the Grand Tetons, the Hudson Valley, Asheville, Washington, D.C., Florida, Costa Rica, Guatamala, Spain, Great Britain, and Iceland.

Contact: North Museum, Franklin & Marshall College, P.O. Box 3003, Lancaster, PA 17604-3003; (717) 291-3941.

NORTHERN OHIO ARCHAEOLOGICAL FIELD SCHOOL
Cuyahoga Community College
Parma, Ohio

Two, four, and six-week summer programs in the Cuyahoga Valley

This program, offered from the last week in June through the first week in August, offers high school and college students and interested adults the opportunity to receive training in archaeological field techniques and proper methods of recording site data. Enrollment is for two, four, or six weeks (for two, four, or six credits). Participants spend five days a week, eight hours daily in the field and process recovered materials in the laboratory of the Cleveland Museum of Natural History.

Specialties: Archaeology field methods.

Faculty: Daniel A. Grossman, Department of Social and Behavioral Sciences, Cuyahoga Community College.

Costs: The cost per credit hour is $25.50 for Cuyahoga County residents, $32.50 for other Ohio residents, and $60.50 for participants from out of state.

Location: Historic 19th century and prehistoric Native American archaeological sites in the Cuyahoga Valley.

Contact: Daniel A. Grossman, Social and Behavioral Sciences, Cuyahoga Community College, Western Campus, 11000 Pleasant Valley Rd., Parma, OH 44130; (216) 987-5492/5504.

NORTHWESTERN UNIVERSITY
Alumni College and Alumni Travel Study Program
Evanston, Illinois

One-week summer program on campus; seven to eighteen-day domestic and international travel study programs

Northwestern University offers a variety of programs for its alumni, friends, and interested adults, including an annual summer **Alumni College** devoted to a specific theme and faculty-accompanied tours to approximately a dozen destinations throughout the year.

Each year's **Alumni College** offers an in-depth exploration of a different theme, such as Religion, The Victorian Age, or The Millennium. Lectures and discussions are scheduled in the mornings and afternoons with evenings reserved for theme-related films and performances. Meals and social hours are shared by participants, College staff, and the more than a dozen faculty members.

Alumni Travel Study Programs range from such domestic locales as the coast of northern New England to international destinations that include the Canary Islands, Holland and Belgium, the Soviet Union, Danube Cruise of Eastern Europe, and Africa. Academic itineraries emphasize the literature, history, and geography of the region and feature on-site exploration and study with University faculty leader.

Specialties: Summer theme program; tours with an academic emphasis.

Faculty: Northwestern University faculty.

Costs, Accommodations: Alumni College tuition is $535, which includes all meals and planned activities. Double occupancy lodging ranges from $160 (residence hall) to $220 (hotel). A $150 deposit ($200 for two) must accompany registration with balance due three weeks prior to program. Cancellations more than eight weeks prior receive full refund. Alumni Travel Study Program costs range from approximately $2,300 to $4,600, which includes round-trip airfare, double occupancy first class accommodations, some meals (all meals on cruises), ground transportation, and scheduled activities. Deposit and refund policies vary. Credit cards (VISA, Master-Card) accepted.

Contact: Alumni College, Office of Special Programs, Andersen Hall, Room 1-117, 2003 Sheridan Rd., Evanston, IL 60208-2650; (800) 346-3768 *or* (708) 491-5250. Alumni Travel Study Programs, Dept. of Alumni Relations, Northwestern University, 1800 Sheridan Rd., Evanston, IL 60208-1800; (800) 682-5867 *or* (708) 491-7200.

OCEANIC SOCIETY EXPEDITIONS
San Francisco, California
One to three-week expeditions worldwide

Since 1972, nonprofit Oceanic Society Expeditions has conducted land and vessel-based ecotours as the environmental travel arm of the Oceanic Society (OS), the only national membership organization dedicated solely to protecting the ocean. The program includes research expeditions that contribute directly to conservation. In 1990, Oceanic expanded its land-based educational natural history trips as a result of The Oceanic Society's joining forces with the Environmental Policy Institute (EPI) and Friends of the Earth (FOE) to build an international citizen's lobby to protect the earth as part of a global environmental strategy. More than 80 water and land expeditions are conducted annually to 34 different itineraries that stress a non-invasive approach to the natural history and wildlife of the regions visited, minimizing impact on habitats and cultures. Average group size is 10 to 15 participants.

Nature Watch Research Expeditions offer the opportunity for hands-on participation in on-going projects to gather data that have applications in wildlife from human-induced mortality and preserving endangered species. **Bahamas: Project Dolphin,** begun in 1984, involves participants in collecting data on dolphin family and social structure, behavior, distribution, and habitat requirements. Activities during more than a dozen one-week summer sessions, each limited to eight participants, include swimming and snorkeling with the dolphins, studying and photographing their behavior, and exploring their underwater environment. Lectures and slide presentations are also featured. **Bio-Acoustics,** the tools and methods of environment sound recordings, are the focus of a project to record the vocalizations of killer whale pods and other animals along the British Columbian coast. Instruction includes shipboard seminars, theoretical discussions, and hands-on field experience using a hydrophone and high frequency stereo tape recorders. In **Southeast Alaska,** participants photograph individual humpback whales for identification, and document behaviors in their feeding grounds. These data become part of an on-going study of humpback whales to determine population numbers and examine this endangered species' relationship to its environment and to other species, including humans.

Specialties: Expeditions and research aimed at protecting wildlife and the environment.

Faculty: A more than 20-member staff of accomplished naturalists, many of whom are actively involved in research.

Costs, Accommodations: Land costs range from $700 to $6,000 for water and land expeditions and from $1,100 to $2,500 for research expeditions, including meals and double occupancy accommodations (single supplement may be available). A 10% surcharge may be added for less than minimum enrollment. A $300 deposit must accompany application with $400 due 120 days prior to departure and balance due 60 days prior. Credit cards (VISA, MasterCard, American Express) accepted for deposit only. Cancellation fee ranges from $50 (more than 180 days prior to departure) to 50% of total (30 to 59 days prior); no refunds thereafter.

Location: In addition to the above, destinations include the Pacific and Caribbean (Australia, Virgin Islands, Dominica, Hawaii, Indonesia and Borneo, and Micronesia), Baja California, South America (the Amazon, Belize, Costa Rica, the Galápagos, and Patagonia), the Arctic, Africa (Botswana, Tanzania, Kenya, and Zaire), and North America (Alaska, the New England coast, and the Pacific Northwest coast).

Contact: Oceanic Society Expeditions, Fort Mason Center, Building E, San Francisco, CA 94123; (800) 326-7491 *or* (415) 441-1106, Fax (415) 474-3395.

ODYSSEYS IN LIFELONG LEARNING
Michigan State University — Alumni Lifelong Education
East Lansing, Michigan
Two-week programs in Oxford, England and other overseas locations

Established in 1983 for alumni and friends of Michigan State University, Odysseys in Lifelong Learning are a series of noncredit travel-to-learn programs that are open to all adults who desire the opportunity to engage in serious study and learn about other cultures. Approximately three to four programs are scheduled annually, sometimes in conjunction with other Big Ten Universities, with enrollment in each limited to 30 to 50 participants.

The annual **Odyssey to Oxford**, offered each summer since 1983 in cooperation with Northwestern University and the University of Oxford, is a two-week residential non-credit study program consisting of morning lecture/discussion courses, related afternoon field trips, and special activities and excursions. Participants can select one of approximately four courses of study, including such titles as Britain Under Thatcher, Theatre in the Age of Shakespeare, A History of European Art, and Historic Houses and Castles. A general course on How to Be a Traveler draws on the literature of travel to help participants gain more meaning and pleasure from their journeys. Special activities include excursions to Coventry Cathedral, Blenheim Palace, and Warwick Castle; a dinner and performance at the Royal Shakespeare Theatre; and plenary lectures by Oxford faculty. Participants are provided with a reading list prior to departure and are encouraged, though not required, to write brief essays in their subjects for critique by the instructor.

Specialties: Study-travel programs.

Faculty: Michigan State University professors and faculty of the other sponsoring universities.

Costs, Accommodations: The Oxford program fee is $2,175, which includes tuition, field trips and excursions, ground transportation, double occupancy lodging (single supplement $200) with private baths, all meals, and planned activities. Oxford participants stay at Rewley House in Wellington Square in Oxford. Other Odysseys range from $1,500 to $2,300. Round-trip airfare is additional. A $300 deposit must accompany reservation with balance due approximately six weeks prior to departure. Cancellations at least ten weeks prior receive full refund less $50 charge; thereafter charge ranges from $150 to $300 plus nonrecoverable costs.

Location: In addition to Oxford, other locations include Florence and Tuscany and the islands of Hawaii, Kauai, and Oahu (1990); and New Zealand, Switzerland, and Oxford (1991).

Contact: Odysseys in Lifelong Learning, Alumni Lifelong Education, 8 Kellogg Center, East Lansing, MI 48824-1022; (517) 355-4562.

OHIO UNIVERSITY-LANCASTER
Lancaster, Ohio

Seven to nineteen-day international trips in March and December

For more than 20 years, Ohio University in Lancaster has sponsored two trips annually for groups that range from 13 to 120 participants. The groups visit such locations as Puerto Vallarta, Italy, Australia, and New Zealand and cruise the Black Sea and Caribbean Islands.

Faculty: Dee Mowry, Associate Professor of Zoology and Biomedicine, accompanies all tours. Other faculty includes Dr. Jean Bryant and Dr. James Bryant.

Costs: Vary, depending on tour.

Contact: Prof. Dee Mowry, Ohio University, 1570 Granville Pike, Route 37 North, Lancaster, OH 43130-1097; (614) 654-6711, ext. 260.

OLD STURBRIDGE VILLAGE (OSV)
SUMMER FIELD SCHOOL IN HISTORICAL ARCHAEOLOGY
Sturbridge, Massachusetts

Seven-week summer program

Since 1979, Old Sturbridge Village and the College of Professional and Continuing Education of Clark University have jointly sponsored the Field School in Historical Archaeology, an opportunity to become involved in the historical and material culture of the early 19th century as well as the methods and techniques of field archaeology. The 20 participants, who need no prior archaeological experience but should have completed at least one year of college, spend the first week at Old Sturbridge Village, an outdoor living history museum recreating a rural New England community of the 1830's. Working with research, curatorial, and interpretation specialists, they become acquainted with the culture and artifacts of the period through lectures, workshops, tours, and problem-solving simulations.

The next six weeks are devoted to the archaeological investigation of the farmstead of an early 19th century Sturbridge farmer, whose house was moved to OSV to become the centerpiece of the living history farm. Archaeological data recovered from the site will strengthen and enrich the exhibit. Participants are involved in excavation, survey, measured drawing, conservation, computer, and other field, lab, and recording activities. Lectures, workshops, seminars, and field trips complement the field and lab work. The

Field School is designed as the equivalent of a two-semester undergraduate or graduate course, with eight semester hours of optional credit available through Clark University in Worcester, Massachusetts.

Specialties: Archeaological investigation of a 19th century New England farmstead.

Faculty: The Field School is under the direction of John Worrell, OSV Director of Research, who directed the previous Field Schools and others in the Middle East. Participants work with archaeologists selected for their professional competence and teaching ability.

Costs, Accommodations: The program fee is $985. College credit is $690 graduate, $515 undergraduate, $140 audit. Housing is available at Clark University.

Contact: John Worrell, Archaeology Field School, Old Sturbridge Village, 1 Old Sturbridge Village Rd., Sturbridge, MA 01566; (508) 347-3362.

OLYMPIC FIELD SEMINARS
Olympic Park Institute (OPI)
Olympic National Park, Washington
Three to five-day summer workshops

Since 1984, the Olympic Field Seminar series has offered programs on a variety of nature-oriented topics. In 1987, the series came under the umbrella of the Olympic Park Institute, a nonprofit educational organization and one of three campuses operated by the Yosemite National Institutes. Approximately 50 courses, scheduled during the spring, summer, and fall, are devoted to subjects that include wildlife, earth sciences, the ancient forest, cultural history, environmental education, botany, and coastal studies.

Typical Field Seminars include The World of Salmon: Past, Present and Future, which explores the importance of salmon in past European and Native American cultures through the retelling of myths and legends. Participants study the salmon stream's habitat and learn how to identify juvenile salmon, steelhead and cutthroat trout. Become Your Own Best Meteorologist combines lectures and field observations to introduce the terminology and concepts of weather and its patterns. Participants learn how to make their own "back pocket weather station". The Ancient Forest examines the complex nature and ecology of the Olympic Peninsula forests, defining old-growth and the interactive components. Northwest Myths and Legends, an examination of the qualities of the Olympic region that inspired stories and shaped world views, offers participants the opportunity to write their own stories in order to understand the origins and purposes of myths and legends. During family voyages that retrace the routes of the early explorers of Puget Sound, participants learn traditional seamanship, story telling, singing, and role playing.

Specialties: Natural and cultural history, environmental education, the arts.

Faculty: Recognized professionals in their respective fields.

Costs, Accommodations: Costs range from $75 to $255 and payment by check or money order should accompany application. A 5% to 8% discount is available to Friends of the Institute (tax-deductible annual membership dues begin at $25 for an individual and $35 for a family). Full refund, less $25 processing fee, is granted cancellations at least four weeks prior; no refunds thereafter. Accommodations are available in new cabins with a modern showerhouse nearby. Meals and meeting space are provided in Rosemary Inn, an historic landmark built in 1914 and now the home of the Institute.

Location: Olympic National Park, a complete ecosystem encompassing 938,000 acres, contains the largest temperate rain forest in the western hemisphere, 60 glaciers, 80 kilometers of roadless ocean coastline, large areas of subalpine meadows, and the largest mixed coniferous forest in the U.S.

Contact: Olympic Park Institute, HC 62 Box 9T, Port Angeles, WA 98362; (206) 928-3720.

OMEGA INSTITUTE FOR HOLISTIC STUDIES
Rhinebeck, New York
Weekend and week-long workshops from mid-June to mid-September

The Institute, founded in 1977, is a nonprofit learning center offering more than 200 workshops on topics in global thinking and social change, the arts, psychology, health, business, spirituality, and preventive medicine. A typical weekend program, Nonviolence and Peacemaking in the Middle East, brings together noted scholars, teachers, and peacemakers for a series of lectures, discussions, and small workshops that address the history, complexities, and possible outcomes of the divisions between the inhabitants of the Holy Lands. The faculty also offers an opportunity to experience the prayers and songs of the Jewish, Christian, and Muslim peoples.

Specialties: Global issues and topics relating to mental, physical, and spiritual health

Faculty: Includes accomplished specialists in their fields.

Costs, Accommodations: Weekend workshop fees range from $125 to $130, week-long workshops from approximately $230 to $300. Camping facilities, dorms, and shared or private cottage rooms are available for $66 to $250. All housing fees are per person and include meals, which are primarily vegetarian. Full refund less a $35 fee is granted for cancellations more than 21 days prior to the workshop. Credit voucher good for one year is granted those who cancel less than 21 days prior. Credit cards (VISA, MasterCard) are accepted.

Location: Omega Institute is located near the village of Rhinebeck on 80 acres of lakefront woodlands and rolling hills in the Hudson River Valley, two hours north of New York City.

Contact: Omega Institute, RD 2, Box 377, Rhinebeck, NY, 12572; (914) 338-6030 (Sept. 22-May 17) *or* (914) 266-4301 (May 20-Sept. 21).

OPERA ODYSSEY
Freeport, New York

Fifteen-day spring opera trips to Germany

Opera Odyssey, founded in 1989, offers two spring opera trips, each including performances at nine opera houses in seven or eight cities, fine dining and post-opera suppers, and excursions to historic and cultural sites.

Specialties: Opera-oriented tours.

Faculty: Tour directors Patrick G. Variano, an orchestral and choral conductor, composer, educator, and founder of the Columbia University Chorale; S. Talbot Thayer, an experienced music educator whose choirs have been invited by the National Music Educators Association to participate at national and regional conventions; and such principal lecturers as Martha Harlem, an American soprano with the Cologne Opera.

Costs, Accommodations: Land costs are $4,195, including most meals, double occupancy deluxe hotel lodging (single supplement available), luxury motorcoach, and best available opera tickets. Round-trip airfare ranges from $511 to $789. A $500 deposit must accompany application with balance due 60 days prior to departure. Full refund less $75 fee is granted cancellations more than 60 days prior; 50% of land package cost is refunded thereafter.

Location: The itinerary includes two to three-day visits in Cologne, Frankfurt, Stuttgart, Nuremburg, and Munich.

Contact: Opera Odyssey, Ltd., 6 Beverly Pkwy., Freeport, NY 11520; (516) 623-1458.

THE OREGON SHAKESPEARE FESTI/VAL (OSF)
Ashland, Oregon

One-week and ten-day summer study programs in Ashland

The Oregon Shakespeare Festival, founded in 1935, sponsors nearly a dozen productions on three stages from February through October and offers two study programs — **Wake Up with Shakespeare** and **OSF Round Table** — during the summer months. A two-week seminar for selected high school juniors and two-week symposia for teachers are also offered.

Wake Up with Shakespeare, a one-week program that starts each Monday from the beginning of July through mid-August, consists of morning preparation and discussion followed by an afternoon or evening performance. Sessions meet from 1 to 5 pm the first day and from 9:30 to 11:30 am the remaining days. **OSF Round Table,** a ten-day June program, features a play a day (except Mondays) plus morning classes, where the focus is on discussion.

Specialties: Shakespearean plays.

Faculty: The Round Table is led by Edward S. Brubaker, who served as director of the Festival Institute. Company members and theatre scholars occasionally assist with the classes.

Costs: Cost, which includes tickets to plays and two-hour backstage tour, is $240 for Wake Up with Shakespeare, $350 for OSF Round Table. Credit cards (VISA, MasterCard, American Express) are accepted.

Location: Ashland is situated in southern Oregon in the foothills of the Siskiyou and Cascade ranges, 350 miles north of San Francisco and 285 miles south of Portland.

Contact: Education Office, The Oregon Shakespeare Festival, Box 158, Ashland, OR 97520; (503) 482-2111.

ORLANDO MUSEUM OF ART
Orlando, Florida
Day trips in Florida; 12-day domestic and international tours

Since 1975, the Orlando Museum of Art has offered local, regional, and international trips to the general community of central Florida and Museum members in particular. Day trips to nearby locales focus on current museum exhibits and art events. Domestic and international tours, scheduled two to four times a year for Museum members, visit such areas of cultural interest as Egypt and Alaska's Inside Passage.

Specialties: Tours with an art/culture focus.

Faculty: Regional tours are accompanied by a member of the museum staff.

Costs, Accommodations: Day trips range from $30 to $40; domestic and international tours range from $2,500 to $4,500, all-inclusive. Museum membership dues begin at $25 per year.

Contact: Orlando Museum of Art, 2416 North Mills Rd., Orlando, FL 32803; (407) 896-4231.

OXFORD AND CAMBRIDGE UNIVERSITY VACATIONS
Miami, Florida
One to two-week programs from June-October

Established in 1983, Oxford-Cambridge University Vacations (UNI-VAC) offers adults of all ages a choice of 35 to 40 summer and fall courses at Oxford and Cambridge Universities in England and Trinity College in Dublin, Ireland. Topics include English literature, history, law, archaeology, and science, with such titles as The Cambridge Concise History of Chaucer's England, The Cambridge Concise History of Great Scientific Discovery, The Concise Oxford History of Modern English Mystery, and The Concise

Oxford History of Shakespeare in England. The programs feature a one-hour lecture each morning, two afternoon tea seminars per week, and motorcoach field trips to course-related sites. Those desiring more academic structure can enroll in the Unihostel programs, which offer a minimum of 10 one-hour lectures per week with fewer field trips. Courses include law history, environmental studies, and archaeology. One-hour private tutorials can also be arranged. Optional activities include river punting, concerts, theatre, and a variety of tours.

Specialties: English literature, history, archaeology, and science.

Faculty: Includes Oxford and Cambridge University lecturers.

Costs, Accommodations: Program costs range from $875 to $3,500, which includes single occupancy college lodging, breakfasts and dinners, welcome reception, farewell dinner, tuition, and course-related field trips. A $250 deposit must accompany reservation with balance due (deposit refundable less $50 fee) at least 10 weeks prior to program. Credit cards (American Express, VISA, MasterCard) accepted.

Location: The programs are held at Brasenose College at the University of Oxford, Corpus Christi College at the University of Cambridge, and Trinity College in Dublin, Ireland.

Contact: Oxford-Cambridge Univac, 9602 N.W. 13th St., Miami, FL 33172; (800) 792-0100 *or* (305) 591-1737.

OXFORD/FLORIDA STATE UNIVERSITY (FSU) SUMMER PROGRAM
Tallahassee, Florida

Three-week summer sessions at Oxford University in England

Since 1983, Oxford and Florida State Universities have offered a joint summer program of courses in English history, literature, music, art, and culture, selected to reflect the interests of adults and advanced college and university students. Sixteen different courses are offered, eight in each of two three-week consecutive sessions from the beginning of July through mid-August. Classes, held each weekday morning and limited to 12 participants, are conducted as informal seminars rather than lectures, with opportunities for individual instruction. Afternoons are devoted to course-related field trips and individual pursuits and weekends are free for travel to nearby locales. All (some) courses carry an option for three semester hours of undergraduate (graduate) credit from Florida State University. Students who do not desire academic credit receive 4.5 Continuing Education Units (CEUs) for each course. Participants are expected to read recommended texts prior to arrival, select a course-related topic for concentrated study, and prepare a short written paper.

Typical course titles include Handel and Purcell, a non-technical introduction to music in England timed to coincide with the annual "Handel in Oxford" music festival; Shakespeare: The Human Insight, an in-depth analysis of the bard's genius for insightfully presenting human character; Queen Victoria and Her Ministers, an examination of the reign of Queen Victoria and the political conflict between Disraeli and Gladstone; English Gardens and Landscape, a study of the development of English garden design with visits to gardens in and around Oxford; and Space and Time, an exploration of space and time in relation to the mysteries of the universe.

Since 1981, Florida State University has also offered an annual **Heritage Tour Abroad**. This summer study tour, limited to 25 participants who are accompanied by an FSU professor, visits a different location each year. Typical itineraries include Istanbul and Holland, Switzerland, and England and France.

Specialties: English history, literature, art, music, and culture.

Faculty: All courses are taught by Oxford University tutors.

Costs, Accommodations: The cost, which includes tuition, single room, and three meals daily, is $2,200 for one three-week session or $4,100 for two consecutive three-week sessions (or a couple enrolled in one three-week session). Course materials and field trips are additional. Students live and study within the walls of historic Christ Church and dine in the College's Great Hall. A $300 deposit must accompany application with balance due on acceptance, by April 25. Fee for written notice of cancellation is $50 prior to April 25; $500 between April 25 and June 15; no refund thereafter.

Facilities: Participants may avail themselves of the resources of the Ashmolean Museum, the Bodleian Library, the University Museum, and the Pitt Rivers Museum. Christ Church, the largest of the Oxford colleges, features the architecture of Sir Christopher Wren.

Contact: Oxford/Florida State University Program, Center for Professional Development and Public Service, R-55, Box V, Florida State University, Tallahassee, FL 32306-2027; (904) 644-7551, Fax (904) 644-2589.

OXFORD HERITAGE STUDY VISITS
Oxford, England
Three-day and one-week programs year-round except December

Each week, Oxford Heritage Study Visits offers a choice of programs of cultural and historic interest that center upon the university city of Oxford. Participants may enroll for a midweek or weekend short course (three days) or a week or more, choosing a different program each week. The Monday to Friday schedule consists of a tutorial or seminar group each morning plus three afternoon study visits to course-related sites, including art galleries, museums, country houses, churches, major public schools, and nearby locales. Programs are available in the fields of art, languages and literature, history, religious heritage, architectural history, and antiques.

Those who enroll in the program, English Literature: The Oxford Writers or Shakespeare, can study such Oxford-connected authors as Tolkien, Lewis Carroll, and Evelyn Waugh or focus on the works of Shakespeare, the

Romantic Poets, or the Nineteenth Century novel. Study visits are arranged to Stratford and to Bath, the setting of many Jane Austen novels. The course, English Art, Architecture, and Antiques, is complemented by study visits to the Art Galleries of Oxford and London. Education in Britain, an examination of public and private schools, Universities and Polytechnics, features visits to colleges, departments, and libraries in the University of Oxford as well as such major area schools as Eton and Harrow. Medieval History, Myth, and Legend, a study of English history from the Dark Ages to the War of Roses, covers such themes as chivalry, art and legend, kingship, and the relationship of church and state. The Great Cathedrals and Churches, an introduction to the history and architecture of the great religious foundations of southern England, includes visits to Glastonbury Abbey and the Cathedrals of Winchester, Salisbury, Hereford, and Gloucester. Conversational language courses are also offered.

Following completion of the program, optional three-day visits are available to Cambridge or the Cotswalds. The Cambridge excursion serves as an introduction to the history, institutions, and art of England's other ancient university city. In the Cotswalds, participants study the importance of the parish church and manor house in the English village and country life.

Specialties: Programs of cultural and historical interest that focus on the city of Oxford.

Faculty: The programs are conducted by specialists and guest lecturers in the fields of art, languages and literature, history, religious heritage, architectural history, and antiques.

Costs, Accommodations: Weekly course fee is $580; accommodations, which may include breakfast, range from $160 to $350 per week (private home, college, or cottage) or $60 to $160 per day (inn, hotel, or guest house). Three-day course or extension is $260. A $100 deposit must accompany registration with balance due three weeks prior; deposit is not refundable within three weeks of scheduled arrival.

Contact: Wilson & Lake International, 330 York St., Ashland, OR 97520; (800) 545-5228, (503) 488-3350, Fax (503) 488-7759 or Oxford Heritage Study Visits, North Parade Chambers, North Parade, 75A Banbury Rd., Oxford OX2 6LX, England; (44) 865-511606.

PARSONS SCHOOL OF DESIGN
SPECIAL SUMMER PROGRAMS
New York, New York
Four week international programs from June-August

Parsons School of Design offers a variety of intensive summer programs that relate to art, architecture, archaeology, crafts, and photography. All programs offer undergraduate credit and many offer graduate credit.

Studies in European Decorative Arts and the History of French Architecture; Modern Paris, sponsored in collaboration with Paris' Musée des Arts Décoratifs each July, focuses on the history of the decorative arts and architecture. Students are required to enroll in two courses (a total of six credits), one dealing with French architecture from the 17th century to 1900, the other investigating the development of the decorative arts in Western Europe from the Renaissance to Art Deco. In addition to privileged access to the galleries of the Musée des Arts Décoratifs, students attend specialized presentations by the museum faculty and visit such course-relevant sites as Versailles, Vaux-le-Vicomte and Fountainbleau. An alternate curriculum, Modern Paris, surveys the development of the city from 1830.

History of Italian Architecture explores the architecture and urban design of Rome, Florence, and Venice through on-site presentations of the major architectural monuments from Roman times to the present. Participants are required to enroll in two courses (a total of six credits), one a survey of Italian architecture, the other an exploration of the principles of architectural language and typologies of buildings through on-site comparative investigation of Roman, Florentine, and Venetian monuments.

History of English Architecture and Decorative Arts 1600-1900, co-sponsored by Parsons and the Cooper-Hewitt Museum, promotes direct experience and knowledge of London architecture and decorative arts collections, including trips to country houses and towns accessible from West End. The curriculum encompasses work at the Victoria and Albert Museum, the National Portrait Gallery, the Sir John Soane Museum, Osterly Park, and daylong visits to Oxford, Brighton, and Greenwich. Participants are required to enroll in two courses (a total of six credits), one on the history of architecture, which emphasizes court and aristocratic patronage, and the other concentrating on the history of English interiors, focusing on furniture history from 1660 to 1880.

Specialties: European art, architecture, and decorative arts.

Faculty: The programs are conducted by Parsons' faculty and local historians and specialists.

Costs, Accommodations: Costs, which range from $3,100 to $4,500, include round-trip airfare from/to New York, tuition, and accommodations. Applicants submit a $30 nonrefundable fee and a $350 deposit on acceptance. Half the total cost is due April 15 with the balance due May 15. Written cancellations prior to May 15 receive full deposit refund, thereafter deposit is forfeited.

Location: Includes Paris, Italy, Great Britain.

Contact: Office of Special Programs, Parsons School of Design, 66 Fifth Ave., New York, NY 10011; (212) 741-8975.

PENN STATE ALUMNI VACATION COLLEGE
The Pennsylvania State University
University Park, Pennsylvania
One-week July on-campus program

This week-long vacation college features a variety of morning faculty lectures, workshops, and discussions, and optional afternoon recreational and educational programs. Speakers on such topics as health, environment, economic policy, recreation, computer use, and biotechnology stress current academic thought and research. Representative afternoon tours include the Biotechnology Center, Breazeale Nuclear Reactor, Davey Observatory, Pasto Agriculture Museum, and such activities as windsurfing, sailing, soaring, golf clinic, and computers. Children's programs include day camps for grades 1 through 7, supervised morning activities for teen-agers, and day care center for infants through five-year-olds.

Specialties: A variety of topics.

Faculty: University faculty members.

Costs, Accommodations: Program registration fee is $185 for adults, $20 to $215 for children and teens. An additional fee is charged for some afternoon events. Credit cards (MasterCard, VISA) accepted. Full payment must accompany application and full refund is granted cancellations more than two weeks prior to session. Cost of residence hall lodging ranges from $77 to $112; meal plan is $71. Off-campus housing is available.

Facilities: The 540-acre campus offers such cultural attractions as The Arts Festival Crafts Center, a resident theater company, and museums of art, anthropology, earth and mineral sciences, and entomology. Additional recreational activities include golf, tennis, racquetball, swimming, hiking, biking, sailing, and trail riding.

Contact: Alumni Vacation College, 409 Keller Conference Center, The Pennsylvania State University, University Park, PA 16802; (814) 863-1743.

PEOPLE TO PEOPLE INTERNATIONAL
Kansas City, Missouri
Two to four-week summer and mid-winter programs

Founded in 1956 by President Dwight Eisenhower to further world peace and understanding through exchanges between private citizens, People to People International has offered Study Abroad Programs in conjunction with the University of Missouri-Kansas City since 1987. Designed for serious, academically oriented students and adults who desire the experience of learning through direct contact with leaders in various fields, the program themes cover major cultural, political, social, business, and educational issues. Enrollment in each program generally ranges from 12 to 20 participants, who can receive three to six academic credits through the University of Missouri. An eight-week summer Internship Program for undergraduate/graduate students is also available.

Approximately a dozen programs are offered during June and July, most targeted to the undergraduate/graduate student or educator. Courses suited to auditing adults include **International Relations: Eastern Europe**, featuring lectures by public officials and professors and visits with U.S. diplomatic staff, academic experts, and citizen groups in Budapest and Prague; **Mexico: Past-Present-Future**, tracing the country's development with tours to historic sites and guest classes at the University of Mexico; and **Costa Rica: Birds—Plants—Animals**, including visits to several nature reserves and national parks. A 12-day noncredit Discover Europe tour, with stops in several cities, can be taken alone or as an extension of a program.

The winter break program features two two-week options to students and interested adults. Typical offerings include Ancient Egypt/Classical Rome and Ireland/England, with sessions on Irish society, Irish music, and a comparison of the newspapers and news reporting in both countries.

Specialties: International study programs that focus on cultural, political, social, business, and educational issues.

Faculty: The University of Missouri-Kansas City provides academic faculty, which is supplemented by professionals in the countries visited.

Costs, Accommodations: Costs for most summer programs range from approximately $2,200 to $3,700, which includes tuition and materials, round-trip airfare from/to the U.S., double or triple occupancy lodging in tourist class hotels or dormitories (single supplement $200 to $450), continental breakfasts and some other meals, and planned activities. A $300 deposit must accompany application with $500 due in mid-February, $1,000 due in mid-April and balance due by early May. Cancellations a least 30 days prior to trip receive full refund; a $200 fee is charged 7 to 30 days prior; no refund thereafter. Winter break courses require a $500 deposit with application and final payment at least six weeks prior to departure. If course is cancelled, applicants forfeit a $100 administrative fee. Those who cancell at least six weeks prior forfeit $250 to $450.

Location: Program locations include Belgium, China, Costa Rica, Czechoslovakia, Egypt, England, France, Germany, Hungary, Ireland, Italy, Mexico, Netherlands, Rome, and Sweden.

Contact: Collegiate Program, People to People International, 501 East Armour, Kansas City, MO 64109; (816) 531-4701.

THE PHILADELPHIA MUSEUM OF ART
Philadelphia, Pennsylvania

One-day to three-week trips in the U.S. and abroad

The Philadelphia Museum of Art offers a variety of tour and travel programs for the general membership and the Friends of the Museum, ranging from day trips to nearby art centers, artists' studios, and private collections to weekend trips in the U.S. and longer trips abroad. Group size is usually limited to 25 to 30 participants.

Day and weekend trips — open to all members — visit such cities as New York, Boston, and Washington, D.C., and feature guided tours of current museum exhibitions. Studio visits offer members the opportunity to drop in on Philadelphia-area artists to talk about their art and working methods. Lunch with artists and tours of their installations are sometimes included. Tours of private collections usually include a seminar or discussion.

Additional day trips and longer domestic and international trips — open to Friends of the Philadelphia Museum of Art — are scheduled throughout the year. In addition to guided tours of architectural highlights and museum collections, these travel programs feature special access to private collections that are not open to the general public.

Specialties: Trips and tours with an art focus.

Faculty: Domestic trips and tours are accompanied by a representative of the Museum. International travel programs are accompanied by a member of the Museum's curatorial or educational staff, who serves as a cultural lecturer throughout the tour.

Costs, Accommodations: Day trips range from $55 to $75 for Members, $85 to $150 for Friends. Domestic travel programs range from $400 to $1,400, which includes round-trip airfare, double occupancy deluxe accommodations (single supplement available), most meals, ground transportation, and planned activities. Costs of international travel vary. Annual membership dues begin at $15 student, $30 individual, $45 household. Annual Friends dues begin at $100 per couple ($40 for ages 35 and younger).

Contact: Bonnie Moxey Coulter, Membership Dept. *or* Helene Voron, Friends, The Philadelphia Museum of Art, Benjamin Franklin Parkway, Box 7646, Philadelphia, PA 19101-7646; (215) 787-5430 (Members) *or* (215) 787-5496 (Friends).

PITT'S INFORMAL PROGRAM (PIP)
University of Pittsburgh
Pittsburgh, Pennsylvania

One-day to three-week domestic and international trips

Since 1978, Pitt's Informal Program has offered travel programs that range from day trips to nearby locales to a variety of international travel opportunities. Approximately 50 to 60 domestic and 7 to 10 international itineraries are offered each year, many preceded by a pre-trip lecture by the tour leader. Group size is limited, depending on tour.

One to five-day domestic travel programs include day trips to historic sites, weekend theatre trips to New York and other locales, and music and art trips that feature museum visits and concerts. International tour destinations may include Kenya, Japan, France, Turkey, Ireland, China, Sweden, and Australia and New Zealand. The annual **London Theatre Tour**, offered each May since 1987, is highlighted by a behind-the-scenes tour, museum visits, and informal after-theatre discussions.

Specialties: A variety of travel programs in the U.S. and abroad, many with an art, music, theatre, or cultural focus.

Faculty: Most trips are accompanied by a University of Pittsburgh professor who excels in the theme of the trip.

Costs, Accommodations: Day trips cost approximately $40, two to five-day domestic excursions range from $250 to $1,000, and international trips range from $1,000 to $4,000. A $100 to $300 deposit secures reservation for domestic and international trips with balance due 30 to 90 days prior to departure. Refund policies vary. Credit cards (VISA, MasterCard) accepted.

Contact: Pitt's Informal Program, 3804 Forbes Ave., Pittsburgh, PA 15260; (412) 648-2560.

THE PLANTAGENET TOURS
Moordown, Bournemouth, England
One to three-week European and African tours year-round

Established in 1982 by Professor Peter Gravgaard, The Plantagenet Tours offers 15 tour itineraries, each scheduled once a year. Each tour focuses on a specific theme, usually historical, literary, or cultural, and is limited to 25 participants. Participants are assisted in obtaining academic credit.

The Isabella Tour to Medieval Andalucia, organized around the story of the reconquest of Spain by the Christians from the Moors, which culminated in the conquest of Granada in 1492 by Queen Isabella and King Ferdinand, includes stops in Madrid, Toledo, Cordoba, Granada, Alhambra, Sevilla, and Lisbon, Portugal. The Joan of Arc Tour from Lorraine to Normandy follows her life from her origins in the East of France to her trial and execution in Rouen. The Elizabeth Tour to Renaissance England, an introduction to the history and culture of the era, provides insight into the life of the court of Queen Elizabeth I and her prominent courtiers through visits to English castles, palaces, and manorhouses. The Literary England Tour features visits to locales associated with noted literary figures, including their homes and birthplaces, the schools they attended, museums exhibiting their work, and the places they wrote about. The Freedom on the March Tour to Eastern Europe visits Warsaw, Budapest, and Berlin and includes lectures on the post-1945 history of Eastern Europe as well as recent events.

Other itineraries include the Karen Blixen Tour to Denmark and Africa, The Philippa Tour to Medieval Portugal, and the Barbarossa Tour to Medieval Germany and Italy.

Specialties: Historical, literary, and cultural theme tours of Europe.

Faculty: Peter Gravgaard, a native of Copenhagen, studied comparative literature at Indiana University and Yale University and taught English literature at the University of Minnesota and Odense University in Denmark.

Costs, Accommodations: Land costs, which range from $995 to $3,758, include double occupancy three-star hotel accommodations (single supplement available), breakfasts and lunches, ground transportation, and planned activities. A $300 (nine-day tour) to $600 (longer tours) deposit must accompany reservation with balance due 90 days prior to first day of tour. Cancellation charge ranges from 15% of total cost (more than 42 days prior) to 60% (less than 15 days prior).

Location: Includes Africa, Denmark, England, France, Germany, Hungary, Italy, Poland, Portugal, and Spain.

Contact: The Plantagenet Tours, 85 The Grove, Moordown, Bournemouth BH9 2TY, England; (800) 521-4556 (toll-free from U.S.) or (44) 202 521895.

POCONO ENVIRONMENTAL EDUCATION CENTER (PEEC)
Dingmans Ferry, Pennsylvania
One and two-day weekend programs

Converted from a Pocono honeymoon resort in 1972, this nonprofit, self-supporting nature study center sponsors **Nature Study Weekends, Birding Weekends**, teacher workshops, photography and creative arts seminars and workshops, Elderhostel programs, and a variety of family vacations. Teacher in-service credit is available for most programs.

Typical **Nature Study Weekend** titles include Winter Wonders, a series of outdoor walks that focus on animal tracking in the snow, identification features of trees and shrubs, searching for dormant insects and spiders, and observing winter bird species, with evening slide programs that cover the diverse methods by which wildlife survive the winter; Nature in Transition, a series of field trips, hikes, and evening slide presentations devoted to the adaptation of plants and animals to seasonal changes in the area's forests, wetlands, and fields; and Whitetail Deer Seminar, a program for naturalists, photographers, and hunters that specializes in this animal's behavior and traits. **Birding Weekends** are strategically scheduled throughout the year to take advantage of such seasonal occurrences as migrations and nesting. Representative topics include In Search of Eagles, a seminar that is part of PEEC's cooperative effort with the National Park Service's on-going research project to determine the number of bald eagles wintering in the area; Warbler Weekend, small group guided walks that emphasize the identification of warblers by sight and sound; and PEEC Christmas Count, a bird count that occurs over one calendar day as part of the National Audubon Society's coast-to-coast annual bird census.

Specialties: Nature study and birdwatching.

Faculty: John Serrao, an interpretative naturalist, photographer, educator, environmental consultant, and author of *The Wild Palisades of the Hudson*; wildlife photographer Leonard Lee Rue III, author of 18 books, including *How I Photograph Wildlife and Nature*; and experienced birdwatchers.

Costs, Accommodations: Program fees, including meals and lodging, range from $45 to $99. A 10% nonrefundable deposit must accompany application. Participants are housed in single room cabins that sleep four to six persons and meals are served buffet style in the Center's dining hall. Membership in PEEC begins at $5 for students, $15 for individuals.

Location, Facilities: The field center is located within the boundaries of the Delaware Water Gap National Recreation Area, 20 miles south of the New York, New Jersey, and Pennsylvania junction, two hours from New York City and three hours from Philadelphia. It consists of 38 acres of residential facilities and 200,000 acres of public lands with fields, forests, ponds, waterfalls, streams, gorges, and 12 miles of hiking trails. Facilities include an indoor pool, arts and crafts center, darkroom, dance floor, library, bookstore, and computer lab.

Contact: Pocono Environmental Education Center, RD 2, Box 1010, Dingmans Ferry, PA 18328; (717) 828-2319.

POINT REYES FIELD SEMINARS
Point Reyes Station, California
One and two-day seminars

This self-supporting year-round program, sponsored by the Point Reyes National Seashore Association and the National Park Service since 1976, offers courses in natural history and birding, the arts, environmental education, and programs especially for families and teachers.

These one and two-day seminars feature such classes as Journey Across Point Reyes, a natural history traverse of the Point Reyes peninsula with discussions of wildflowers, reproduction of ferns, earthquake geology, and weather; Tidepooling, an exploration of the diverse life that exists at the water's edge; Tracking, a study of such clues as prints and scat to reveal the habits and habitats of many of the region's elusive wildlife; and Beginning Birding, which focuses on species identification using behavioral and plumage characteristics.

Specialties: Natural history.

Faculty: Specialists in natural history subjects, including biology, botany, zoology, entomology, and ornithology.

Costs, Accommodations: Costs range from $20 to $75. When activities continue into the evening, the fee includes dormitory accommodations at the Clem Miller Environmental Education Center or the Chimney Rock Lifeboat Station. Full refund less $10 fee is granted cancellations more than 15 working days prior to seminar; 50% refund less $10 is granted 11 to 15 working days prior; no refund thereafter. Those who cancel more than 10 days prior can opt for a seminar credit, good for one year, in lieu of refund. College credit ($30 per unit) may be earned for some courses.

Location: Point Reyes National Seashore is 50 miles north of San Francisco.

Contact: Point Reyes Field Seminars, Point Reyes National Seashore Assn., Bear Valley Rd., Point Reyes Station, CA 94956; (415) 663-1200.

PROJECT OCEAN SEARCH (P.O.S.) EXPEDITIONS
The Cousteau Society
Norfolk, Virginia

Approximately two fourteen-day projects each summer at an island locale

Begun in 1973, Project Ocean Search (P.O.S.) is a series of intensive sea/land field-study programs conducted by The Cousteau Society to promote appreciation and understanding of nature and the value of natural resources. Each year a limited number of participants (30 or less) from diverse age groups and backgrounds join a Cousteau team on expeditions to a remote island area. Daily activities include scuba dives that emphasize different aspects of natural history, hiking and exploration of the island, and afternoon lectures that cover such subjects as coral reef and fish ecology, island culture, resource management, marine mammals, history of diving, and art and literature of the sea. Evening audio-visual presentations focus on the relationship of humankind to the environment. While no scientific background is necessary, scuba diving experience is strongly recommended for full participation. Each session of P.O.S. includes instruction in underwater photography conducted by a Nikon expert and Costeau staff members.

Specialties: Natural history and ecology.

Faculty: Includes Jean-Michel Cousteau, ecologist Richard Murphy, a team of marine scientists, and Cousteau Society lecturers and divers.

Costs, Accommodations: Cost, which includes housing (tents or shelters) and board, averages $150 per day. Participants supply their own sleeping gear and eating utensils, depending on location.

Location: Typical locations include the Fijian island of Vanua Levu; Hilton Head, South Carolina; Catalina and Santa Cruz Islands, California; Wuvulu Island, north of Papua New Guinea; and Moskito Island in the British Virgin Islands.

Contact: Project Ocean Search, 930 W. 21st St., Norfolk, VA 23517; (804) 627-1144.

PROSPECT ART AND MUSIC TOURS
European Travel Management
Westport, Connecticut

Two to twenty-five-day tours worldwide

Prospect Music and Art Ltd., based in London, offers more than 150 tours annually, each limited to 10 to 25 participants.

Two to five-day **cultural tours** offered throughout England include the three-day Shakespeare in Stratford, which features two plays, the opportunity to study one play in depth during two three-hour and one 90-minute study sessions, and a two-hour review and critique after the performance.

Art tours, which include slide-illustrated lectures by the tour leader, feature visits to regions noted for their art, architecture, and archaeology as well as their literary and cultural heritage. **Music and opera tours** are scheduled to festivals and other musical events.

Specialties: Art and music tours.

Faculty: More than 60 art historians, archaeologists, and music scholars who are selected for their expertise and communication skills.

Costs, Accommodations: Tours in England range from £170 to £475, other tours range from £375 to £2,750, which includes transportation from/to Great Britain, double occupancy first class accommodations (single supplement available), breakfasts and some other meals, and admission fees. Nonrefundable £75 to £100 deposit must accompany booking with balance due eight weeks prior to departure. Within six weeks of departure, cancellation penalty ranges from 30% of total (29 to 42 days prior) to 80% of total (less than eight days prior).

Location: Art tours are scheduled to 24 countries, Music and Opera tours to more than 25 destinations, including Belgium, Czechoslovakia, Denmark, France, Germany, Holland, Hungary, Iberia, Indonesia, Ireland, Italy, Jordan, the Soviet Union, Spain, Switzerland, Syria, Thailand, Turkey, the United States, and Vienna.

Contact: European Travel Management, 235 Post Rd. West, Westport, CT 06880; (203) 454-0090, Fax (203) 454-8840 *or* Prospect Music & Art Ltd., 454-458 Chiswick High Rd., London W4 5TT, England; (44) 81-995-2163/2151.

QUESTERS WORLDWIDE NATURE TOURS
New York, New York
Eleven-day to four-week domestic and international tours

Established in 1973, Questers offers more than 30 tour itineraries in the United States, Central and South America, the Caribbean, Europe, Asia, Africa, and the South Pacific. The focus of each tour, which is limited to 20 participants, is on the natural history of the country or region visited. Local cultures, customs, archaeological sites, and points of interest are emphasized.

Specialties: Tours with a natural history focus.

Faculty: Tour directors are naturalists with a particular expertise in one area and general knowledge in other subjects of nature study. Local guides often accompany field trips and excursions.

Costs, Accommodations: Tour costs, which include airfare, first class or best available hotel and game lodge accommodations where appropriate, meals, and surface transportation, range from approximately $2,100 to $7,770; single supplement is available. A surcharge of 10% of land cost may be levied in the event of less than minimum enrollment (15 persons). A $300 deposit must accompany application with balance due 60 days prior to departure. Cancellation penalty ranges from $50 (more than 60 days prior) to 80% of cost (14 to 44 days prior); no refunds thereafter.

Location: Summer itineraries include Alaska, the Pacific Northwest, the High Arctic, Brazil, Iceland, Scotland, Norway, France, Switzerland, Greece, and Eastern Europe. Winter itineraries include Hawaii, Mexico, Costa Rica, Venezuela, the Amazon, the Galapagos Islands and Ecuador, Chile, Argentina, the Himalayas, East Africa, Australia, and New Zealand.

Contact: Questers Worldwide Nature Tours, 257 Park Ave. South, New York, NY 10010-7369; (800) 468-8668 *or* (212) 673-3120, Fax (212) 473-0178.

RECURSOS DE SANTA FE
Santa Fe, New Mexico

Two-day to two-week seminars and study tours in the Southwest and Central America

Founded in 1984 as a nonprofit organization dedicated to promoting an appreciation of the Greater Southwest, Recursos de Santa Fe offers a variety of programs that focus on art, archaeology, native and regional culture, and natural history. Representative titles include Skylight Conversations on Contemporary Art, which consists of background discussions, conversations with artists in their studios, and visits to local museums, galleries, native pueblos and villages, and archaeological sites; Indian Art of the Central Plains, a series of discussions and illustrations of the art hertitage of these nomadic peoples; and Georgia O'Keeffe, a reappraisal of this important artist that focuses on her artistic and psychological development, her reactions to criticism, the context within which she painted, and the people who influenced her work and her life. Several **Natural History Study Trips** are planned to various ecosystems.

Specialties: Seminars and study tours that focus on natural history, art, and archaeology.

Faculty: Includes co-founder and director Ellen Bradbury, former director of the New Mexico Museum of Fine Art, and co-founder and director of programs Ginger Richardson. Seminars and study tours are conducted by experienced art historians, curators, museum staff members and directors, artists, scholars, naturalists, and archaeologists.

Costs, Accommodations: Seminar costs are approximately $125 per day, $325 for a three-day program, $525 including double-occupancy lodging, and $1,000 to $1,500 for trips to Mexico.

Location: Seminars are held at hotels in Santa Fe, a well-known artistic center with a rich heritage of adobe architecture and art. Local cultural attractions include museums, musical events, and repertory theater. Natural History Study Trip destinations include Costa Rica, Baja California, Big Bend National Park, and the Sonoran Desert.

Contact: Recursos de Santa Fe, 826 Camino de Monte Rey A-3, Santa Fe, NM 87501; (505) 982-9301.

RED COAT TOURS
Lethbridge, Alberta, Canada
Five to seven-day tours each week from May to October

Established in 1990, Red Coat Tours offers a series of programs, each limited to 20 participants, that specialize in reliving history by following the routes of early explorers. Typical itineraries include the original route of the Mounties, when they traveled west to bring law and order, and the 1858 routes of two of the first explorers through the Canadian Rockies. Each participant receives a book that contains excerpts of the original journals and has room for them to pen their own observations when visiting the same location.

Specialties: Historical tours.

Faculty: Tour leader Bruce Haig, B.Ed. B.A., is recipient of several awards, including the Canada Celebration Award, AHRF Heritage Service Award, Heritage Canada Award, Hilroy Innovations in Canadian Education Award, and the Historical Society of Alberta Award.

Costs: Approximately C$125 per day. A cancellation charge is assessed withdrawals within 45 days. Credit cards (VISA, Mastercard) accepted.

Contact: Red Coat Tours, 1710D-31 St. N., Lethbridge, AB T1H 5H1, Canada; (403) 327-4099.

ROCKLAND COMMUNITY COLLEGE (RCC)
Center for International Studies
Suffern, New York

Three-week wintersession and two-week summer sessions abroad

Since 1968, Rockland Community College's Center for International Studies has offered a **Wintersession in London Program** and also sponsors a variety of study tours to other countries during the summer. Three college credits are available for each program.

The three-week January **Wintersession in London Program,** which is open to both students and adults, consists of nine seminars that usually vary each year, supplemented by an itinerary of relevant visits, tours, and other activities. Representative seminar titles include Broadcasting in Britain, which features on-the-scene visits to the Museum of the Moving Image, the BBC, ABC-TV's London office, and such commercial outlets as Thames, London Weekend, and Granada; Criminal Justice Seminar, an exploration of the historical development, procedures, and policies of the English system, with visits to the Old Bailey, courts, and prisons to hear lectures by experienced personnel; Literary England Seminar, focusing on major British writers through both their work and visits to important locations connected with them; History of England, a tour of the principal historical sites supplemented by lectures and museum visits; and Performing Arts in London, including musical and non-musical theatre performances, a backstage tour, meetings with performers and directors, and an excursion to historical sites in Cambridge.

Typical summer study tours include Seminar in Comparative Cultures, which compares and contrasts the cultures, history, and people of Spain and Morocco; European Integration: Challenges and Opportunities, an examination of the barrier-free trade policies proposed for the EEC with visits to EEC Headquarters and the U.S. Mission in Brussels and businesses in West Germany and Paris; and Criminal Justice Seminar in Israel, an opportunity to learn about the development, procedures, and policies of the Israeli system.

Specialities: Study tours that focus on a variety of topics, including broadcasting, criminal justice, literature, and theatre.

Faculty: Members of the Rockland Community College faculty.

Costs, Accommodations: Costs, which include round-trip airfare, double occupancy accommodations (some singles available), breakfasts, and day excursions, are $968 for the London Wintersession program and $1,355 to $1,715 for the summer study tours. Tuition is additional ($170 for New York State residents). Deposit and refund policies vary.

Contact: Center for International Studies, Rockland Community College, 145 College Rd., Suffern, NY 10901; (914) 356-4650.

LA SABRANENQUE RESTORATION PROJECTS
Saint Victor la Coste, France
Two and three-week summer sessions

Since 1969 the nonprofit La Sabranenque has been working with volunteers in southern France on projects aimed toward the preservation, restoration and revitalization of villages, simple monuments, and rural sites. They restored an entire old village dating from medieval times and, in 1981, expanded to Italy through a collaboration with Italian preservation organizations. Having won national awards and prizes, their goal is to restore, reconstruct, re-use, and revitalize abandoned historic sites as well as give participants an opportunity to work together on creative projects. Two and three-week sessions run from June 1 to August 30 with each session limited to 20 to 35 participants, of whom 10 are North Americans.

The work is diverse, involving training of the eye and hand through the use of local raw materials and manual tools and techniques. Participants are integrated into continuing projects and work within a small team on a precise part, the type of work depending on the project's stage of completion. Work may include stone masonry, stone-cutting for window and door openings, carpentry for ceilings and roofs, floor and roof tiling, path paving, and dry stone walling. At least one day during each session is spent visiting the surrounding region. La Sabranenque also offers three-month intensive French language programs in spring and fall.

Specialties: Restoration of monuments and villages.

Faculty: Restoration technicians include architects, master carpenters, professors, photographers, and students.

Costs, Accommodations: Cost, which includes housing, full board, transportation within France and Italy, and all activities, is $450 for the two-week sessions, $780 to $830 for the three-week sessions. Participants live in modern, restored houses.

Location: The two-week sessions are in Saint Victor la Coste, in the South of France near Avignon. The three-week projects begin with 10 days of training and participation in Saint Victor la Coste. The team then works on a restoration project in Montescaglioso, Gnallo, or Settefonti, Italy.

Contact: La Sabranenque Restoration Projects, c/o Jacqueline C. Simon, 217 High Park Blvd., Buffalo, NY 14226; (716) 836-8698 *or* rue de la Tour de l'Oume, 30290 Saint Victor la Coste, France; (33) 66 50 05 05.

SACRED SITES AND SACRED SCIENCE IN ANCIENT EGYPT
Saugerties, New York
15-day tours of Egypt

Since 1985, Egyptologist John Anthony West has conducted approximately four 15-day tours a year to Egypt, including visits to major sites in Cairo, Giza, Sakkara, Memphis, Abydos, Dendera, Luxor, West Bank, the Valley of the Kings, Karnak, Aswan, and Abu Simbel. Designed for 15 to 36 serious travelers, the tours focus on the meaning and significance of ancient Egyptian architecture, art, religion, and science, and examine the various theories surrounding the tombs, temples, and pyramids.

Specialties: Egyptology.

Faculty: Independent Egyptologist John Anthony West is author of *The Traveler's Key to Ancient Egypt* and *Serpent in the Sky: The High Wisdom of Ancient Egypt,* an examination of the work of the late mathematician, philosopher, and Orientalist R.A. Schwaller de Lubicz, who published a three-volume text documenting his Symbolist interpretation of ancient Egypt.

Costs, Accommodations: The cost of approximately $2,900 includes roundtrip transportation from/to New York, deluxe or best available accommodations, most meals, ground transportation, and planned activities, including a desert camel trek. A $500 deposit must accompany reservation with balance due 60 days prior to departure. Cancellations more than 45 days prior receive full refund less $50; no refunds thereafter.

Contact: Sphinx Tours, 721 Fifth Ave., #38B, New York, NY 10022; (212) 832-3120 *or* John Anthony West, 1517 Manorville Rd., Saugerties, NY 12477; (518) 678-9580.

SAINT MARY'S COLLEGE SUMMER PROGRAMS
Notre Dame, Indiana

One-month travel programs in London and Rome

Each year Saint Mary's College sponsors two one-month summer study programs, one to London and one to Rome, that are designed for both college students, who can earn up to six hours of academic credit in each program, as well as interested adults. Part of each program consists of visits to places of historical and cultural interest and part is devoted to course study. Each course is offered for two or three credits, with the third credit available through a research paper written after the trip. Participants in the London program, from the third week in May to the third week in June, can also join part or all of the Rome program, which runs from mid-June to mid-July. Informational meetings, not a prerequisite, are held in the fall and spring.

The London program, offered annually since 1974, features five-day sightseeing excursions in Ireland, Scotland, and Paris, and two weeks of study in London, during which classes are held in the mornings and trips to major points of interest are scheduled most afternoons. Approximately a half dozen courses are offered on such subjects as The British View of Nature, which examines the contributions of the United Kingdom to the understanding of natural history; Survey of International Business and Economics, a study of business factors that affect international trade; Study Tour: Great Britain and Ireland, with lectures and discussions on the history of the areas visited; and The City in Modern European History, focusing on the cities of Dublin, Edinburgh, London, and Paris at various stages of their development. All courses feature visits to relevant sites and full-day trips are scheduled to Stratford-Upon-Avon, Oxford and Blenheim Palace, and other locales.

The Rome program, offered annually since 1977, is for those who wish to investigate more complex European problems and gain historical insight into political, social, and economic issues. The trip features organized travel through France, Germany, Switzerland, and Italy, with a ten-day stay in Rome devoted to a choice of courses, including Social Problems in Cross Cultural Perspective and lectures and tours conducted at places of interest to the historical and cultural development of Western Europe, with emphasis on Rome. Classes are held in the Saint Mary's College Rome Program building and at monuments and galleries.

Specialties: Cultural, historical, and economic aspects of Europe, with emphasis on London and Rome.

Faculty: Program coordinators are Dr. Anthony A. Black, Professor of History at Saint Mary's College and a specialist in European history, and Dr. Portia Prebys, a Saint Mary's College alumna, resident of Italy for more than 20 years, and a specialist in Italian history, culture, and language. Other instructors include Professors David Sever, Donald Horning, Lauren Strach, Charles Poinsatte, and Charles Martucci.

Costs, Accommodations: The $2,795 cost of the London program includes air travel from/to New York, ground transportation in Europe, all breakfasts and three dinners, and admissions to scheduled points of interest. A $100 airfare supplement is charged nonstudents. A $100 deposit, refundable until April 1, secures a reservation until April 23 with airfare payable by April 12 and balance due by May 2. The $3,655 cost (plus $100 airfare supplement for those over age 26) of the Rome program includes air travel from/to New York, ground transportation in Europe, and all breakfasts and dinners. A $100 deposit, runfundable until May 1, secures a reservation until May 26. Cost per credit hour is $100.

Contact: Professor Anthony R. Black, Saint Mary's College, Notre Dame, IN 46556-5001; (219) 284-4460 weekdays, (219) 272-3726 evenings and weekends.

SAN DIEGO MUSEUM OF ART (SDMA)
San Diego, California
Four-day to one-month domestic and international tours

The San Diego Museum of Art sponsors eight to ten tours annually for its members. Trips within the U.S. range from four to six days and include visits to private collections and artists' studios and guided tours of museums and galleries. Trips abroad feature informal cultural talks and sightseeing at major attractions with emphasis on museums, galleries, palaces, and churches. Most tours are limited to 20 to 35 participants.

Specialties: Tours with an art focus.

Faculty: Each tour is accompanied by a representative of the museum, usually a member of the curatorial staff who has helped plan the intinerary.

Costs, Accommodations: Four to six-day trips within the U.S. range from $900 to $1,000, two-week trips abroad range from $3,500 to $5,000 (single supplement usually available), which includes a museum donation, round-trip airfare from/to San Diego, ground transportation, lodging, scheduled activities, and most meals. A $250 to $500 deposit secures a reservation. Annual SDMA membership dues are $30 for an individual, $45 for a couple.

Location: Tour destinations within the U.S. include Taos and Washington, D.C. Tour destinations abroad include India, Eastern Europe, the Aegean Sea, England, Italy, and the Danube River. The Museum is located in the center of Balboa Park near downtown San Diego, within walking distance of the San Diego Zoo.

Contact: Membership/Travel Coordinator, San Diego Museum of Art, P.O. Box 2107, San Diego, CA 92112-2107; (619) 232-7931, ext. 160.

SAN DIEGO NATURAL HISTORY MUSEUM
San Diego, California
One to two-week West Coast trips year-round

The San Diego Natural History Museum sponsors a variety of trips with a natural history emphasis. Typical programs include a one-week exploration of the geological and biological islands in the Sea of Cortez and a nine-day boat trip to examine the flora, fauna, and geology of Baja California, featuring a three-day encounter with the gray whales of San Ignacio Lagoon. Some trips are organized by the museum, others are planned by travel companies.

Specialties: Natural history excursions.

Faculty: Museum staff and qualified naturalists.

Costs, Accommodations: Costs of the described trips range from $750 to $1,100, which includes membership dues ($20 individual, $30 family).

Contact: Education Dept., San Diego Natural History Museum, P.O. Box 1390, San Diego, CA 92112; (619) 232-3821.

SAN DIEGO STATE UNIVERSITY (SDSU)
TRAVEL STUDY PROGRAMS
College of Extended Studies
San Diego, California
Ten-day to three-week international study tours

Each year, the SDSU College of Extended Studies sponsors approximately 18 to 20 travel study programs that utilize a variety of instruction methods, including lectures, seminars, discussions, field trips, and individual study projects.

Typical itineraries include Galápagos Islands & Ecuador, an exploration of the islands' unique flora and fauna and the various Ecuadorian cultures; A Kenya Adventure, focusing on African bird and wildlife; and Hawaii, an introduction to the region's cultural and natural history.

In cooperation with the Classical Alliance of the Western States (CAWS), SDSU also offers several tours that are available for academic credit in **Humanities through Extension.** Representative credit programs include A Turkish Odyssey: Classical, Byzantine, and Ottoman Turkey with Greece, which highlights the art and archaeology of the northeastern Mediterranean; Hapsburg Capitals: Vienna, Prague, Budapest, an in-depth cultural and art history tour of the capitals of the old Austro-Hungarian Empire; and Spain — Fusion of Culture and History.

Specialties: Travel study programs that focus on a variety of topics, including natural history, humanities, and culture.

Faculty: All programs are escorted by University faculty members who are familiar with the area's cultural opportunities. Resident specialist lecturers are also utilized.

Costs: Tour costs range from approximately $1,700 to 3,400. Deposit requirements and refund policies vary.

Location: In addition to the above, may include Alaska, Australia, the Dominican Republic, Egypt, Morocco, the Soviet Union, and South America.

Contact: SDSU Extended Studies Travel Programs, 5630 Hardy Ave., San Diego, CA 92182; (619) 594-2645.

SAN JOSE STATE UNIVERSITY (SJSU)
INTERNATIONAL TRAVEL PROGRAMS
Continuing Education
San Jose, California

Two to six-week international programs

San Jose State University's Continuing Education Department offers 15 to 25 travel and language study programs annually for students and adults. A variety of instructional methods are used, including lecture, discussion, field trips, seminars, and individual study projects, and participants are expected to participate in and complete pre-travel reading and academic assignments. Some trips feature classes at universities in the regions visited and degree and/or professional credit is offered for all programs. Group size is limited to 5 to 40 participants, depending upon program.

During the **Summer Session in London,** a six-week summer program offered in cooperation with Middlesex Polytechnic, students spend about ten hours a week in classes, usually three mornings or afternoons, in groups of about 15. Most teaching is on a seminar basis but lectures and tutorials are also scheduled. Students select one or two of a variety of courses relating to the humanities, social sciences, art and design, and performing arts and participate in such optional activities as weekend excursions to Paris, Amsterdam, and Edinburgh; day trips to nearby historical sites of interest; and half-day and evening visits to landmarks and London theatres.

Great British Sports, a summer series planned for 1991, focuses on important traditional British sports from an historical, sociological, and geographical perspective. The programs feature attendance at major sporting events, such as Wimbledon (tennis), Lords (cricket), and the British Open (golf), visits to sports museums and playing sites such as Wembley Stadium, and lecture/discussion relating to the place of sport in the British context and its historic world influence.

Specialties: Travel-study tours to international destinations.

Faculty: All programs are conducted by SJSU faculty. Students in the Summer Session in London study with British faculty.

Costs, Accommodations: Costs range from approximately $2,100 to $3,500, which includes round-trip airfare, double occupancy accommodations (single supplement usually available), meals, ground transportation, and scheduled activities. Tuition is additional. A $100 to $300 deposit must accompany reservation with balance due two months prior to departure. Cancellations less than two months prior forfeit deposit and nonrecoverable costs.

Location: Students in the Summer Session in London live and attend classes at Middlesex Polytechnic Trent Park Campus, a half-hour Underground trip from downtown London. Other travel study program itineraries may include the Galápagos Islands and Ecuador, East Africa, Nepal, Thailand and Hong Kong, Brazil, the Soviet Union, Alaska, and Japan.

Contact: Travel Programs, Office of Continuing Education, San Jose State University, San Jose, CA 95192-0135; (408) 924-2680.

SEAFARERS EXPEDITIONS
Bangor, Maine
Three to twelve-day international expeditions year-round

Established in 1982, Seafarers Expeditions offers approximately ten trips annually to regions of marine wildlife activity. Itineraries include the Central Azores, an opportunity to learn about the geological phenomena of the area's semi-active volcanoes, and the Mingan Islands/Gulf of St. Lawrence, where participants work with the Mingan Island Cetacean Research Study.

Specialties: Marine wildlife, including whales, dolphins, and polar bears.

Faculty: Expeditions are accompanied by a member of Seafarers' eight-member staff of naturalists and biologists as well as local experts.

Costs, Accommodations: Costs range from $595 to $2,995, which includes double occupancy lodging (single supplement available), meals, ground transportation, boats, and may include airfare. A $200 deposit must accompany reservation.

Location: In addition to the above, includes Newfoundland, the Bay of Fundy, Nova Scotia, Tortola, Dominica, and Venezuela.

Contact: Seafarers Expeditions, P.O. Box 691, Bangor, ME 04401-9862; (207) 942-7942.

SEMESTER AT SEA
Institute for Shipboard Education
University of Pittsburgh
Pittsburgh, Pennsylvania
Fourteen-week global semesters in spring and fall

Established as the University of the Seven Seas in 1963 and sponsored by the University of Pittsburgh since 1980, Semester at Sea offers two programs each academic year, from late January to early May and from mid-September to late December. Designed to be a special global semester in a student's undergraduate career, each program accommodates approximately 500 students, 40 to 50 of whom are senior adults seeking personal enrichment. The University of Pittsburgh approves the academic program and faculty credentials and grants academic credit while the Institute for Shipboard Education arranges field programs in ports of call and faculty-developed practica to complement the academic portion.

The purpose of the program is to provide participants with insight and background for interpreting international problems, understanding different cultures, and learning various disciplines. Students are required to enroll in at least four courses (12 semester hours) and attend daily classes, which average 20 to 30 students, while at sea. Adults may also enroll in classes, depending upon the capacity of the classroom and the instructor's willingness to admit them. More than 50 courses are offered in approximately 17 disciplines, including anthropology, biological sciences, business, economics, fine arts, geography, geology, history, literature, music, philosophy, political science, psychology, religious studies, sociology, and theatre arts. A special seminar for adults, which is usually offered, consists of a series of lectures focused on broad issues of cultural, political, economic, scientific, and artistic interest.

About half of the semester is spent at sea and half in the countries of call, with three to seven-day stays in each of eight to ten countries. Field activities in each of the ports, designed to complement the academic portion, are of three types: Standard, Faculty-Developed, and Independent Field Practica. Standard Practica are broadly related to the nature of the voyage and include travel to sites of cultural, historical, and political interest with activities such as diplomatic briefings, university visits, meetings with government officials, and tours of corporate and manufacturing facilities, museums, and rural villages. Extended overnight trips to the People's Republic of China, India, and the Soviet Union may also be available. Faculty-Developed Practica relate in-port practical experiences with on-ship academic course work and Independent Field Practica are initiated and developed on an individual basis between the student and a faculty member. Students also have opportunities for independent travel.

Specialties: Global education.

Faculty: The 20 or so faculty members are drawn from undergraduate institutions nationally. Faculty and courses are approved by the College of Arts and Sciences and credits earned are University of Pittsburgh credits.

Costs, Accommodations: Tuition, room, board, and passage ranges from $8,775 to $12,375, depending upon accommodations. An additional $2,500 is recommended for in-country travel and spending money. A $25 nonrefundable fee must accompany application with $1,000 deposit due on acceptance and balance due 60 days prior to departure. Cancellations at least 45 days prior receive full refund. Financial aid is available in the form of scholarships and a work grant program.

Location, Facilities: Semester at Sea is conducted aboard the 18,000-ton S.S. Universe, a fully air-conditioned and stabilized ocean liner that contains classrooms, laboratories, study lounges, a 10,000-volume library, audiovisual and closed-circuit television equipment, theater, student union, bookstore, swimming pool, darkroom, and hospital. Ports of call include cities in Japan, Taiwan, Malaysia, India, the Soviet Union, Turkey, Yugoslavia, and Morocco.

Contact: Semester At Sea/I.S.E., University of Pittsburgh, 811 William Pitt Union, Pittsburgh, PA 15260; (800) 854-0195 *or* (412) 648-7490.

SHAKESPEARE AT STRATFORD
Western Washington University
Bellingham, Washington
Two-week July program in England

Since 1979, Western Washington University, in collaboration with The Shakespeare Institute of the University of Birmingham, England, has sponsored a two-week tour for 14 to 40 Shakespeare enthusiasts of all ages. The program's purpose is to enhance the appreciation and understanding of the bard's poetry and drama through interpretive readings, lectures, discussions, attendance at the Royal Shakespeare Theatre, and visits to the Shakespeare Properties, the English countryside, and historic sites relating to the Elizabethan and Tudor periods. Four units of academic credit are available.

Specialties: The poetry and drama of Shakespeare.

Faculty: Tour leader and originator Dr. Arthur Solomon, a retired professor of Western Washington University, is a former Shakespearean actor and director with the Margaret Webster Shakespeare Company and a founder of the Antioch Area Theatre. Lectures are also presented by Dr. Robert Smallwood, Educational Director of the Shakespeare Birthplace Trust and teaching fellow at the University of Birmingham; Fellows of the Shakespeare Institute; and members of the Royal Shakespeare Theatre Company.

Costs, Accommodations: The $2,300 cost includes round-trip airfare from/ to Seattle, guest house accommodations, and all other expenses except lunches and one dinner in London. A $500 deposit must accompany registration with balance due by June 1. Cancellations after June 1 receive a $1,000 refund.

Location: The program, which is based in Stratford-Upon-Avon, features visits to Warwick and Kenilworth castles, Coventry Cathedral, an excursion to the Cotswolds, and at least one day in London.

Contact: Shakespeare-At-Stratford, Dept. of Communication, Western Washington University, Bellingham, WA 98225-5996.

SITE SEEING TOURS
National Building Museum (NBM)
Washington, D.C.
One-day local tours

Founded in 1980 under a congressional mandate to celebrate American achievements in building and encourage excellence in the building arts, the National Building Museum offers one-day SITE SEEING tours that focus on local buildings or areas of unusual interest. Typical tours include Best

Addresses: A Tour of Washington's Distinguished Apartment Houses, a seven-hour bus tour to landmark and historic apartment houses with discussions of neighborhood architectural development, height limitations, zoning laws, climate, and the transitory population; Escaping the Box: Washington's Twelve Best New Office Buildings; How To Read a Building Stone, which examines the types of building stone used in the Mall's buildings and monuments; and Dulles Airport Terminal, an exploration of Eero Saarinen's architectural landmark. Additional short tours of the Museum and important area buildings currently under construction or restoration are also scheduled. The NBM, a private, nonprofit institution housed in the landmark Pension Building, also sponsors exhibitions, educational programs, concerts, an annual festival, and various publications, including the quarterly journal, *Blueprints*.

Specialties: The building arts: architecture, design, planning, crafts.

Faculty: Includes members of the Museum staff and local experts.

Costs: SITE SEEING tours range from $11 ($8 for members) to $60 ($45). Annual NBM membership dues begin at $25.

Contact: National Building Museum, Judiciary Square, N.W., Washington, DC 20001; (202) 272-2448.

SITKA CENTER FOR ART AND ECOLOGY
Otis, Oregon

One and two-day natural science workshops from May-August

Founded in 1970 as a learning center for art, music and the ecology of the central Oregon coast, the Sitka Center for Art and Ecology offers more than 30 spring and summer workshops and seminars in natural science, photography, arts, crafts, and other creative media. Workshop enrollment is limited to 10 to 20 participants of all levels and daily sessions are usually scheduled from 10 am until 4 pm. A varied program of evening events includes concerts, lecture/slide shows, demonstrations, films, and an annual open-house.

Typical natural science workshop titles include Old Growth Forests, a walking tour that focuses on the structure and processes of forest ecosystems, what keeps them healthy, and the role of forests in the global ecosystem; Stuck in the Sand, an exploration of life between the tides from the tiniest Copepod to the large mussel — their behaviors, patterns of living, and how they feed; and Organic Farming, which covers the growing of plants from seed through transplant, fertilization, and harvest and also addresses environmental topics on pesticides.

Specialties: Natural sciences and ecology.

Faculty: Instructors are experienced ecologists, botanists, and biologists.

Costs, Accommodations: Class fee, which ranges from $10 to $20 per day, must accompany registration. Friends of Sitka family sponsors, which begin at $35, receive a 10% workshop discount. A full refund, less $5, is granted cancellations more than one week prior; no refunds thereafter. There is no on-campus housing, however accommodations for approximately $30 per day are available at nearby hotels, motels, and lodges.

Location: The Center, located in Otis along Oregon's central coast, is situated on the slopes of Cascade Head, bordering the Salmon River estuary.

Contact: Sitka Center for Art & Ecology, P.O. Box 65, Otis, OR 97368; (503) 994-5485.

SKIDMORE COLLEGE SUMMER PROGRAMS
Office of Special Programs
Saratoga Springs, New York

Two -week May study program in Florence

Since 1988, Skidmore College has offered a two-week study and vacation program of lectures and field trips in Florence, limited to approximately 17 participants who are accompanied by a college staff member. Designed to explore the the art and culture of Italy, the courses provide a background to the history, art, and architecture of Medieval and Renaissance Tuscany. Lectures are supplemented by on-site teaching at historic landmarks, churches, and museums plus planned excursions to such locales as Siena, San Gamignano, and Pisa.

Specialties: A variety of topics including art, history, and culture.

Faculty: Skidmore College faculty members.

Costs, Accommodations: Cost of the two-week program in Florence is $2,775, which includes round-trip airfare from/to New York, double occu-pancy pensione housing (single supplement available), all meals, ground transportation, and local excursions. A $250 nonrefundable deposit must accompany application with balance due four weeks prior to departure. Credit cards (VISA, MasterCard) accepted.

Contact: Skidmore College, Office of Special Programs, Saratoga Springs, NY 12866; (518) 584-5000.

SMITHSONIAN NATIONAL ASSOCIATE PROGRAM
Smithsonian Institution
Washington, D.C.

Three-day to four-week domestic and international study programs

The Smithsonian National Associate Program, which provides educa-tional opportunities for Associates and the general public, began offering **Study Tours and Seminars** in 1970 and **Research Expeditions** in 1987. Domestic and international tours for families and special programs for Contributing Members are also offered. More than 180 programs are scheduled annually throughout the world, reflecting the interests and concerns of the Smithsonian Institution and providing a combination of study, discovery, adventure, and vacation. The number of participants ranges from 15 for specialized tours to 200 for some cruises.

Study Tours and Seminars range from rugged rafting and hiking experiences to river and ocean cruises, cultural tours, and in-depth university courses. Lectures, behind-the-scenes tours, and presentations by local experts are a feature of many of the programs. Domestic three and four-day weekend study tours are scheduled to major cities that include New York, Chicago, and Detroit, and such natural phenomena as the Grand Canyon. A representative domestic study tour, Pueblo Indians of the Rio Grande Valley, includes lectures on Indian cultures, Southwestern arts and crafts, and Pueblo land issues, as well as guided museum tours and demonstrations by local artists and craftspeople. Some tours focus on a specific event, such as Van Gogh's World: A Symphony of Color, a 100th anniversary tour of museums and sites relating to the artist's life and work in Amsterdam, Paris, and Arles; and The Battle of Britain, a commemorative 50th anniversary tour that includes visits to renowned collections of aircraft that took part in key battles and opportunities to meet military experts and World War II British pilots. Interlude tours focus on the culture and history of a single city while Countryside Study Programs offer in-depth study of a specific region, such as Wales, Provence, or Austria's Tyrol.

Seminars offer a greater emphasis on academic quality with courses, lectures, and discussions, complemented by field excursions to related sites. The Oxford Seminar, a two-week program organized jointly with Oxford University each summer since 1979, offers a plenary program of lectures, visits, and social events. Participants select from a variety of options in which they study, with a specialist tutor, one aspect of English heritage. Classroom discussions cover such topics as literature, history, archaeology, landscape, and architecture. The Florence Seminar features two courses — The History of Florence and Great Monuments of Florence — that combine lectures on the economic, political, and social aspects of Florentine history with visits to important monuments. The Smithsonian Seminar in Egypt traces the country's history and cultural development during morning lectures at the American University in Cairo and afternoon excursions to monuments and historic sites. Three and four-day domestic **Smithsonian Seminars** highlight permanent collections and special exhibitions at Smithsonian museums and introduce Associates to the work of Smithsonian research stations around the U.S. Typical subjects include American coins and currency, animal communication, astronomy, and various periods of art.

Research Expeditions offer participants the opportunity to contribute their labor and financial support to projects led by Smithsonian scientists, curators, and research associates that result in exhibitions, publications, and collections for the Institution. Volunteers aid Smithsonian scholars in projects such as archaeology, volcanology, photographic documentation, folk culture interviewing, wildlife ecology, and archival research. No previous experience is needed. A typical project, Costa Rican Volcano: Reshaping the Landscape, focuses on the geology and botany of the active Arenal Volcano. Volunteers interested in volcanology concentrate on monitoring eruptions and studying volcanic samples using sensitive photographic, audio, and seismographic equipment. Those interested in botany study the impact of lava and ash debris on the region's vegetation by concentrating on specimen collection and cataloguing, as well as monitoring the effects of acid rain on local plant life. Academic credit may be available.

Tours exclusively for Contributing Members include the **Smithsonian Focus** and **Treasures** tours, which offer the opportunity to investigate collections in a number of Smithsonian museums, to make behind-the-scenes visits to observe exhibitions in preparation, and to talk in-depth with Smithsonian conservators, curators, and museum directors. These limited-enrollment tours feature candlelit dining in museum settings and accommodations in a first-class Washington hotel.

Specialties: A wide variety of study tours, seminars, and research expeditions that focus on the culture, history, and science of the regions visited.

Faculty: Tours and seminars are conducted by U.S. academicians and local experts chosen for both their knowledge and their ability to communicate effectively with lay audiences. A Smithsonian representative accompanies each program to coordinate activities. All Research Expeditions are led by a Smithsonian scientist or curator.

Costs, Accommodations: Approximate costs are from $600 to $1,600 for three to ten-day domestic programs, $2,800 to $5,200 (includes airfare) for 10 to 15-day international programs, and from $1,000 to $1,500 (contribution) for one to two-week research expeditions, which include accommodations, some meals, and all scheduled activities. A deposit ranging from $200 to $700 is required with balance due 60 days prior to program. Refund policies vary. Membership is $20 for Associates, which includes a subscription to the monthly *Smithsonian* magazine, and begins at $60 for Contributing Members. *The Smithsonian Traveler*, a free biannual newsletter, highlights upcoming programs.

Contact: Smithsonian Study Tours and Seminars, 1100 Jefferson Dr. S.W., Room 3045, Smithsonian Institution, Washington, D.C. 20560; (202) 357-4700 *or* Smithsonian Research Expeditions, 490 L'Enfant Plaza, S.W., Suite 4210, Washington, DC 20560; (202) 287-3210.

SOCIETY EXPEDITIONS CRUISES, INC.
Seattle, Washington
Twelve to thirty-day international expeditions

Since 1974, Society Expeditions has offered adventure travel to exotic destinations. It operates two expedition ships, the 139-passenger *World Discoverer* and the 96-passenger *Society Explorer*, both specially equipped for access to out-of-the-way islands, narrow jungle tributaries, and polar exploration. Approximately 50 cruises are scheduled year-round, each offering onboard seminars and daily wrap-up sessions. Participants receive a reading list and notebook about their destination before the expedition and a log of their travels when they return.

Approximately twelve expeditions are scheduled annually to Antarctica, each featuring visits to scientific research stations established by a half-dozen countries. Stops at the South Georgia Islands, the Falkland Islands, and the Chilean Fjords may also be included.

Specialties: Travel to unusual destinations with emphasis on the region's history, wildlife, and culture.

Faculty: Distinguished historians, anthropologists, marine biologists, ornithologists, and other experts in the regions visited.

Costs, Accommodations: Cruise and land costs range from $3,990 to $14,250, including pre- and post-cruise deluxe accommodations, on-board outside cabin with private bath, all meals, shipboard gratuities, and all cruise activities. A 25% deposit must accompany reservation with an additional 25% due 150 days prior to departure and balance due 90 days prior. Cancellation penalty ranges from $100 (more than 89 days prior to departure) to 50% of cruise cost (30 to 59 days prior); no refund thereafter.

Location: Antarctica (November-February), Polynesia (March and April), Melanesia (May), Indonesia and Malaysia (June-September), New Guinea (May and September), South America and the Amazon (March, April, May, October, and November), the Caribbean and Atlantic (May), Greenland and the Canadian Arctic (August), Hudson Bay (July), Newfoundland (June and September), and Australia/New Zealand (October-December).

Contact: Society Expeditions Cruises, Inc., 3131 Elliott Ave., Suite 700, Seattle, WA 98121; (800) 426-7794 *or* (206) 285-9400, Fax (206) 285-7917.

SPECIAL ODYSSEYS
Medina, Washington
Seven to ten-day trips to the High Arctic and the South Pole

Special Odysseys operates year-round sponsoring nine itineraries to the northernmost (the Arctic islands and inland seas north of the latitude that parallels the mainland coast) and southernmost parts of the world, with most trips limited to 12 to 14 participants. Lectures and discussions relate to the wildlife, culture, and natural phenomena unique to these regions.

The Auroral Odyssey, an opportunity to view the Northern Lights during one of the greatest display periods in 100 years, includes lectures on astronomy and mythology, photographic instruction, and telescope viewing, as well as ice floe cruising and opportunities to observe arctic animals. **The History of Arctic Exploration Odyssey** visits sites that span the period of the Musk Ox Trail of the Thule and Dorset periods of 1,000 to 3,000 years ago. **Arctic Wildlife Odyssey**, specifically designed for amateur and professional naturalists who enjoy firsthand viewing and photographing of wildlife and birds, includes discussions of the area's customs, historical background, and culture of the Inuit people (Eskimos). **Arctic Marine Mammals and Ornithology Odyssey**, for those especially interested in wildlife and birds, features observation of unique marine mammals and seabirds at the Arctic floe edge, where wildlife is plentiful.

Two itineraries — **North Pole** and **South Pole Odyssey** — offer participants the opportunity to travel to the top or bottom of the world. Lectures on history and the natural sciences are included in both programs.

Specialties: The wildlife, history, culture, and natural phenomena of the High Arctic region and the South Pole.

Faculty: All trips are accompanied by scientists and educators with Arctic experience, including astonomers, historians, geographers, archaeologists, and anthropologists.

Costs, Accommodations: Most trips range in cost from $2,800 to $4,000, which includes double occupancy lodging (single supplement available) in the best available facilities, meals, and transportation during the trip. The North Pole trip is $7,900 and the South Pole trip is $30,000. A $300 to $500 deposit ($1,000 for North Pole, $10,000 for South Pole) must accompany reservation with balance due 120 days prior to departure. Fee for cancellation more than 120 days prior is $200 ($500 for North Pole, $5,000 for South Pole), no refunds thereafter.

Contact: Special Odysseys, P.O. Box 37, Medina, WA 98039; (206) 455-1960.

SPECIALITY TOURS
Durham City, Northumbria, England

Weekend and five-day tours

Since 1986, Speciality Tours has offered approximately 14 tours of Great Britain that emphasize archaeology and social history. Enrollment in each is limited to 35 participants.

Typical five-day excursions to Northumbria include What's News in Archaeology?, which explores the application of new and experimental techniques and affords participants the opportunity to make and fire prehistoric-style pottery; Riches From the Land, a study of industrial archaeology that focuses on agricultural change and mining in the North East; and Ancient Landscapes in Our National Parks, an examination of the remains of prehistoric societies that are preserved in the northern National Parks. Five-day excursions are also scheduled to Wessex, Durham and Scotland. Weekend tours include such locales as York, Lincoln, and Bath.

Specialties: Tours that focus on archaeology and social history.

Faculty: Include tour operators Lucy Walker, an archaeologist, and Diane Williamson, an anthropologist/prehistorian, and a staff of guides with such varied backgrounds as archaeology, sociology, history, landscape restoration, and interior design.

Costs, Accommodations: Costs, which include room, full board, and coach travel, range from £189 to £198 for five-day trips, £98 to £115 for weekends;

single supplement may be available. Accommodations range from residential college housing to hotels. A nonrefundable £20 deposit must accompany registration with balance due four weeks prior. Refund for cancellations within four weeks ranges from 60% (two to four weeks prior) to 20% (less than two weeks prior).

Contact: Speciality Tours, 13 Nevilledale Terr., Durham City, DH1 4QG, England; (44) 91 384 7962/386 5358.

SPRINGFIELD LIBRARY AND MUSEUMS ASSOCIATION
Springfield, Massachusetts
One-day to two-week trips in the U.S. and abroad

The Springfield Library and Museums Association offers a variety of trips that reflect the diversity of its members, which include the Springfield Museum of Fine Arts, the George Walter Vincent Smith Art Museum, the Springfield Science Museum, the Connecticut Valley Historical Museum, and the Springfield City Library. The travel program is divided into two areas. **Art on the Go** trips, scheduled two or three times a month for both members and nonmembers, are primarily day trips to museums in New England and New York, with occasional excursions to Montreal and Washington, D.C.

The extended travel program, established in 1989 for members only, features three or four trips annually to cultural centers in the U.S. and Canada, as well as France, Egypt, Greece, Italy, Sicily, Eastern Europe, and Japan. The itineraries are varied, providing insight into the literary, historical, scientific, and artistic aspects of each locale. Tours are often planned to coincide with a museum or library exhibit and pre-travel orientation lectures are also a part of the program.

Specialties: Travel to museums and cultural centers.

Faculty: In addition to a museum professional with relevant expertise, the tours are accompanied by Charles and Irene Hayward, operators of Hayward Cultural Tours for 18 years and leaders of more than 35 international trips.

Costs: Day trips range from $45 to $55 for members, $55 to $65 for nonmembers. Longer trips within the U.S. and Canada range from $400 to $1,300. Costs vary for trips abroad.

Contact: Springfield Library and Museums Travel Program, 49 Chestnut St., Springfield, MA 01103; (413) 736-8956.

STANFORD UNIVERSITY ALUMNI ASSOCIATION
Stanford Summer College and Travel/Study Programs
Stanford, California

One-week mid-August program on campus; one to three-week domestic and international travel programs

Stanford University offers a variety of programs for alumni, friends, and interested adults, including an annual **Summer College** devoted to a specific theme and 25 to 30 faculty-accompanied tours each year.

The annual **Summer College**, first held in 1966 and now attended by 125 to 200 participants, offers an in-depth exploration of a different theme each year. Typical themes include Perspectives on a Changing World, China, The Brain, and The Power and Politics of Religion.

Travel/Study Programs present several types of itineraries: Colleges (shipboard programs); Seminars, Safaris, Excursions, and Symposia, (land-based trips for groups of 20 to 35 participants); Budget Seminars (shorter, less-structured trips); and Outdoor Trips (provide adventure and a physical challenge). All trips feature an educational program of lectures, presentations, and informal discussions. Oft-repeated shipboard programs include the spring College on the Mississippi and the late summer Danube College, which visits seven central and eastern European countries. Popular land-based trips are the September Oxford/Stanford Seminar, two weeks of study at Brasenose College with excursions to nearby locales; the July Africa Safari, which features talks by well-known naturalists; the Seminar in the Southwest, an opportunity to visit Hopi potters and basket makers, Zuni silversmiths, and Navajo weavers; Renaissance Symposium in Tuscany, which focuses on Italian history, culture, and current events and includes guided tours of private collections; and Budget Seminar in Paris, a one-week off-season program with lectures, receptions, and a State Department briefing. Physically challenging trips with an academic focus include the Salmon River Expedition, an eight-day dory trip that offers adults and children ages nine and over the opportunity to learn about the wildlife and geology of the Pacific Northwest.

Specialties: A variety of topics, including the humanities, science, history, and politics of the regions visited.

Faculty: Stanford University faculty members and guest specialists.

Costs, Accommodations: Cost of the Summer College is $975 single, $1,875 double, which includes books, all meals, and a single room in one of Stanford's newest student residence buildings. Nonresident rates are $660 for one, $1,220 for a couple, which includes books and lunches. A $100 deposit must accompany registration with balance due two months prior to program. Cancellations more than one month prior receive full refund less $50, no refunds thereafter. Approximate land costs of Travel/Study Programs range from $3,000 to $6,000 for Colleges, $2,500 to $6,000 for Seminars, $1,600 to $2,900 for Budget Seminars (includes airfare), and $1,000 to $3,600 for Outdoor Trips. Deposit and refund policies vary. Stanford Summer College and Travel/Study Programs are open to alumni, their families and friends, and to non-alumni friends of the University. Membership in the Stanford Alumni Association is open to the public. Non-alumni are eligible to join on a life membership basis, or simply pay a non-member rate of $55 for the Summer College or $50 for the Travel/Study programs.

Location: The Summer College is held on the Stanford University campus. Travel/Study programs have traveled to six continents and almost 40 countries. In addition to the above, destinations include Alaska, Australia, Austria, China, Egypt, the Galápagos Islands, Germany and Poland, the Greek Isles and Turkey, Holland, India and Nepal, Japan, Norway, the Seine, the Soviet Union, Spain and Portugal.

Contact: Monica L. Seghers, Program Director (Summer College) *or* Mev Hoberg, Assistant to the Director (Travel/Study Programs), Stanford Alumni Association, Bowman Alumni House, Stanford, CA 94305-4005; (415) 723-2027 (Summer College) *or* (415) 725-1093 (Travel/Study).

STERLING AND FRANCINE CLARK ART INSTITUTE
Williamstown, Massachusetts
One-day to two-week tours year-round in the U.S. and abroad

Since 1984, the Institute has sponsored programs for its members that include one-day bus trips to nearby museums and historic sites, scheduled every two to three months; three to four-day domestic trips to such art centers as Charleston, South Carolina, offered about once a year; and international tours to a variety of European cities, including London, Paris, Prague, Vienna, and Budapest, approximately once every 18 months. Groups range from 15 to 40 participants. A lecture series at the Institute, with previews of sites to be visited, precedes international tours. The itineraries include guided museum visits with informal talks relating to the tour theme and walking tours through historic areas. Cultural evening events are also planned.

Specialties: Tours with an art focus.

Faculty: Includes John H. Brooks, Associate Director; Mary Jo Carpenter, Director of Membership and Public Relations; Fred Stocking, Professor of English at Williams College; and travel writer Willa Petschek.

Costs, Accommodations: From $50 to $60 for day trips to $3,000 for international tours. Superior double occupancy accommodations, round-trip airfare, and most meals are included in the cost. Participants must be Friends of Clark. Annual dues begin at $5 student, $15 individual, $25 family.

Contact: Sterling and Francine Clark Art Institute, 225 South St., Box 8, Williamstown, MA 01267; (413) 458-9545.

SUMMER ACADEMY STUDY HOLIDAYS
AT BRITISH UNIVERSITIES
Great Britain

One-week programs from July-September

Established in 1986 and open to anyone age 16 or over, Summer Academy offers more than 70 study holidays at nine universities throughout mainland Britain. The range of topics includes arts and literature, the countryside, lifestyles, and heritage. Each course consists of 10 to 15 hours of instruction as well as related field trips, discussion groups, video sessions, lectures, and play readings.

Typical course titles include The Landscape in Literature, tracing the development of literary representation of the English landscape; Thomas Hardy and Wessex, and exploration of the writer's craft and his environment, with field trips to sites that inspired him; Understanding Scenery, a demonstration of how scenery evolves from underlying rock structures and natural processes; Hadrian's Wall and the Roman Army, including a visit to the Wall and examination of reconstructions and archaeological evidence; Museums, a behind-the-scenes look at several museums; and Creation, an interdisciplinary course dealing with cosmology, the origins of suns and planets, how humanity emerged, and creation as perceived through the arts. A series of lifestyles courses focus on the history and present-day culture of European countries, including Greece, France, Spain, and Italy.

Specialties: A variety of topics relating to European cultures and English arts, literature, countryside, lifestyles, and heritage.

Faculty: Professors and educators selected for their teaching ability and expertise.

Costs, Accommodations: Program costs, which range from £208 to £248, include tuition and course-related excursions, full board and accommodations for seven days, and non-course activities. Participants are lodged in single and twin university dormitories. A nonrefundable £40 deposit must accompany application with balance due at least eight weeks prior to course. Cancellation penalty within eight weeks ranges from 30% of total cost (more than four weeks prior) to 60% of total (less than two weeks prior).

Location: The nine course locations are the University of Edinburgh, the University of Kent at Canterbury, the University of East Anglia, the University of Exeter, the University of Swansea, the University of Sheffield, the University of Liverpool at Chester College, the University of Southampton at Sparsholt College, and the University of Durham.

Contact: Summer Academy, School of Continuing Education, The University, Canterbury, Kent CT2 7NX, England; (44) 227 470402.

SUMMER PROGRAM IN ITALY
Rosemont College and Villanova University
Rosemont, Pennsylvania
One-month program from May-June

Since 1972, Rosemont College and Villanova University have co-sponsored an interdisciplinary program in art and Italian studies with emphasis on late Medieval-Renaissance culture and art. The program, which is accredited by the Middle States Commission on Higher Education, is open to approximately 80 adults and students who may enroll for personal enrichment or up to six college credits. Participants can choose from more than a half-dozen courses, including such titles as History of Italian Renaissance Art, which investigates Italian art, architecture, and sculpture from 1300 to 1520 and features visits to museums in Siena, Florence, Venice, and Rome; History of Italian Cities (1250-1520), with emphasis on the political and institutional growth economy and culture of the Italian city-states; and Dante and His Times (taught in English or Italian), which considers his *Divine Comedy* in the light of universal, literary, moral, religious, and political implications. Other course offerings include watercolor landscape painting, Italian language, and independent study. Course content is adapted to meet the needs and levels of the participants as well as prevailing cultural influences.

Specialties: Italy, particularly late Medieval-Renaissance culture and art.

Faculty: Program Director Leda Giannuzzi Jaworski, Chair, Italian Studies, Associate Professor of Italian at Rosemont College; program founder George T. Radan, Professor of Art History at Villanova University; Richard G. Cannuli, Assistant Professor, Department of Art and Art History at Villanova University; and Richard Donagher, Professor of History at Rosemont College.

Costs, Accommodations: The program cost of $2,225 includes double occupancy room and board, course fees, ground transportation, and receptions in the U.S. and Italy. Group air fare is available on Alitalia. Lodging and classrooms are at the family-owned Hotel Vico Alto in Siena. Application, accompanied by $75 nonrefundable fee, is due by the last week of February. A $700 deposit is due March 15 with balance payable by April 20. Three semester credits are available for each course at no additional cost. Students who register for credit may enroll in no more than two courses and audit additional courses.

Location: Siena, a Medieval city in the center of Tuscany, borders on the hills of Chianti to the north and the clay fields to the south. The program includes field trips to Venice, Verona, Florence, San Gimignano, Assisi, Todi, Orvieto, and a two-day stay in Rome.

Contact: Dr. Leda Giannuzzi Jaworski, Italy Program Director, Italian Studies, Rosemont College, Rosemont, PA 19010; (215) 527-0200, ext. 423 *or* 325 (days) or (215) 667-4547 (evenings and weekends).

SUMMER PROGRAMS IN POLAND
American Institute of Polish Culture, Inc.
Miami, Florida

Four and six-week programs in July and August

The American Institute of Polish Culture offers individuals from age 18 to 80 the opportunity to spend four or six weeks at a major Polish university to study one of a half dozen courses that are offered in Polish history, culture, business, economics, and international trade. Lectures are held in the mornings and afternoon activities include meetings, tours, and social events. A short tour of Poland is planned at the end of the semester. All courses are taught in English and persons interested in learning Polish are placed in a class at the level of their knowledge of the language. Three semester credit hours are available for the four-week program, six credits for six weeks.

Specialties: Polish culture, business, economics, language, foreign trade.

Faculty: Faculty of the sponsoring universities.

Costs, Accommodations: Costs, which include tuition, books, dormitory lodging, and three meals daily in the student cafeteria, are $600 for four weeks, $700 for six weeks. A nonrefundable deposit of $50 must accompany application with balance due six weeks prior to departure. Round-trip airfare from/to major U.S. cities is approximately $1,000.

Location: Jagiellonian University and Krakow Academy of Economics in Krakow, Gdansk Technical University, Catholic University in Lublin, and the Mickiewicz University in Poznan.

Contact: The American Institute of Polish Culture, Inc., 1440 79th St. Causeway, #117, Miami, FL 33141; (305) 864-2349.

SUSQUEHANNA UNIVERSITY SUMMER PROGRAMS
Office of International Education
Selinsgrove, Pennsylvania

Eighteen-day to five-week summer programs in Europe

Susquehanna University "Learning Traveler" summer programs for adults include a three-week educational tour in Great Britain, offered since 1983, and an eighteen-day European cultural tour, offered since 1985. These tours are an outgrowth of the five-week Oxford Summer Session, which has been offered since 1966, and the four-week London Mini-Term in British Theatre, begun in 1983. Both are open to students and adults with the latter comprising about 10% of enrollment.

Each year's Britain tour, exclusively for adults, focuses on a specific theme and locale, such as Scotland Wild & Woolly: The Scottish Highlands & Islands (1990), Legends and Literature of Devon and Cornwall: Sea, Sand, and Moors (1991), and Landscapes and Literature of South Wales and Ireland (1992). The eighteen-day European cultural tour scheduled in August, also for adults only, visits Italy in odd-numbered years and the drama and music festivals of Germany, Austria, and Switzerland in even-numbered years. Group size is limited to 16 to 20 participants, preferably over 30 years of age. Travel is by nine and twelve-passenger minibuses. Handicapped persons are welcome if they bring a companion to assist them.

The five-week **Oxford Summer Session**, scheduled from early July to early August and limited to 50 students and adults, offers academic programs in Business and Economics and in the Liberal Arts (Social Sciences and Humanities). Each student in the liberal arts program selects two courses, one of which is British History, Politics, and Society in the 20th Century or British Literature of the 20th Century. The second course is selected from five choices that include Novels and Poetry of Thomas Hardy, Modern British Politics, Britain Before the Mayflower: History and Culture, and The English Country House in Oxfordshire. Three or four credits are available for each course (adults may audit). Mornings are devoted to lectures, which are supplemented by twice weekly afternoon seminars, and optional excursions are scheduled some weekends. A three-week **Pre-Oxford Excursion** includes nine days in London, three days in Stratford, three days in Edinburgh, and two days in York, with guided tours of architectural and historical sites in each city. A one-week **Post-Oxford Excursion** features a guided tour of Paris and visits to Versailles Palace and Chartres Cathedral.

The four-week **London Mini-Term in British Theatre**, which precedes the **Oxford Summer Session** and is limited to 15 students and adults, focuses on representative British plays currently offered on the London, Stratford, and regional stages. Students attend approximately 16 plays that are selected to illustrate periods in the history of British theatre and various types of productions, from the West End to the "fringe". Class sessions are devoted to text analysis, study of historical settings, critiques, and special seminars conducted by performers, producers, directors, and critics. Excursions are scheduled to Canterbury, Windsor Castle, Hampton Court Palace, and the Houses of Parliament and the program concludes with a weekend attending theatre productions in Stratford. Six semester hours of credit are available.

Specialties: Educational tours of Europe; liberal arts study at Oxford; British theatre.

Faculty: Robert Bradford, Director of the Office of International Education, Susquehanna University, and Stan Myers, Professor of Psychology at Washington & Jefferson College, lead the Britain and European tours. The Oxford Summer Session courses are taught by prominent British and Oxford scholars and the British Theatre Mini-Term is conducted by Dr. Cynthia Eland, a former actress on the London stage.

Costs, Accommodations: Approximate costs are $2,525 for the Britain tour, $2,200 for the European tour, $3,950 for the Oxford Summer Session, and $1,975 for the London Mini-Term in British Theatre, which includes round-trip airfare, double occupancy hotel accommodations (single supplement may be available for $175 to $195), all breakfasts and most other meals, ground transportation, and all planned activities. Costs of the Pre- and Post-Oxford excursions are $950 and $450 respectively, which includes transportation in Europe, bed and breakfast accommodations, and planned activities. A pro-rated reduction is granted those who must join the Britain and European tours late or leave early. For Britain and European tours, a $200 deposit must accompany registration with balance due six weeks prior to departure. Written cancellations received at least ten weeks prior receive full refund less $25. Cancellation charge thereafter ranges from $200 (six to ten weeks prior) to full cost less $500 (within two weeks of departure) unless space can be filled, in which case full refund less $100 is granted. For the Oxford Summer Session and London Mini-Term, a 10% deposit is required by March 1, nonrefundable after April 15, with balance due May 15.

Contact: Robert L. Bradford, Director, Office of International Education, Susquehanna University, Selinsgrove, PA 17870; (717) 372-4254 *or* (717) 374-0101, ext. 4254.

SWAN HELLENIC CRUISES AND TOURS
Esplanade Tours
Boston, Massachusetts
Eight-day to three-week international cruises

Through its U.S. sales agent, Esplanade Tours, Swan Hellenic Cruises offers more than 150 cruises and tours annually worldwide. All are accompanied by guest experts who give lectures and conduct informal get-togethers.

Approximately 20 cruises take place aboard the 5,100-ton vessel Orpheus, which accommodates 250 passengers as well as four or five guest lecturers in the fields of ornithology, botany, geology, astronomy, geography, and music. Passengers, who are met in London, can select itineraries that include the Mediterranean, the Aegean, southern Greece and the islands, the Turkish coastline, Scandinavia, Britain's northerly islands, France, Italy and the Iberian peninsua, the Levant, the Black Sea, and through the Suez Canal to the Red Sea. Almost 50 itineraries are **Art Treasures Tours** that explore locations in Europe, North Africa and the Eastern Mediterranean, the Indian Sub-Continent, China, the Far East, and the Americas. **Natural history tours** range through six continents, including Antarctica, and follow interests that include botany, ornithology, and wildlife. Three itineraries explore the Nile River, including 600-mile cruises along the length of the Nile between Cairo and Aswan, cruises that concentrate on the Upper Nile, and shorter trips that combine a five-day cruise between Luxor and Aswan with three nights in Cairo. Special ornithological cruises with the Royal Society for the Protection of the Birds link Egyptian history with contemporary bird life.

Specialties: Tours and cruises with an art, cultural, historical, and/or natural history focus.

Faculty: All cruises and tours are accompanied by guest lecturers who are experts in their fields.

Costs, Accommodations: All-inclusive costs range from $1,715 to $8,715, which includes deluxe or first class accommodations. Deposit, payment, and refund policies vary.

Contact: Swan Hellenic, Esplanade Tours, 581 Boylston St., Boston, MA 02116; (800) 426-5492 *or* (617) 266-7465.

SYRACUSE UNIVERSITY
Travel and Study/Alumni University
Syracuse, New York
Weekend to three-week programs in the U.S. and abroad

Syracuse University's Division of International Programs Abroad (DIPA) and division of Alumni Programs offer eight to ten programs, mostly during the summer months.

Travel and Study, sponsored by DIPA as Syracuse's educational travel program for students of all ages and interests, offers about a half dozen trips each summer to international destinations. Each trip features visits to both well and little-known attractions, special site visits, meetings with experts in various fields, and lectures by professors. Enrollment is limited and three undergraduate or graduate academic credits are available for some trips. Typical itineraries include The Journey of Vincent Van Gogh, with visits to special events and exhibits in Amsterdam, The Hague, Paris, Arles, and Saint-Remy; The Medieval Pilgrimage Routes, a re-creation of the 12th century religious journey from southern France to Santiago de Compostela, with stops at 16 major artistic and historic sites and 36 lectures and colloquia; and The Soviet Union From the Ground Up, an intensive tour of Moscow, Tbilisi, and Tallinn preceded by a week in London studying Soviet domestic politics. DIPA also sponsors a variety of accredited summer programs overseas for graduate and undergraduate students.

Specialties: In-depth study programs.

Faculty: All programs and trips are led by Syracuse University faculty or distinguished DIPA adjuncts.

Costs, Accommodations: Travel and Study international trip costs range from $2,200 to $3,800, including round-trip airfare from/to New York, double occupancy lodging (single supplement may be available), ground transportation, continental breakfasts and some other meals, and planned activities. Tuition is additional. A $350 deposit must accompany registration with balance due 60 days prior to departure. Written cancellations received more than 60 days prior receive full refund less $50. Cancellation penalty ranges from 30% of land costs (30 to 60 days prior) to 50% of land package (less than seven days prior).

Contact: Syracuse University, Division of International Programs Abroad, Summer Programs Office, 119 Euclid Ave., Syracuse, NY 13244-4170; (315) 443-9420/9421 *or* Syracuse University Alumni Programs, 820 Comstock Ave., Syracuse, NY 13244-5040; (315) 443-3516.

TECH ROME
Louisiana Tech University
Ruston, Louisiana
Six-week summer program in Rome

Since 1967, Louisiana Tech University has offered an annual May-July travel-study program that is open to 75 college students, high school seniors, and post-college adults, who are required to complete an admission form and be admitted to Louisiana Tech. More than 40 courses are offered in business, archaeology, architecture, art and art history, biology, education, engineering, English, fashion, health and physical education, history, human ecology, family and child studies, independent studies, Italian language, life sciences, photography, and speech. A normal course load is 10 hours, including mandatory enrollment in History of the Arts and Activity, which includes all guided tours, lectures, and field trips to Naples, Pompeii, Assisi, Tivoli, Pisa, and Florence. Optional excursions are scheduled to the Isle of Capri, Greece, Paris, Switzerland, and Venice.

Specialties: Travel and study in Rome.

Faculty: Approximately 10 Louisiana Tech faculty members, most of whom have Ph.D.s and several years of experience with the program.

Costs, Accommodations: The cost of $3,889 includes tuition, round-trip airfare, lodging in two, three, or four-bedded rooms, meals, ground transportation, and planned activities and excursions. Optional excursions range from $142 to $640. A $200 deposit secures a space with balance due April 20. Cancellations prior to April 20 receive full refund; thereafter penalty ranges from 20% of balance (April 20 to 30) to 60% of balance (after May 22). Credit cards (VISA, MasterCard) accepted. Financial assistance is available.

Location, Facilities: The Louisiana Tech Rome campus is in a facility in central Rome, within two blocks of the Circus Maximus, the Arch of Janus, and the Capitoline. Facilities include dormitories, classrooms, dining areas, assembly rooms, and recreational areas.

Contact: Louisiana Tech Rome, P.O. Box 3172, Ruston, LA 71272; (800) 346-8324 *or* (318) 257-4854.

TEXAS CAMEL CORPS (TCC)
Witte Museum, San Antonio Museum Association (SAMA)
San Antonio, Texas
One-day to three-week trips in the U.S. and abroad

Established in 1985 by ten San Antonio Museum supporters as the San Antonio Museum Association's Field Research and Adventure Travel Group, the Texas Camel Corps sponsors 20 to 30 travel programs annually, ranging from local day and weekend trips to longer tours and research expeditions in the United States, Mexico, and abroad. Groups usually range from 10 to 20 participants, who meet several times prior to longer trips in order to become acquainted and discuss the forthcoming program. On longer trips, participants are sometimes encouraged to study one particular aspect of the country to be visited, such as the wildlife, architecture, or culture. Although Museum membership is not required, members receive such benefits as a bimonthly newsletter with advance notice of trips, first priority on space, and discounts. The TCC also holds monthly meetings at which guest lecturers present programs on natural history, anthropology, and archaeology.

Typical day and weekend trips include Whooping Cranes, an annual February/March pilgrimage to Corpus Christi Bay in South Texas to view America's tallest bird at its winter home in Aransas National Wildlife Refuge; Lower Pecos Rock Shelters, a fall visit to the Prehistoric Indian Rock Shelters in West Texas with tours of the museum and rock shelters at Seminole Canyon State Historical Park; and Bald Eagles at Lake Buchanan, a cruise on the Buchanan and Colorado Rivers with opportunities to view the Southern Bald Eagle in its natural habitat. The one-week Big Bend Prehistory Trip, a research expedition, involves participants in preliminary surveys of prehistoric settlement in Big Bend National Park. Two to three-week international trip destinations include Brazil, Costa Rica, Egypt, England, Galapagos, India and Nepal, Madagascar, and Peru.

Specialties: Travel programs with an art, wildlife, natural history, or cultural focus.

Faculty: TCC Travel Director and tour leader Ian P. McCord was trained as an actor and taught theatre at the university level. A freelance tour guide for more than ten years, he has conducted more than 100 natural history and anthropology tours. Faculty may also include an expert in the field of academic specialty.

Costs, Accommodations: Fees, which are payable by check or major credit card, range from $28 to $365 for day and weekend trips, $750 to $850 for one-week domestic trips, and $2,500 to $4,000 for international travel. Deposit and refund policies vary. SAMA membership dues are $35 individual, $60 family, $35 senior citizen; TCC membership (requires SAMA membership) dues range from $20 to $100.

Contact: Ian P. McCord, Director of Travel, Texas Camel Corps, Witte Museum, P.O. Box 2601, San Antonio, TX 78299-2601; (512) 226-5544, ext. 215.

THE TEXTILE MUSEUM STUDY TOURS
Washington, D.C.

Fourteen to sixteen-day international tours

Since 1984, The Textile Museum has offered its members study tours abroad that focus on the textiles and weavings of the regions visited. Approximately three tours are scheduled annually, each limited to 20 to 30 to participants and featuring guided tours of museums and manufacturing facilities, visits to private collections, and weaving demonstrations.

Typical itineraries include a Nile cruise and tour of Coptic textiles, focusing on old and contemporary weavings and Egyptian antiquities; an Indonesian cruise preceded by visits to Bali and Java to visit weaving centers and private collections of antique batik and ikat textiles; and Eastern Europe, including museums and private rug collections in Poland, Czechoslovakia, Hungary, and both East and West Berlin.

Specialties: Study tours with a focus on weaving and textiles.

Faculty: Museum lecturers and staff members and guest scholars.

Costs, Accommodations: Costs, which include round-trip airfare, double occupancy first class or best available lodging (single supplement available), most meals, and tax-deductible donation, range from approximately $3,700 to $3,900. A $600 deposit is usually required with application and balance due 60 days prior to departure. Refund policies vary.

Contact: The Textile Museum Study Tours, 2320 "S" St. N.W., Washington, DC 20008; (703) 920-0228.

TRAVELEARN
Lakeville, Pennsylvania
Twelve to twenty-four-day programs in Alaska and abroad

Established in the mid-1970's, Travelearn offers 11 year-round travel/ study itineraries for adult learners. All programs include on-site lectures, seminars, and field experiences as well as opportunities to meet local people and visits to special sites and facilities. Group size is usually limited to 15 to 20 participants and college credits are available.

Specialties: Travel/study programs.

Faculty: All programs are escorted by college faculty who are specialists in the fields of study encompassed within each program and knowledgeable about the cultural opportunities available in the region visited. Resident specialist lecturers are also utilized.

Costs, Accommodations: Costs range from $1,495 to $3,995, including round-trip airfare, double occupancy lodging in first class or best available hotels, ground transportation, and most meals. A $300 deposit must accompany reservation with balance due 60 days prior to departure. Cancellations more than three months prior forfeit $50. Credit cards (VISA, MasterCard) accepted.

Location: Tour destinations include Alaska, Australia, China, the Dominican Republic, Egypt, the Galápagos Islands and Ecuador, Kenya, Morocco, Nepal, South America, and the Soviet Union and Eastern Europe.

Contact: Professor Edwin Williams, Director, Travelearn, P.O. Box 315, Lakeville, PA 18438; (717) 226-9114.

TRAVELING SEMINAR IN HISTORY
Francis Marion College
Florence, South Carolina

Two to three-week European tour in June-July

Since 1971, history professor Joseph T. Stukes, Ph.D., has conducted European history tours, limited to 15 to 45 participants, that combine travel and study. Although designed primarily for college students seeking academic credit, nonstudents are accepted on a space available basis. The itinerary and theme changes each year, with the countries and locales selected for their historical significance and beauty. A typical three-week tour includes visits to Switzerland, Liechtenstein, Germany, Austria, and Hungary, with academic emphasis on such subjects as Europe since 1945, the creation of modern Germany, the Hapsburg Dynasty, comparative political systems, and Viennese music of the 19th century. Students seeking three to six hours undergraduate credit in history must complete pre-departure assignments, on-continent reports, a coursebook, and a post-return examination.

Specialties: European history.

Faculty: Joseph T. Stukes, Ph.D., is Chairman of the History Department, Francis Marion College. Other tour leaders include Norman G. Raiford of Greenville Technical College and Betty E. Riddle.

Costs, Accommodations: Cost, which includes transatlantic airfare from/to Atlanta, on-continent transportation, double occupancy accommodations (single supplement available) in three-star hotels or better, and continental breakfasts and some dinners, is approximately $2,500 for two weeks, $3,000 for three weeks. Tuition is approximately $80 per semester hour. A $1,500 deposit by February 15 reserves a space and balance is due May 1.

Contact: Joseph T. Stukes, Francis Marion College, Florence, SC 29501; (803) 661-1550.

TROPICAL MARINE BIOLOGY
Long Island University (LIU) Southampton Campus
Southampton, New York

Three-and-a-half to four weeks during January intersession

Since 1979, Long Island University (LIU) has offered a four-credit field trip course to study special tropical marine habitats. Approximately the first half of the course is devoted to learning about the organisms and their ecology and the second half to collecting observations for a modest independent research project. Lectures and demonstrations explain details of the complex ecosystems and additional major activities include reef-walking, snorkeling, underwater photography, and optional scuba diving. A small library and field microscopes are available to carry out detailed on-shore observations.

Specialties: Marine biology, ichthyology, phycology, malacology.

Faculty: Drs. Stephen T. Tettelbach, Larry B. Liddle, and Howard M. Reisman of LIU's Biology and Marine Science faculty.

Cost, Accommodations: Program cost of approximately $3,150 includes tuition, airfare, room, board, and surface transportation; scuba diving is extra.

Location: The location, which changes each year, has included the Fiji Islands, New Caledonia, the Great Barrier Reef, the Solomon Islands, Vanuatu, Guam, Palau, Tahiti, and Rarotonga.

Contact: Stephen T. Tettelbach, Ph.D., Natural Science Division, Southampton Campus, Long Island University, Southampton, NY 11968; (516) 283-4000.

TULANE UNIVERSITY SUMMER SCHOOL
New Orleans, Louisiana

Four and six-week programs in Cambridge, Paris, Tokyo, Colorado, and Louisiana

Since 1978, Tulane University Summer School has offered a variety of annual travel and study programs that are open to students and adults. These include six-week programs abroad in Cambridge, Paris, and Tokyo, the four-week **Astronomy in Colorado** program in July, and the six-week **Archaeological Summer Field School** in St. Joseph, Louisiana, in May and June.

The six-week **Summer Abroad in Cambridge**, first held in 1988, is open to 15 to 23 students who attend morning classes and have afternoons free for study and individual pursuits. Students are required to select two courses (eight credits) of four that are offered: Contemporary British Fiction, Women in Fiction Since 1800, Women and the Arts, and Seminar in the History of Art: British Art and Architecture. Classes are scheduled from 9 to 10:30 am and 11 to 12:30 pm on weekdays and include field trips to museums and other cultural attractions that relate to the courses.

Summer Abroad in Paris, first held in 1983, is open to 20 to 38 students, who attend morning classes with afternoons and weekends reserved for group and class field trips and individual pursuits. Students are required to select two courses (eight credits) of six that are offered: Art Survey, Modern Art: David to Cezanne, European Governments, Special Topics: The Political Psychology of Dictatorship and Democracy, and two French language and grammar courses. Classes are scheduled from 9 to 10:45 am and 11:15 am to 1 pm on weekdays. Excursions to Chartres, Giverny, and an overnight trip to Mont St. Michel on the Normandy coast are also featured.

Summer Abroad in Tokyo, held in cooperation with Sophia University since 1987, is open to 12 to 16 students who begin the program with a six-day tour of Kyoto and Nara. Students are required to select two courses (eight credits) of 12 that include Survey of Japanese Art, Survey of Japanese Literature, Japanese Religions, Management in Japan, and Contemporary Chinese Society and Politics. Classes are scheduled from 8:30 to 9:50 am, 10 to 11:20 am, and 11:30 am to 12:50 pm. Afternoon field trips include a tour of Tokyo and visits to Meiji Shrine, National Diet, Stock Exchange, Supreme Court of Justice, and Kabuki Theater.

Astronomy in Colorado, intended for non-scientists and held in conjunction with Tulane University's Department of Physics and Astronomy since 1984, provides instruction in astronomy both as a modern scientific discipline and as a science whose roots can be traced to prehistoric times. Observation is emphasized and current topics and discoveries are introduced in an informal environment. Students are required to enroll in Descriptive Astronomy and Archaeoastronomy (four credits each), which are part of Tulane's regular astronomy curriculum. A three-day field trip to an important archaeoastronomical site is also featured.

The **Archaeological Summer Field School** offers participants, who must be in excellent physical condition and need not have any academic or prior excavation experience in anthropology or archaeology, the opportunity to work on burial sites dating from 400 to 1100 A.D. Two four-credit courses are offered: Archaeological Field Methods, a practical course consisting of field work, class lectures, laboratory processing, and analysis, and Archaeology of Southeastern United States, primarily a lecture course with tours of relevant sites in the area.

Specialties: Astronomy, archaeology, and topics relating to the cultures of Britain, France, and Japan.

Faculty: All programs are taught by members of the faculty of Tulane University.

Costs, Accommodations: Program costs are $3,250 for Cambridge, $3,725 for Paris, $5,545 for Tokyo, $1,700 for astronomy, and $1,915 for archaeology, including double occupancy lodging, eight undergraduate credits, planned activities, and round-trip airfare for trips abroad. Deposit and refund policies vary.

Location, Facilities: Students at the university town of Cambridge, located an hour's drive from London, live and attend classes at Girton College, which has a swimming pool and squash and tennis courts. Students in the Paris program live in the B.V.J. Quartier Latin Hostel in the Latin Quarter on the Left Bank, about a 20-minute walk from classes in the sixth *arrondissement*. Students in Tokyo are housed in the kitchen-equipped International Student Dormitories in Ikebukuro in a business, shopping, and entertainment complex a short subway commute from the Ichigaya Campus of Sophia University, where classes are held. Students in the astronomy program stay at Mt. Crested Butte, a resort community two miles from Crested Butte, situated at an altitude of 9,300 feet. Students in the archaeology program are housed at the Tensas Academy, a small Christian school in St. Joseph, a rural community approximately 50 miles from Natchez, Mississippi.

Contact: Ms. Amy E. Pick, Summer School, 125 Gibson Hall, Tulane University, New Orleans, LA 70118-5698; (504) 865-5555.

UCLA INTERNATIONAL TRAVEL STUDY PROGRAMS
UCLA Extension
Los Angeles, California

Ten-day to six-week international programs

UCLA Extension offers more than a dozen international travel study programs a year, most during the summer months, for undergraduate and graduate students and adults. Many programs are devoted to study of a specific subject and some are offered annually, such as the **Cambridge/UCLA Program** and the **UCLA/London Program**.

The **Cambridge/UCLA Program**, jointly sponsored by the University of Cambridge Board of Extra-mural Studies and UCLA Extension since 1981, consists of courses in literature, history, politics, archaeology, and the arts. Participants can choose one of nine courses that are offered during each of two three-week summer sessions that run consecutively from early July to mid-August. Weekday mornings and some afternoons are occupied by lectures or related field trips and optional excursions are scheduled on weekends. Classes, which are limited to 15 students, are supplemented by guest lectures, special field trips, individual discussion of work in progress, and lectures on the history and traditions of Cambridge and topics of broader interest. Typical course titles include The Architecture of England, from the Norman Conquest to the Victorian Era; Landscapes and Gardens, a survey of English gardens from the Middle Ages to the present; Dickens and the Victorian Age, with detailed study of three major novels; The Thatcher Years, an examination of political, economic, and social trends; Churchill and His Times, which includes field trips to places of interest; and Shakespeare's Tragedies, viewed through a modern perspective with a field trip to Stratford-Upon-Avon. Four quarter units (2-3/4 semester units) of credit are available for each course.

The **London/UCLA Program**, held since 1986 in cooperation with Sotheby's, the British Museum, the Victoria and Albert Museum, the Royal Shakespeare Company, the British American Drama Academy, and Newcastle upon Tyne Polytechnic, offers approximately a dozen two and three-week summer programs with an in-depth arts focus. Participants can earn six quarter units (four semester units) of credit for three-week courses, four quarter units (2-2/3 semester units) for two-week courses. Typical titles include Assessing Works of Art, a three-week program based on Sotheby's yearlong Works of Art course; The Royal Shakespeare Company: An Inside View, including meetings and discussions with members of the acting, directorial, and technical teams whose performances they attend; The Art of London's Past, which features visits to several museums and galleries; Vienna 1900: The Age of Art Nouveau, a travel study course with a five-day tour of Vienna and privileged access to museums and private collections; and English Country Houses and Gardens From Within, a detailed study of a historic house in its setting.

Other travel study programs include Tropical Ecology: The Amazon, an Amazon River and basin tour that includes visits to the Tampobata Nature Reserve, Amazon habitats, Cuzco, and Machu Picchu; Art, Architecture, and Interior Design Study Tour to Byzantium: From Istanbul to Venice, arranged with the cooperation of curators, historians, architects, and designers; China Kaleidoscope: The Art & Lifestyles of the Ethnic Minority Cultures, a tour of China's ethnic regions and villages; and Antarctica, Falklands, and South Georgia Island: Exploration of the Last Frontier (Jan., 1991), which includes trips to visit scientists at American, British, Chilean, Argentinean, Polish, or Russian research bases.

Specialties: A variety of topics, including literature, history, politics, archaeology, landscape design, science, and the arts.

Faculty: The Cambridge/UCLA Program courses are taught by a distinguished faculty of tutors from Cambridge and other British institutions. The London/UCLA Programs are instructed by directors and specialists from the cooperating institutions. Other study tours are led by scholars with expertise in the subject and region visited.

Costs, Accommodations: Cost of the Cambridge/UCLA Program is $2,695 for one three-week session, $5,140 for two consecutive sessions, which includes tuition, single dormitory room (some doubles available) in Trinity Hall, all meals, and course-related field trips. Cost of the London/UCLA Program ranges from $1,975 to $3,500, which includes tuition, tutorials, and course-related field trips for courses based in London and may include accommodations and meals. Dormitory lodging, if not included, ranges from $393 to $834. A $250 deposit ($400 for two sessions) must accompany application with balance due by March 30. Cancellation penalty is $100 prior to March 15, $250 from March 15 to 30, no refund thereafter. Other study tour costs average $3,500 to $4,500 all-inclusive. Credit cards (MasterCard, VISA) accepted.

Location: In addition to the above, itineraries include the Yucatan Peninsula, Egypt, Hungary, Indonesia, and other international destinations .

Contact: John G. Watson, UCLA Extension, Marketing Dept., 10995 LeConte Ave., Ste. 315, Los Angeles, CA 90024; (213) 825-1901, Fax (213) 206-5123.

UCSD EXTENSION TRAVEL/STUDY PROGRAMS
University of California-San Diego
San Diego, California

Two-day to three-week domestic and international travel programs

Begun in 1983, UCSD Extension's travel/study program now offers approximately ten escorted tours for 20 to 40 participants as well as a residential credit program at the University of Innsbruck, Austria.

Typical itineraries include the Yucatan Peninsula, a study of the the area's economic and political conditions combined with visits to the Mayan ruins and sites of its colonial past; Greece and Turkey, a tour/cruise that focuses on the classical past of Greece; Spain and Portugal, an in-depth introduction to historic and modern-day Iberia, with emphasis on geography, history, art, folklore, and gastronomy; and Death Valley, an examination of the region's geology and natural history, including faults and folds, mountain-building, fossils, rock identification, plant ecology, star-gazing, and the desert adaptation of fish, birds, and other animal life. The University also schedules a series of slide preview/orientation meetings for several of the tours, providing an opportunity to become acquainted with the program directors.

The **European Centre**, a three-week residential credit program held at the 300-year-old University of Innsbruck, is limited to 90 adults who want to study Western culture while living in a Central European alpine environment. Participants choose one of a half dozen courses that are each limited to 15 students. Typical courses include A Cultural History of Europe, a combination of lectures and discussions dealing with the interrelationship of political history, architecture, art, music, and philosophy; The Music of Austria, a survey of music with discussion and analysis of the music of Haydn and Mozart from the Viennese classical period to the compositions of Mahler; and Early 20th Century Austrian Literature, including the works of Arthur Schnitzler, Hugo V. Hofmannsthal, and Franz Kafka, with emphasis on psychoanalysis of Sigmund Freud. Students attend classes each weekday morning at the Leopold-Franzens University and afternoons are devoted to course-related field trips. Day trips are also scheduled. A distinguished lecture series, featuring Senator George McGovern, is held in the evenings. Three hours of academic credit are granted for each course. Those who enroll for credit take mid-term and final examinations and all who satisfactorily complete the program are awarded a European Centre Certificate.

Specialties: Travel programs that focus on a variety of subjects, including the arts, humanities, natural history, and the natural sciences.

Faculty: Educators and specialists in the areas visited.

Costs, Accommodations: Land costs for domestic travel programs range from $235 to $1,320 and total costs for foreign programs range from $1,300 to $3,250; single supplement available. Deposit and refund policy varies with each trip. The $1,985 cost of the European Centre Program includes accommodations at a university residence facility, some meals, and afternoon and day field trips. A $200 deposit must accompany application with a $750 payment due approximately five months prior and balance four months prior. Full refund, less $50 fee, is granted cancellations more than four months prior; thereafter cancellation fee ranges from $750 to nonrecoverable costs.

Contact: Education Dept., UCSD Extension, X-001, University of California-San Diego, La Jolla, CA 92093-0176; (619) 534-3440.

UNIVERSITY OF BRITISH COLUMBIA (UBC)
CENTRE FOR CONTINUING EDUCATION
Vancouver, British Columbia, Canada

One-day to three-week domestic and international travel programs

Since the late 1960's, The University of British Columbia has offered noncredit educational travel programs, usually limited to 10 to 22 adult participants (16 years and older), that consist of one to seven-day regional field trips and longer term trips abroad.

Typical field excursions include Coastal Villages: A Voyage Into the Past, in which participants live and travel aboard a sailing yacht and study central coastal villages of diverse ethnic, cultural, and historical significance; and Dempster Highway Adventure: The True North, a camping expedition along this unpaved road in Canada's northland to study the indigenous birds and wildlife. Some day and weekend trips focus on the Petroglyphs of Gabriola and the Gray Whales during their spring northward migration.

Representative international travel programs include Art Tour of London and Paris, with visits to selected museums and private galleries; India: The Mythic Landscape, featuring sites that are central to India's mythological literature and focusing on the importance of myth to the country's art, music, and ritual; Scottish Heritage: A Cultural and Historical Perspective, which consists of morning lectures that trace Scotland's history and the work of its major writers and philosophers, supplemented by afternoon field trips.

Specialties: History, art, literature, culture, natural history, sociology.

Faculty: UBC faculty members and specialists in the various fields of study.

Costs, Accommodations: Day trips are approximately C$60 and field trips range from C$355 to C$2,385. Foreign travel programs range from C$1,780 to C$4,875 and include airfare, double occupancy hotel accommodations (single supplement available), some meals, and local transportation. A C$400 deposit must accompany application with balance due 60 days prior to departure. Cancellations more than 60 days prior receive full refund less C$100; recoverable costs are refundable thereafter.

Location: In addition to above, locations may include New York City, London, Paris, Italy, Sicily, Germany, Austria, Spain, and Korea.

Contact: Centre for Continuing Education, The University of British Columbia, 5997 Iona Dr., Vancouver, BC V6T 2A4, Canada; (604) 222-2181, Fax (604) 222-5283.

UNIVERSITY OF CALIFORNIA BERKELEY
University Extension
Berkeley, California

Two to three-week summer programs abroad

The University of California at Berkeley offers a variety of educational travel opportunities for adults, including the annual **Oxford/Berkeley Program** and about a half-dozen **Travel with Scholars** programs to international destinations. Most programs offer academic credit and require advance reading and active participation by enrollees.

The **Oxford/Berkeley Program**, sponsored jointly with the Department for External Studies of the University of Oxford since 1970, consists of two consecutive three-week sessions during July and August. Students, who must have completed two years of college and can enroll in one or both sessions, select one of a dozen courses selected to reflect the interests of participants and the resources of Oxford. Representative titles include Chaucer and the Middle Ages, British Art from Hogarth to Whistler, Reason and Morality, Shakespeare: The Tragedies, and Literature and the Unconscious. Enrollment in each course is limited to 12, to encourage active classroom discussion and close contact with the tutor. All students are required to participate fully in the course, which includes preparatory readings, written assignments, and excursions to relevant sites. Classes are scheduled weekday mornings, while afternoons and weekends are free for study and individual pursuits. Evenings are reserved for lectures by distinguished British scholars. Three upper division undergraduate semester units are available for each session.

Travel with Scholars programs offer in-depth exploration of sites of cultural and historical interest. Most of the programs feature an academic component of daily lectures or classes, followed by visits to the places studied. In a typical three-week program, The Paris Program, participants choose one of five liberal arts courses that focus on the city's unique cultural, social, and political heritage. Morning classes are supplemented by two subject-related field trips each week and evenings are devoted to lectures, receptions, and a group excursion. Kyoto: Heart of Japanese Culture combines a two-week residential study program in Kyoto with a week-long tour of culturally important sites in Japan. Inside the London Theater Scene, a three-week program offered in cooperation with the National Theatre of Great Britain, features talks by leading British actors, directors, designers, and playwrights and a dozen theatrical performances.

Specialties: In-depth study programs at the University of Oxford and other international locations.

Faculty: The Oxford/Berkeley Program courses are taught by faculty of the University of Oxford. The Travel with Scholars programs are conducted by professors and specialists in the regions studied.

Costs, Accommodations: The cost of the Oxford/Berkeley Program is $2,250 for one session, $4,100 for both, which includes tuition, single room at Worcester College, and full board. Field trips range from $30 to $100. A

$200 ($300 for both sessions) deposit must accompany application, along with a statement of educational background, reason for applying, and course-related experience. Balance is due upon acceptance, no later than ten weeks prior to program. Cancellation penalty is $50 for written notice more than four months prior, $200 from ten weeks to four months prior, no refunds thereafter. Travel with Scholars programs range from $2,250 to $3,500, which includes tuition, double occupancy accommodations (single supplement available), ground transportation, breakfasts and most dinners, and scheduled activities. Participants in some programs are lodged in college residence halls. A $250 deposit must accompany enrollment; balance due dates and refund policies vary. Credit cards (MasterCard, VISA) can be used to pay for all programs.

Location: The Oxford/Berkeley Program is held at Worcester College, which has its own gardens, lake, playing field, and grass tennis courts. Participants have access to the city and university libraries, the Bodleian Library, and the Ashmolean Museum. In addition to the above, other Travel with Scholar destinations may include France, Venice, and Scotland.

Contact: Lynne Kaufman, Program Director, Travel/Study Dept. 3A, UC Berkeley Extension Center, 55 Laguna St., San Francisco, CA 94102; (415) 642-8840.

UNIVERSITY OF CAMBRIDGE SUMMER STUDY PROGRAM
Office of Cooperating Colleges
Erie, Pennsylvania
Two week July program in Cambridge, England

Originated in 1985, the annual University of Cambridge Summer Study Program is designed for adults who are interested in an in-depth study of a particular subject. Five courses are offered, each limited to 15 students and selected to reflect the interests of adults and the resources of the University of Cambridge, England. Lectures and field trips are scheduled every week-day morning and some afternoons, with evenings and weekends free for leisure activities or optional general interest lectures and excursions. Classes are supplemented by guest lectures, excursions to historic sites, and optional weekend field trips. Graduate or undergraduate credit is available.

Typical course titles include British Secret Services, a study of the successes and failures of 20th-century British intelligence and the interaction between politics and the security services; Life in the Middle Ages, a survey of Medieval England that focuses on the period's art, architecture, religious life, social structure, and institutions; Shakespeare's World, an introduction to Shakespeare's theatre and its social, cultural, and political influence; The Nineteenth-Century Novel, which examines the novel as a reflection of British society and its values during this time; and The English Country House, a consideration of the settings, architecture, and furnishings of some of Britain's stately homes and their relation to the owners' status and lifestyles.

The Summer Study Program originated in 1985 through Villa Maria College and has since been sponsored by the Office of Cooperating Colleges, which includes Gannon University, Villa Maria College, Case Western Reserve University, Allegheny College, and Mercyhurst College.

Specialties: A variety of topics with emphasis on English history and culture.

Faculty: All courses are planned and taught by Cambridge faculty, supplemented by guest lecturers.

Costs, Accommodations: The $1,995 tuition fee includes two meals daily, room, course-related field trips, and general lectures. A $250 fee must accompany application with balance due upon notification of admission. Full refund less $100 to $250 charge is granted cancellations more than 90 days prior; no refunds thereafter. Service fee is $50 for undergraduate credit, $100 for graduate credit. Accommodations, meals, and instruction are provided at Emmanuel College, home of the Wren Chapel and one of the University's 35 colleges. Housing is in dormitory-style single rooms overlooking a landscaped garden. Round-trip bus service from London airports, for those who wish to travel with the group, is available for a nonrefundable $50 fee.

Facilities: Participants have access to historic libraries, museums, art galleries, and grass tennis courts at Emmanuel College.

Contact: Dr. Joann Painter, Office of Cooperating Colleges, 714 Sassafras St., Erie, PA 16501; (814) 456-0757.

THE UNIVERSITY OF CHICAGO'S SUMMER THEATRE STUDY TOURS
Office of Continuing Education
Chicago, Illinois

Four to seven-day tours to Ontario, Canada

Since 1971, the University of Chicago's Office of Continuing Education has offered summer study tours to the Stratford Festival and Shaw Festival, where 20 to 47 participants have the opportunity to attend four to six performances of works by classical and modern playwrights. Four tours are offered during the summer, most over a long weekend, each with a different selection of plays. An introductory seminar to the historical, literary, and theatrical aspects of the plays is held prior to departure and the tour concludes with an interpretation and discussion of the performances. Faculty-led seminars, informal gatherings, and backstage tours are scheduled during the weekend and Festival-sponsored events such as meetings with actors and directors, exhibitions, and lunchtime presentations are also offered.

Specialties: Theatre study tours featuring the works of Shakespeare, Shaw, and other playwrights.

Faculty: Each tour is led by a University of Chicago faculty member, who conducts seminars and accompanies the group to all performances.

Costs, Accommodations: Costs, which range from $515 to $900, include tuition, fine hotel accommodations, Chicago/Stratford bus transportation and lunches en route, theatre tickets, planned activities, play and travel notes, and a Festival tote bag. A $100 deposit must accompany reservation with balance due six weeks prior to departure. Credit cards (VISA, MasterCard) accepted. Cancellations more than six weeks prior receive a full refund less $45; no refunds thereafter.

Location: The Festivals are held in the Canadian towns of Stratford and Niagara-on-the-Lake, Ontario, a nine to ten-hour bus ride from Chicago.

Contact: Summer Theatre Study Tours, The University of Chicago Office of Continuing Education, 5835 S. Kimbark Ave., Chicago, IL 60637; (312) 702-1722.

UNIVERSITY COLLEGE DUBLIN (UCD) INTERNATIONAL SUMMER SCHOOL
Dublin, Ireland

Seventeen-day summer course

Since it was first offered, in 1949, the purpose of the UCD International Summer School has been to present a broad survey of Irish history, heritage, tradition, and contemporary culture. The program is open to students and adults who are already familiar with Ireland as well as those with no previous knowledge of the country. Each year a different aspect is studied, providing an examination of Irish tradition in archaeology, literature, history, folklore, drama, politics, architecture, and the arts. Included are lectures, seminars, theatre and museum visits, musical events, and two two-day field trips to historic and archaeological sites outside of Dublin. Receptions and panel discussions by prominent experts are also a part of the program. Three academic credits are available and participants receive a transcript of 60 hours of attendance.

Specialties: The history, heritage and contemporary culture of Ireland.

Faculty: Approximately 30 distinguished Irish scholars, artists, writers, and public figures.

Costs, Accommodations: Tuition only is IR£350; accommodations range from IR£136 for campus lodging in Roebuck Castle to IR£187 for single room bed and breakfast in a private home. Full payment must accompany application by June 1.

Location, Facilities: University College Dublin, the largest university college in Ireland, is situated at Belfield about three miles from the center of the city. On-campus facilities include a library, bank, indoor sports center, tennis courts, and playing fields.

Contact: UCD Summer School, Newman House, 86 St. Stephen's Green, Dublin 2, Ireland; (353) 1-752004, Fax (353) 1-694409.

UNIVERSITY COLLEGE OF NORTH WALES (UCNW)
Bangor, Gwynedd, United Kingdom
One-day to one-week spring and summer courses in Wales

The University of Wales, Bangor, offers a variety of Study Breaks that offer adults the opportunity to learn about the landscape, archeaology, wildlife, and history of North Wales.

Rambling in Snowdonia, offered for three weeks during July and August, consists of lectures and guided walks through Snowdonia National Park. The theme changes daily and participants can enroll for any number of days. A one-week course, **Snowdonia: Its Landscape and People,** investigates the environment, cultural character, and economic development of Snowdonia. The program combines a series of lectures with field visits that relate to the region's structure and geology, glaciation and topography, fauna, flora, and ecology, Medieval heritage, culture and language, and economic patterns and issues. **Creative Gardening,** a one-week summer course, offers a combination of lectures and practical sessions covering the principals and practices of gardening, soils and fertilizers, plant propagation, and pest and disease control. Students also learn how to plan fruit, flower, and vegetable gardens. Two one-week courses, **The Story of the Celts,** trace the origins of the Celts with field visits to archaeological sites, the castles at Caernarfon and Beaumaris, a quarry museum, and the boyhood home of David Lloyd George.

Specialties: The landscape, archeaology, wildlife, and history of North Wales.

Faculty: Courses are taught by botanists, geologists, geographers, historians, archaeologists, and other specialists.

Costs, Accommodations: Costs range from £32 per day to £230 for a one-week course, which includes full board, lodging, tuition, and VAT. Weekly nonresident tuition is £105. Lodging is provided in Neuadd John Morris-Jones, UCNW's oldest residence hall, which has been refurbished and offers single and twin rooms with washbasins.

Location: Bangor is situated in between Snowdonia to the south and Anglesey, on the coast, to the north, about a four-and-a-half-hour drive northwest of London. International flights arrive at Manchester, Birmingham, and Liverpool airports, approximately a two-hour drive.

Contact: Conference Office, University of Wales, Bangor, Gwynedd, LL57 2DG, United Kingdom; (44) 248 351151, ext. 2560.

UNIVERSITY OF MINNESOTA, DULUTH
SUMMER STUDY IN ENGLAND
Duluth, Minnesota

Four-week program in July-August

Since 1984, the University of Minnesota, Duluth, in cooperation with the University of Birmingham in England, has conducted a four-week summer study program for college students and adults. Participants select one of four courses, each limited to 25 students, that meet for two to three hours daily, Monday through Thursday. Course-related field trips are scheduled during off-class hours and three-day weekends are free for individual travel. Academic credit is available.

Typical course topics include British Mysteries in a Landscape, an interdisciplinary course that combines readings of British mysteries with tours of characteristic mystery settings; Great Britain and Germany Today: from Adversaries to Partners in the New Europe, a comparison of the recent history and development of Great Britain and West Germany with field trips to parliament and the German consulate and a week in Germany visiting government, university, business, and historic sites; Geology, Scenery and the Industrial Revolutions in the West Midlands, a study of the rock types and industrial history of this region; and The Architecture of the English Country House, 1450-1900, which examines the development of a variety of structures, from the medieval fortified manor to the comfortable Edwardian house.

Specialties: British studies.

Faculty: Courses are taught by faculty of the University of Minnesota and the University of Birmingham.

Costs, Accommodations: Land costs range from $1,575 to $1,800, which includes tuition, course-related field trips, single room accommodations at High Hall on the University of Birmingham campus, and some meals. A nonrefundable $100 deposit must accompany enrollment with 50% of balance due three months prior to departure and remaining balance due six weeks prior.

Location: Birmingham, a hub of industrial, commercial, and cultural activity located in the heart of Britain, is 90 minutes northwest of London. The college campus is situated near the Botanical Gardens and about a mile and a half from Birmingham City Centre.

Contact: Summer Study in England, Continuing Education and Extension, University of Minnesota, Duluth, 10 University Dr., Duluth, MN 55812-2496; (218) 726-6193.

THE UNIVERSITY MUSEUM OF ARCHAEOLOGY
AND ANTHROPOLOGY
The University of Pennsylvania
Philadelphia, Pennsylvania
Seven to sixteen-day tours to Mexico, Canada, and abroad

Since 1967, the Women's Committee of the University Museum has planned tours that relate to current exhibitions and ongoing research projects. Approximately four trips are planned annually, each limited to 30 museum members. Typical tour itineraries include Southeast Asia: Buddhist Splendors and Tribal Traditions, which features visits to Bangkok, Borobadur, the Dayak region of Borneo, and Torajaland; Empires of Greatness: Splendors of Pre-Columbian Central Mexico, focusing on a variety of environments, cultures, and time periods of pre-history, with emphasis on recent fieldwork; and Eastern Turkey: A Historic Drama of Four Thousand Years, including an exclusive visit to Gordion, which has been excavated and studied by The University Museum for more than 30 years.

Specialties: Tours with an anthropological or archaeological focus.

Faculty: Each tour is accompanied by a University Museum curatorial staff member who is an expert in the region visited.

Costs, Accommodations: Tour prices vary, with $2,500 to $3,000 the average for a two-week tour abroad. Museum membership is required and begins at $35 individual, $40 family. A donation is included in the price of the tour.

Location: In addition to the above, includes Toronto, Guatamala, and India.

Contact: Women's Committee Tours, The University Museum of Archaeology and Anthropology, The University of Pennsylvania, 33rd and Spruce Streets, Philadelphia, PA 19104-6324; (215) 898-9202.

UNIVERSITY OF NEW ORLEANS (UNO)
INTERNATIONAL STUDY PROGRAMS
New Orleans, Louisiana
Three to six-week summer programs in Austria and Italy

The University of New Orleans offers a variety of programs for high school students, undergraduate and graduate students desiring academic credit, and adults seeking personal enrichment. Programs for adults include **The European Centre**, a three-week educational experience in July co-sponsored by UNO and the University of Innsbruck in Innsbruck, Austria, and two programs at **The Ezra Pound Center** in Northern Italy: a one-month course in anthropology in June and three weeks in July devoted to the study of the works of Ezra Pound.

The goal of **The European Centre** is to involve adults in an active and creative learning experience, broadening their knowledge of Western culture. The program is limited to 90 participants, who choose one of a half dozen courses that are each limited to 15 students. Typical courses include A Cultural History of Europe, a combination of lectures and discussions dealing with the inter-relationship of political history, architecture, art, music, and philosophy; The Music of Austria, a survey of music with discussion and analysis of the music of Haydn and Mozart from the Viennese classical period to the compositions of Mahler; and Early 20th Century Austrian Literature, including the works of Arthur Schnitzler, Hugo v. Hofmannsthal, and Franz Kafka, with emphasis on psychoanalysis of Sigmund Freud. Students attend classes each weekday morning at the Leopold-Franzens University and afternoons are devoted to course-related field trips. Day trips to Munich, Oberammergau, Salzburg, or the South Tyrol are also scheduled. A distinguished lecture series, featuring Senator George McGovern, is held in the evenings. Three hours of academic credit are granted for each course. Those who enroll for credit take mid-term and final examinations and all who satisfactorily complete the program receive a European Centre Certificate.

The Ezra Pound Center in nothern Italy is the location for the anthropology program, offered since 1987, and the literature program, first offered in 1990. The Center is housed in the Brunnenburg Castle, Pound's residence in his later years and now the home of his grandson, anthropologist Dr. Siegfried de Rachewiltz. The Castle houses a museum of ceremonial and agricultural artifacts from the Tyrolean area and Africa as well as extensive Pound archives. Each program is limited to 14 participants, who can earn 3 semester credit hours. The anthropology course, **From Cottage to Castle: Field Study in an Alpine Village**, features a weekend trip to Venice as well as excursions to the surrounding area. During the literature course students read, study, and discuss Pound's shorter poems, selections from his life's work, *The Cantos*, selected translations, and important critical essays. A highlight of the program is a three-day trip to Venice and Verona, where Pound spent many years.

Specialties: The history, music, art, literature, and culture of central Europe; anthropology; the literature of Ezra Pound.

Faculty: Classes at The European Centre are conducted by faculty from the U.S. and Europe. The anthropology course is taught by Professor Paul Magnarella of the University of Florida and the literature course is taught by University of New Orleans Associate Professor of English John Gery, a poet and critic. Visiting lecturers include Dr. de Rachewiltz, Pound's daughter Mary de Rachewiltz, and his biographer Noel Stock.

Costs, Accommodations: The European Centre program cost of $1,985 includes tuition, accommodations with private bath at the International Student House at the University of Innsbruck, continental breakfasts and lunches on weekdays, use of campus athletic facilities, and scheduled excursions. Round-trip airfare from/to New Orleans or New York and weekend field trips to South Tyrol and Venice are additional. A $200 deposit must accompany application with $750 due March 1 and balance due April 2. Cancellations prior to April 2 receive full refund less $50 fee; a $750 fee is charged from April 2 to May 1, and additional nonrecoverable costs are assessed thereafter. The cost of the anthropology (literature) program is $1,399 ($1,299), which includes tuition, accommodations in a renovated 17th century farm house within the castle complex, most meals, field trips, and other scheduled activities. Round-trip airfare to/from Europe is not included. A $100 deposit must accompany application with balance due April 15. Cancellations received prior to April 15 forfeit a $50 cancellation fee, thereafter fee is $200 plus nonrecoverable expenses.

Location, Facilities: Situated in Austria's Tyrolean Alps on the banks of the Inn River, the University of Innsbruck is a ten-minute walk from the "old city" and convenient to Munich, Salzburg, Vienna, Zurich, Lucerne, Venice, Florence, and Rome. Recreational facilities include tennis courts, a weight room, gymnasium, and swimming pool. Mountain hikes and summer skiing are available on weekends and fitness courses, golf, and saunas are situated nearby. Brunnenburg Castle is in Italy's South Tyrol region, which borders on Austria and Switzerland in the Alps. Located on a mountainside, it overlooks Merano and is accessible by rail from Florence, Innsbruck, Siena, Venice, and Nice.

Contact: Office of International Study Programs, University of New Orleans, P.O. Box 1215, New Orleans, LA 70148; (504) 286-7116.

UNIVERSITY OF OXFORD
Department for External Studies
Oxford, England
One-week to six-week on-campus and international programs

The Department for External Studies of the University of Oxford has been arranging residential summer courses since 1888 and currently enrolls more than 1,000 students from 24 countries in programs arranged by the Department, often in conjunction with another university. On-campus programs include the three-week **Oxford University Summer School for Adults,** one-week **Oxford Local History and Archaeology Summer Schools,** and two and three-week programs co-sponsored by such institutions in the United States as the University of California at Berkeley (page 177), Florida State University (page 129), Michigan State and Northwestern Universities (page 123), and the Smithsonian Institution (page 153). Three or four **Study Tours** are also offered during the year.

The annual **Oxford University Summer School for Adults,** offered from mid-July to early August, seeks to introduce students to the full-time experience of serious academic study in Oxford. The more than 200 enrollees choose one of eight to ten seminars on a wide range of subjects that are offered during each of the program's three weeks. Typical seminar titles include Mahler in Vienna, Human Communication, Modern Soviet Fiction, The Industrial Revolution, and Film as Art. Before arriving at Oxford students will have worked on an initial reading list and written a project. During the session they produce a second project related to their subject and based on private study. In addition to daily seminars, two individual tutorials per week, and private study, the schedule includes general lectures for all students and an informal social program, which features a visit to the Shakespeare Memorial Theatre at Stratford, visits to local theatres, museums, and concerts, tours of Oxford, and discussions and presentations at the school.

The **Oxford Local History and Archaeology Summer School**, offered since 1988, aims to provide intensive small group teaching in local history and practical archaeology. Two one-week sessions scheduled during August, each limited to 10 participants, cover such topics as place-name studies, computing techniques, excavation techniques, Anglo-Saxon and Medieval towns, prehistory, documentary sources, archaeological pottery, and topography. A typical day is likely to include two morning workshops or equivalent field work, followed by private study time devoted to a practical project. Guest lectures, field trips, and informal social programs are also offered.

Ten to twelve-day **Study Tours** focus on the history, politics, and culture of such locations as the Soviet Union, France, and Spain and Portugal. A typical itinerary, The Albigensian Crusade, retraces the path followed by the Crusaders and gives students the opportunity to absorb some of the culture and traditions of the French Midi.

Other programs include an annual four-week summer course in **Yiddish Language and Literature** and a six-week summer school for final year undergraduate students, graduate students, and teachers, titled **Britain: Literature, History, and Society from 1870.**

Specialties: A variety of subjects relating to the humanities, history, culture, politics, and archaeology.

Faculty: Programs are conducted primarily by University of Oxford faculty members.

Costs, Accommodations: Weekly cost for Summer Schools ranges from £200 to £350 (includes full board). Students are lodged in single or shared rooms in Rewley House, where the department is based, or in Oxford Colleges. Study Tours range from £565 to £880.

Location: Oxford is approximately a one-hour drive northwest of London.

Contact: Summer Schools Secretary, Dept. for External Studies, University of Oxford, 1 Wellington Square, Oxford OX1 2JA, England; (44) 865 270396.

UNIVERSITY OF THE PACIFIC (UOP)
Lifelong Learning
Stockton, California

Four to sixteen-day domestic and international programs

The University of the Pacific's Office of Lifelong Learning offers a variety of programs for adults and families, including one-week summer family camps and study tours in the U.S. and abroad.

The Pacific Alumni Camp, offered three times each summer for 30 to 40 families, features morning lectures and crafts classes and afternoon nature walks. Domestic and international tours, which offer two or three credits of extended education credit, include lectures and other educational activities.

During a typical domestic travel program, the Sierra Cascades Geological Adventure, participants learn about the history, ecology, and geology of the region north of Lake Tahoe and participate in a geological project that will be included in a textbook. An international trip, the Israel Study Tour, features an evening lecture at a Kibbutz, visits with small groups in the homes of Israeli Jerusalemites, and informal discussions with archaeologists and Palestinians.

Specialties: A variety of on-campus, domestic, and international tours.

Faculty: Instructors and tour leaders are UOP faculty members and other experts.

Costs, Accommodations: The family camp cost is $355 for adults and $40 to $248 for children, which includes meals, programs, and accommodations at the Feather River Inn in Blairsden, California. A $100 nonrefundable deposit must accompany registration with balance due at least six weeks prior to program. Credit cards (VISA, MasterCard) accepted. Travel program costs, deposits, and refund policies vary.

Contact: Office of Lifelong Learning, University of the Pacific, Stockton, CA 95211; (209) 946-2424.

UNIVERSITY RESEARCH EXPEDITIONS PROGRAM (UREP)
University of California
Berkeley, California

Two to three-week domestic and international research expeditions

Established in 1976 as a self-supporting unit of the University of California, UREP's purpose is to bring the public and scientific community together and encourage greater communication and sharing of information and skills. Although the program is open to all, the five to ten volunteers on each research team are selected on the basis of their suitability for the project. Wilderness experiences, observation skills, and drawing, photography, and diving ability are helpful, as well as adaptability to other people and cultures. College students may qualify for academic credit through their own institutions. Approximately 30 different research expeditions are conducted annually, each scheduled from one to four times during the year, inquiring into such areas as animal behavior, anthropology/sociology, archaeology/paleontology, arts, botany/ecology, and marine studies. Volunteers receive full details on project objectives, field techniques, and recommended readings, and all projects begin with an on-site orientation and offer on-going instruction in field methods.

Typical animal behavior projects include Wildlife of the White Mountains, devoted to proper management of the area's natural resources through a detailed survey of its indigenous reptiles, birds, and small mammals; and Wings over Kakamega: Birds of the Rain Forest, which examines the dynamics of mating rituals of the Yellow-Shouldered Widowbird as well as the factors involved in the regeneration of forest trees. Anthropology/ sociology expeditions include Distant Shores: Why Cape Verdeans Immigrate, a survey of cultural causes and consequences of this West African nation's immigration, in which small teams, working with an interpreter, observe and interview local families; and two projects conducted in cooperation with UNICEF: AIDS and Homeless Youth in Brazil and Thy Daily Bread: Children's Nutrition in Brazil. Archaeology/paleontology projects include Chinese Pioneers of the California Gold Rush, which focuses on understanding the everyday lives of these pioneers, their social organization, and the significance of their settlement within the larger Chinese community; and Dawn of the Dinosaurs, a layer-by-layer study of an ancient pond in Arizona, searching for remains of its fossil vertebrates. A typical arts topic is Festive Costumes of Highland Bolivia, an analysis of Andean costumes for regional differences and a documentation of this vanishing art form. Botany/ ecology projects include Seeing the Forest for the Trees: An Ecuadorian Rain Forest, a continuation of a detailed inventory of plant species in the Maquipucuna Tropical Reserve, designed to expedite land management and ecological plans for the area; and Stronger Crops, Higher Yields: Natural Methods for African Farms, a study of natural methods of pest control such as the timing and combination of crop cultivation. Coral Communities of the Sea of Cortez, a marine studies program, examines the effect of several environmental factors on the distribution of marine invertebrates inhabiting the Cabo Pulmo coral reef.

Specialties: Animal behavior, anthropology/sociology, archaeology/paleontology, arts, botany/ecology/ marine studies.

Faculty: All leaders are University of California professors or Ph.D. candidates.

Costs, Accommodations: UREP volunteers participate in the costs of field and research expenses as well as the costs of planning and implementation. Expedition costs, including accommodations, ground transportation, group camping and field gear, and research equipment and supplies, range from $665 to $1,535. All costs are tax-deductible charitable contributions to the extent allowed by law. A nonrefundable $200 initial contribution must accompany application with balance due 90 days prior to departure. Written cancellations received more than 90 days prior are granted a refund only if space can be filled. A limited number of teacher and student scholarships are available.

Location: UREP expeditions are worldwide.

Contact: University Research Expeditions Program (UREP), University of California, Berkeley, CA 94720; (415) 642-6586.

UNIVERSITY OF ROCHESTER
Alumni Association
Rochester, New York

One to two-week domestic and international trips

Since 1977, the University of Rochester Alumni Association has offered trips to popular destinations throughout the world. Approximately six to ten trips are scheduled annually, with 20 to 30 participants.

Specialties: International travel.

Faculty: Some trips are accompanied by a University of Rochester faculty member who conducts informal lectures.

Costs, Accommodations: Costs, which include round-trip airfare, double occupancy first class accommodations (single supplement available), meals, ground transportation, and planned activities, range from $1,500 to $4,500. Deposits and refund policies vary. Participants who are not affiliated with the University of Rochester are asked to make a tax-deductible $50 contribution to the University.

Location: Destinations include the Alps, London and Paris, the South Pacific, the Amazon, the Caribbean, the Canary Islands, the Soviet Union, and Alaska.

Contact: Fairbank Alumni House, University of Rochester, Rochester, NY 14620; (716) 275-3684.

UNIVERSITY OF SOUTH FLORIDA (USF)
TRAVEL- STUDY PROGRAMS
Division of Special Programs/Travel Study
Tampa, Florida

Two to six-week residential and travel-study programs abroad

In 1983, the University of South Florida's Division of Special Programs began offering a variety of annual residential and travel-study programs that are open to both students and adults. All offer academic credit.

Residential programs, which range from three to six weeks, are held in the summer in Cambridge, Edinburgh, Italy, Paris, and Spain, and year-round in Costa Rica and Venezuela. The **University of Cambridge,** in conjunction with the Florida Consortium of Colleges and Universities, offers three three-week programs that focus on English literature, art, and history — **English Literature Summer School, Art History Summer School,** and **History Summer School** — and the **International Summer School,** a four-week term followed by a two-week term that offers the opportunity to choose from more than 50 different courses relating to English heritage and culture. Students in Term I attend Special Subject lecture-discussion classes and a General Lecture program. Those in Term II study at a more advanced level a wide range of subjects during in-depth 90-minute sessions. Optional excursions to East Anglia, London, Oxford, Stratford-Upon-Avon, and other places of interest are scheduled on weekends. Six to nine academic credits can be earned in each session.

Three and six-week programs at the **University of Edinburgh** offer participants the opportunity to study Scottish literature, 20th century English literature, or British social history. The extracurricular program features guided tours of Edinburgh, evenings of music and poetry in the Scottish tradition, and excursions to other parts of Scotland. Three to six academic credits are available.

USF in Italy, a one-month program at the Italian University for Foreigners in Perugia, offers four-credit courses in Italian Civilization and Culture and the History and Art of Italy. Language courses and studio arts courses in drawing, painting, sculpture, and photography are also available. Weekly excursions are scheduled to Siena, Florence, Venice, Ravenna, Assisi, and Rome. **Contemporary French Culture**, a study and travel program offered in July, consists of four weeks of on-site study in Paris with afternoon and weekend excursions to historic and cultural centers in the provinces.

Travel-study programs, limited to 20 participants, are offered each summer to Asia, France, England, Ireland, and the Soviet Union, and during wintersession break to Egypt. Summer tours to Africa and Greece are scheduled every few years. During the six weeks prior to each program, the tour leader conducts a series of weekly on-campus lectures on the history, culture, and other aspects of the regions to be visited. Three academic credits are available for each lecture program.

Specialties: Culture and heritage of countries in Europe, Asia, Africa, and South America.

Faculty: All tour leaders are regular USF faculty or adjuncts. They are required to be knowledgeable about the countries visited.

Costs, Accommodations: Residential program costs range from $970 to $2,400, which includes tuition, room or apartment, planned excursions, and may include meals. Cost of academic credit is additional. Costs of travel-study programs range from $1,900 to $4,000, which includes round-trip airfare, double occupancy lodging, most meals, ground transportation, scheduled activities, pre-tour lecture series, and academic credit.

Location: Residential programs in Costa Rica, England, France, Italy, Scotland, Spain, and Venezuela; travel-study programs to East Africa, Egypt, Germany, Great Britain, Greece, Ireland, the South Pacific, and the Soviet Union.

Contact: Division of Special Programs/Travel-Study, LLL 012, University of South Florida, Tampa, FL 33620-8700; (813) 974-3218.

THE UNIVERSITY OF TEXAS AT AUSTIN STUDIES ON TOUR
Division of Continuing Education/Thompson Conference Center
Austin, Texas

Eight-day and two-week summer travel study programs in Europe

Since 1983, The University of Texas at Austin Division of Continuing Education has offered in-depth summer programs for adults that focus on both the academic and travel aspects of study abroad. The five annual programs are **UT/Cambridge, UT/Paris, UT/Scotland, UT/Spain**, and **From D-Day to the Rhine.**

The two-week **UT/Cambridge Program**, offered jointly with the Board of Extra-mural Studies of the University of Cambridge since 1985 and limited to 130 participants, consists of morning and early afternoon small-group classes, half and full-day field trips, and optional evening lectures and concerts. Students select one of ten courses offered in a variety of topics including Romans and Saxons in Britain, The English Novel in the 20th Century, British Painting from Hogarth to Hockney, Churchill and the Second World War, Shakespeare: Play and Performance, and From Alchemy to Atoms: A History of British Science. A course description and reading list are provided in advance. While there are no prerequisites and written work is optional, preparatory reading, participation in class discussion, and completion of written assignments under instructor supervision enhance the program's benefits. Optional weekend excursions are scheduled to such sites as the villages of East Anglia and Stratford-Upon-Avon, which includes a performance at the Royal Shakespeare Theatre. Students live and attend classes at Clare College, established in 1326 and one of the oldest of the 31 Cambridge colleges.

The two-week **UT/Paris Program — From Revelry to Revolution**, offered jointly with the Formation Permanente Adultes of the American University of Paris since 1989 and limited to 30 participants, consists of morning classes and on-site afternoon lectures at course-related sites in the Paris area and four days of lecture-visits in the Loire Valley. Lecture topics include Flamboyant Gothic and Early Renaissance Styles, Aristocratic Life in the Garden of France, The Affluence of the Nobility on the Eve of the Revolution, The Rise of Absolute Monarchy, and The End of the Ancien Regime. Students attend classes at the American University of Paris and are lodged in first-class hotels throughout the program.

The eight-day **UT/Scotland Program — Heritage and Culture**, offered jointly with the University of Edinburgh since 1988 and limited to 34 participants, consists of morning, afternoon, and/or evening classes, a city tour of Edinburgh, and full and half-day field trips to such locations as Ingliston, Stirling, The Trossachs, Hopetoun, and St. Andrews. Lecture topics cover the history, geography, language, art, architecture, politics, and economy of Scotland. Students are housed in Mylne's Court, an historic student residence hall of the University of Edinburgh located less than a block from Edinburgh Castle.

From D-Day to the Rhine, offered since 1987 and limited to 40 participants, is a two-week study of major World War II European battlefields, with special emphasis on Normandy and the Battle of the Bulge. The program begins with excursions to London museums and presentations by British specialists and continues by bus to sites of principal battles during the Allied advance to the German heartland, including Utah Beach, Omaha Beach, Pointe du Hoc, Paris, Rheims, Bastogne, Malmedy, Siegfried Line, and Remagen Bridge. Books, maps, and reading lists are provided and lectures are given en route. Participants are lodged in first-class hotels.

Spain: Crucible of Cultures, to be offered in 1991 and limited to 30 participants, is a two-week study of the country's history, art, literature, and folklore traditions. The course emphasizes Spain's unique development, derived from its separation from the rest of Europe by the Pyrenees and the mixing of Celtic, Roman, Visigoth, Moorish, and Catholic cultures.

Specialties: Travel study in England, France, Scotland, and Spain; travel study of World War II European battlefields.

Faculty: The programs in Cambridge, Paris, Scotland, and Spain are taught by the faculty of the co-sponsoring institution. From D-Day to the Rhine is taught by a six-member faculty of distinguished authors and historians, including Charles B. MacDonald, Michael R.D. Foot, Ralph Bennett, Martin Blumenson, William C.C. Cavanagh, and Thomas M. Hatfield.

Costs, Accommodations: Approximate land costs are $2,395 for Cambridge, $2,595 for Paris and Spain, $1,595 for Scotland, and $3,000 for D-Day, which includes tuition, lodging, most meals, and scheduled activities and excursions. A $400 deposit must accompany reservation ($300 is refundable until a predetermined date) with balance due by May 1. No refunds granted after May 1. Earlybird discounts are offered until late January and credit cards (VISA, MasterCard) are accepted for all programs except D-Day.

Contact: Studies on Tour, Division of Continuing Education, The University of Texas at Austin, P.O. Box 7879, Austin, TX 78713-7879; (512) 471-3124, Fax (512) 471-9677.

THE UNIVERSITY OF WARWICK SUMMER SCHOOL
Coventry, England

Four weeks in July

Established in 1965, the University of Warwick offers a summer school British studies program specifically designed for students from abroad and taught by members of the Warwick academic staff. Most participants are from the U.S. and Canada with 80% undergraduates and the rest graduate students, teachers, and interested adults. Students can enroll in one of approximately ten courses, all intensively academic and selected because of the advantage to studying them in England, where field trips, excursions, and guest lectures augment classroom learning. Each course is limited to 15 students and consists of at least 45 class contact hours with an additional 20 contact hours derived from special lectures, field trips specific to the course, and excursions involving all students in the program. Four units of academic credit are offered for each course.

Typical courses include British Politics and Society in the Age of Thatcher, which analyzes current politics in the broad historical and social context and includes field trips to institutions that range from the local planning office to Parliament; Victorian Art and Architecture, taught on location with field trips to galleries and buildings; and The English Detective and Mystery Novel, ranging from the 19th century to the present, with visits to The Fens, Norwich, Oxford, Shrewsbury, Scotland Yard's Black Museum, and other locales used by noted authors. Students have the opportunity to write papers on the critical appreciation of one writer, an exploration of one theme, and an original piece of detective fiction. Shakespeare in Performance examines the bard's work in light of a variety of traditions and interpretations and features six Royal Shakespeare Company performances, workshops and discussions with RSC actors and directors, visits backstage, and excursions to Warwick Castle and Kenilworth. Programs for all students include a performance of a Shakespeare play and lectures on such topics as The City of Coventry, English Literature and English Life, and How England Got Its Government.

Specialties: A range of British studies.

Faculty: All courses are designed and taught by full-time members of the University of Warwick faculty and are derived from the regular academic curriculum. The twelve-member summer school staff is headed by David Mervin, Ph.D., Senior Lecturer in the Department of Politics and author of *The Presidency and Ronald Reagan.*

Costs, Accommodations: The fee for each course is $1,695, which includes tuition, field trips and excursions, accommodations, and all meals except weekday lunches. A $150 nonrefundable deposit must accompany application by two months prior to session with balance due one month prior. Several $500 scholarships are awarded, based on academic merit and financial need, to those who apply at least three months prior. Private rooms are provided on campus.

Location, Facilities: The University is situated on a 500-acre campus between Coventry and Kenilworth, surrounded by fields and woodlands on three sides. Centrally located in England, it's 70 minutes by rail from London, 15 miles from Stratford-Upon-Avon, and accessible by day trip to Bath, Stonehenge, Oxford, Cambridge, and York. Program participants can avail themselves of all University facilities and services, including the library, swimming pool, squash and tennis courts, and track.

Contact: Dr. David Mervin, Director, University of Warwick Summer School, Coventry CV4 7AL, England; (44) 203-5231133, Fax (44) 203-461606.

UNIVERSITY OF WASHINGTON EXTENSION TRAVEL-STUDY PROGRAM
Seattle, Washington

Twelve-day to three-week programs in the U.S. and abroad

Established in 1968, the University of Washington Extension offers four to eight domestic and international educational tours annually for the traveler who wants to experience other places and cultures in depth. Enrollment is limited to 20 to 40 participants, depending on tour. A preliminary reading list is provided upon registration and tour orientation meetings are scheduled before departure.

A popular tour, London Theater and Concert Halls, includes 12 theatrical and musical events, from performances by the Royal Shakespeare Company and full orchestral productions to brand-new plays and small ensemble groups. Lectures are a part of the program and each morning features a discussion of the previous evening's event and preview of the next. Native Cultures of the American Southwest: The Hopi and Navajo focuses on the prehistoric, historic and contemporary Indian life of the Southwest. Participants are introduced to the area's native prehistory; make specially arranged visits with museum curators, Indian traders, and Hopi elders; and tour villages, historic sites, and museums. Information from traditional scholarly investigation in the disciplines of archaeology, anthropology, history, and ethno-history is presented by tour leaders. The Acropolis of Athens and Its Immediate Surroundings, an intensive exploration of the Acropolis, includes a visit to the Athenian Agora and the temples of Artemis at Brauron and Poseidon at Sounion and lectures throughout the program that cover Acropolis history, origins of the polis, Greek religion and drama, sculptures of the Acropolis, Pericles, and the Golden Age, and the Legacy of Greece in Western civilization.

Specialties: In-depth educational tours to domestic and international locations.

Faculty: Distinguished University of Washington faculty and other scholars plan the itineraries and lead each tour.

Costs, Accommodations: Land costs, which include tuition, double occupancy lodging (single supplement available), some meals, ground transportation, and tickets and admissions to planned activities, range from $1,600 to $2,300. A $200 deposit must accompany reservation with half of balance due ten weeks prior to departure and remaining amount due five weeks prior. Credit cards (VISA, MasterCard) accepted. Written cancellations more than 90 days prior forfeit $100; penalty thereafter ranges from $200 (45 to 90 days prior) to 25% refund (less than 30 days prior).

Contact: UW Extension Travel-Study Program, University of Washington, Seattle, WA 98195; (206) 543-2300, Fax (206) 685-9359.

UNIVERSITY OF WISCONSIN SEMINARS
Madison, Wisconsin

Weekend and three-week seminars year-round in Europe, North Africa, China, and Madison, Wisconsin

Each year, the University of Wisconsin-Madison and University of Wisconsin-Extension sponsor more than a half-dozen international seminars abroad and about the same number of weekend seminars on campus. The programs are designed to provide an enjoyable learning experience that helps participants better understand other people and cultures. Continuing education units (CEUs) are available for each seminar.

International seminars range in length from 17 to 25 days and include briefings at embassies and by journalists, governmental leaders, and local experts. The Medieval Seminar, offered annually since 1977, focuses on the history, art, and architecture of English locales, with visits to small villages, parish churches, museums, and little-known medieval sites. An annual pilgrimage to the cradle of western civilization, covering the classical, Byzantine, and modern aspects of Greece and Turkey, includes excursions to Salonika, Pella, Delphi, Athens, Corinth, Mycenae, Epidaurus, an Aegean cruise, Knossos, Izmir, Sardix, Ephesus, Pergamum, Troy, and Istanbul. Other seminars may include Arab Morocco and Moorish Spain, which visits Rabat, Mednes, Fez, and Marrakesh; Performing Arts Experiences in Ireland, Wales, England, and Scotland, featuring lectures and performances at the Royal Festival Hall and Barbican Center in London, the Royal Shakespeare Company Swan Theatre in Stratford-Upon-Avon, and the International Festival of Music and Drama in Edinburgh; Eastern Europe: Fifty Years After, with stops in Sofia, Bucharest, Prague, Budapest, Warsaw, Krakow, and East and West Berlin; and The Three Faces of China, including Taiwan, Hong Kong, and the People's Republic of China. Participants receive 4 CEUs for each seminar.

Weekend seminars, held at St. Benedict Center on the Madison campus, begin with dinner on Friday and conclude at 4 pm Saturday. A variety of topics are covered and typical titles include Retreat to the Medieval World, Jerusalem: From Solomon to Teddy Kolleck, Eastern Europe: What Is Happening Behind the Iron Curtain?, and A Revolution Revisited, which explores the impact of the French Revolution on Western civilization. A certificate of participation and equivalency clock hours are available as well as 0.7 CEUs.

Specialties: A variety of topics relating to history, culture, and politics.

Faculty: Robert Schacht, Director, International Seminars, has traveled extensively throughout Eastern Europe and the United Arab Republic. Other University of Wisconsin faculty members/tour leaders include Professor Jane T. Schulenburg of the Department of Liberal Studies, Professor Christopher Kleinhenz of the Departments of French and Italian, and Professor Richard N. Ringler of the Departments of Scandinavian Studies and English.

Costs, Accommodations: Costs of the international seminars, including airfare from/to the U.S., double occupancy lodging (single supplement available), most meals, excursions, admissions, and the academic program, range from approximately $2,800 to $4,300. Registration fee for the weekend seminars is $30 with an 80% refund for cancellations. Meals alone are $24, meals and lodging are $47 single, $77 for two.

Contact: Robert Schacht, Director, International Seminars, 624 Lowell Hall, 610 Langdon St., Madison, WI 53703; (608) 263-2774.

UTAH STATE UNIVERSITY
Department of Languages and Philosophy
Logan, Utah
17-day summer travel-study program to the Soviet Union

Since 1975, Utah State University's Department of Languages and Philosophy has sponsored an annual travel-study program to the Soviet Union, usually in June. The program is limited to 40 students and adults and features visits to the Kremlin and Red Square in Moscow, the Hermitage in Leningrad, and three or four other cities, which are different each year. University credit in Russian language and culture is available and orientation sessions consisting of films, slides, and lectures precede the trip.

Specialties: Travel-study in the Soviet Union.

Faculty: Tour directors are Dr. Kent E. Robson, Head of the Department of Languages and Philosophy, and Dr. Lynn R. Eliason, Professor of German and Russian. Both speak Russian and have visited the country more than a dozen times.

Costs, Accommodations: Cost of approximately $2,875 includes round-trip airfare from/to Salt Lake City, first class hotel accommodations, meals, and planned activities. A $200 deposit must accompany reservation with balance due 60 days prior to departure. Cancellations more than 60 days prior receive full refund.

Contact: Dr. Kent E. Robson *or* Dr. Lynn R. Eliason, Dept. of Languages and Philosophy, Utah State University, Logan, UT 84322-0720; (801) 750-1209.

A VERMONT INQUIRY
Hawk Inn and Mountain Resort
Plymouth, Vermont
Three-day sessions from January-October

Established in 1988, A Vermont Inquiry sponsors approximately 40 three-day seminars annually on a variety of subjects, including art, music, history, philosophy, poetry, and current affairs. Each discussion-oriented session is limited to 14 participants and devoted to one topic, which is covered during four morning and evening seminars, a total of nine hours of class time. Afternoons are free for resort activities and leisure. Participants, who are not expected to have prior knowledge of the topic, are provided with two instructor-selected books in advance of the program.

Seminar topics, which range from entertaining to intellectually challenging, include Conceptualizing Love, an exploration of writings, philosophies, and contemporary ideas; Classical Music Weekend — Listening to Haydn's Sonatas, the development of listening skills and their application to the works of other classical composers; How the Supreme Court Interprets the Constitution, a non-legalistic look at dilemmas and analysis of specific cases; Understanding the Cold War Through Popular Film, an examination of East-West relations of the post-war period by viewing films made during this era; and Dreams, Nightmares and Poetry, a review of major clinical and theoretical writing on dreams with a discussion of participants' dreams and poems that incorporate dream-like visions.

Specialties: A variety of topics relating to art, music, history, philosophy, poetry, and current affairs.

Faculty: A Vermont Inquiry founder and director is Vermont State College professor Neal Gersony. All faculty members are professors from New England-area colleges and universities, including Dartmouth, Middlebury, Williams, University of Vermont, Harvard, Columbia, and University of Massachusetts.

Costs, Accommodations: The seminar cost of $395 includes two dinners and breakfasts, double occupancy lodging (single supplement $100), tuition, books, and use of resort facilities. Nonresident fee is $275 (includes meals) and nonparticipant guest fee is $65 (plus $495 for participant). A $295 deposit ($340 single) must accompany registration with balance due on arrival. Credit cards (VISA, MasterCard) accepted. Cancellations at least 15 days prior receive a 90% refund or can apply full deposit to a later session.

Location, Facilities: Hawk Inn & Mountain Resort, rated Four-Star by the Mobil Travel Service, is accessible from airports in Burlington and Rutland, Vermont, and Lebanon, New Hampshire. Facilities include tennis, swimming, boating, skiing, horseback riding, and hiking. Specially equipped rooms are available for handicapped persons.

Contact: A Vermont Inquiry, Hawk Inn & Mountain Resort, Route 100, Box 64, Plymouth, VT 05056; (800) 451-4109 *or* (802) 672-3811.

VIRGINIA COMMONWEALTH UNIVERSITY (VCU)
Richmond, Virginia

Two to six-week spring-summer study tours abroad

Virginia Commonwealth University sponsers eight to ten study programs for students and adults during the months of May through August, each offering the opportunity to earn one to six academic credits. The programs are sponsored by various departments of the University with approximately half emphasizing language or studio art instruction and the others focusing on the culture and history of the host country.

Typical cultural/history programs include the London Theatre Tour, an annual event since 1982, featuring performances at Stratford-Upon-Avon, the Royal National Theatre, and West End theatres; Ancient Egypt and Nile Cruise, including reading assignments and lectures; and Minorities in the Russian Empire, with visits to Leningrad, Kiev, Yerevan, Tbilisi, Sevan, Ordzhonikidze, and Helsinki.

Specialties: Culture, history, language, and art of the host countries.

Faculty: All tours are led by VCA faculty, assisted by faculty in host countries.

Costs, Accommodations: Cultural/history programs range from $2,100 to $2,900, which includes round-trip airfare from/to the U.S., air and ground transportation en route, double occupancy accommodations (single supplement available), most meals, tickets and entrance fees, and tuition. A $250 deposit must accompany enrollment with the balance due in two installments. Full refund is granted cancellations more than three months prior to departure.

Location: Includes Egypt, the Soviet Union, and Western Europe.

Contact: Office of International Education, Virginia Commonwealth University, 827 W. Franklin St., Richmond, VA 23284-2041; (804) 367-8471.

VOLUNTEERS FOR PEACE (VFP)
INTERNATIONAL WORKCAMPS
Belmont, Vermont

Two to three-week summer workcamps in the U.S. and abroad

Established in 1981, the nonprofit membership Volunteers for Peace, Inc., sponsors more than 800 workcamps — short-term "peace corps" — annually in 33 countries. The program is open to anyone 18 or over, with the average age being 22, and most participants register for a number of consecutive workcamps in the same or different countries, thereby spending several months abroad. Workcamps are sponsored by a United Nations sanctioned organization in a host country, but coordinated by people in a local community. Generally, 10 to 20 people from four or more countries arrive on a given day in the host community. The work, which is casual and requires no special skills or foreign language facility, may involve construction, restoration, agriculture, maintenance, environmental, or social projects.   Many workcamps provide instruction relating to the project. Communication, sharing, and adapting are emphasized and participants have the opportunity to discuss issues of common concern, pursue free-time activities, and visit nearby places of interest.

Typical workcamps, which run from June to September, include a three-week program in the Soviet Union in which participants assist Soviet students with archaeological excavations in Vladimir. Day trips to ancient cities on the "Golden Ring" are also scheduled. A reforestation effort in Costa Rica includes a three-day intensive course in ecology and visits to the Presidential Palace and Soviet Embassy. During a three-week program in Norway, volunteers set up a biological/ecological garden while studying ecology and nature protection in relation to modern agriculture and hydro-electric power. The Federated Republic of Germany and Service Civil International (FRG/ SCI) sponsor study tours that include an overview of the different political movements in Germany and the present situation of the peace movement in all of Europe.

Specialties: International work/learn programs that promote goodwill through people-to-people exchange and community service.

Costs, Accommodations: Placement is on a first-come, first-served basis and most registrants respond by early May. Registration, which includes meals and accommodations, is $90 for most workcamps, $100 for those in Eastern Europe, and $400 to $700 for those in the USSR. Transportation to/ from the workcamp is not included. Full registration ($50 deposit for Soviet workcamps) must accompany reservation form and cancellations prior to June 1 receive a $25 refund. Those who submit a brief report of their experience by October 1 receive a $10 refund. Participants may be housed in a school, church, private home, or community center and living arrangements are generally cooperative, with workcampers coordinating and sharing such activities as food preparation, work, and entertainment. A $10 tax deductible contribution, which is deductible from workcamp registration fee, covers annual membership in VFP and the annual International Workcamp Directory, published in April. Credit card (VISA, MasterCard) payments accepted.

Location: Includes 13 states in the U.S., Austria, Belgium, Bulgaria, Canada, Czechoslovakia, Denmark, West Germany, East Germany, Finland, France, Ghana, Greece, Hungary, Ireland, Northern Ireland, Israel, Italy, Morocco, The Netherlands, Nicaragua, Norway, Poland, Spain, Sweden, Switzerland, Tunisia, Turkey, England, Wales, Scotland, the USSR, and Yugoslavia. Some workcamps are accessible to handicapped persons.

Contact: VFP International Workcamps, 43 Tiffany Rd., Belmont, VT 05730; (802) 259-2759, Fax (802) 259-2922.

VOYAGERS INTERNATIONAL
Ithaca, New York
Two to three-week international trips

Voyagers International offers a variety of year-round natural history, ornithology, cultural, and photography trips to Central and South America, East Africa, Asia, and the South Pacific. Some trips are organized for special groups, such as the American Birding Association, the Cornell Lab of Ornithology, the National Association of Biology Teachers, and the Audubon Societies of various states, but all are open to anyone who shares the interests of the group.

Specialties: Natural history, culture, ornithology, photography.

Faculty: Accomplished naturalists and birders, including Kenya birder Don Turner, Ecuadorian birder Paul Greenfield, naturalists Simon Nevill, Walt

Anderson, Milan Bull, and Douglas Pratt, author of *A Field Guide to the Birds of Hawaii and the Tropical Pacific.*

Costs, Accommodations: Costs average $2,200 to $4,000, including air and ground transportation, double occupancy accommodations (single supplement may be available), and most meals. A $400 deposit must accompany booking with balance payable 60 days prior to departure. Cancellation penalty ranges from $50 (more than 120 days prior) to 25% to 50% of land costs (less than 60 days prior).

Location: Destinations include Australia and New Zealand, Belize, Costa Rica, Kenya, Tanzania, Galápagos, Indonesia, and Malaysia.

Contact: Voyagers International, P.O. Box 915, Ithaca, NY 14851; (607) 257-3091.

WAINWRIGHT HOUSE
Rye, New York
One to five-day year-round programs

Wainwright House is a nonprofit, nonsectarian educational conference enter that has offered programs to the public since 1941 and currently offers more than 200 adult programs a year. Four institutes provide seminars, conferences, and on-going courses in the fields of health, psychology, business leadership, global issues, spirituality, and the arts. Group size ranges from 1 to 150 participants, depending upon the program.

A typical program, The U.N.: Ideal, Reality and Future, offers five days of contact with United Nations personnel, beginning with orientation at Wainwright House and followed by three days of briefings and a tour at U.N. headquarters in New York City. The last day is devoted to final briefings at Wainwright House.

Specialties: Global issues and topics relating to mental, physical, and spiritual health.

Faculty: The U.N. program is conducted by U.N. and associated personnel. Other programs are conducted by accomplished specialists in their fields.

Costs, Accommodations: Costs range from $45 for a a one-day program to $100 for a weekend workshop. The cost of the U.N. program is $125, which includes bus transportation. Lodging rate is $25 for a dormitory room; meals are $5 for breakfast, $7 for lunch, $10 for dinner. Credit cards (MasterCard, VISA) accepted. A 50% deposit must accompany registration. Cancellations at least one week prior to program receive full refund less $10 fee. Membership in Wainwright House (not required to attend programs) is $60 per year.

Location: Wainwright House is situated in Rye, a regular stop on the Metro North train.

Contact: Wainwright House, 260 Stuyvesant Ave., Rye, NY 10580; (914) 967-6080.

WASHINGTON AND LEE UNIVERSITY ALUMNI COLLEGE
Lexington, Virginia
One to two-week summer and fall programs on-campus and abroad

Washington and Lee University's Alumni College sponsors educational programs, both on-campus and abroad, that are open to alumni, parents, and friends, as well as a four-week summer academic and recreational program designed for college-bound high school seniors.

Three one-week campus sessions for adults, each devoted to a specific theme, are held in July. Representative titles include Spain: From Ferdinand to Franco, which covers the age of colonial expansion beginning in the 16th century through the political struggles that led to the Civil War, with special emphasis on the art of Velazquez and Goya, the Inquisition, Cortez and Montezuma, and Hemingway; Whodunits: Reflections on the Art of Mystery, an exploration of the history, art, and culture of the mystery genre, with readings of works by such writers as Hammett, Chandler, Leonard, and Hillerman, and an inside view of the craft of mystery writing; and Our Global Environment: Can We save the Future?, an inquiry into such areas of environmental crisis as pollution and natural resource depletion, alternative energy systems, and the effects of global warming, acid precipitation, and the ozone hole.

Four or five educational travel programs, including one or two that are follow-up tours to a campus session the previous summer, are scheduled from June through October. Typical programs include Alaska's Coastal Wilderness, a ten-day natural history cruise; A Voyage to Bavaria and the Oberammergau Passion Play; Celts and Kilts: Ireland and Scotland Through the Ages; and Wings Over the Nile, a 13-day safari/Nile cruise.

Specialties: A variety of topics relating to a specific theme.

Faculty: Includes members of the Washington and Lee University faculty, distinguished faculty of other colleges and universities, and specialists in various fields.

Costs, Accommodations: Cost of the campus sessions, which includes dormitory lodging and meals, is $1,050 couple, $650 single, $300 juniors (under age 20). A $100 deposit must accompany registration. Cost of travel programs abroad, including transportation, most meals, and double occupancy accommodations (single supplement available), ranges from approximately $3,000 to $3,850. A $450 to $800 deposit must accompany application with balance due 60 days prior to departure. Full refund, less $50 to $100 fee, is granted cancellations more than 90 days prior; thereafter, penalties vary.

Contact: Dr. Robert Fure, Director, Office of Special Programs, Washington and Lee University, Lexington, VA 24450; (703) 463-8723.

WENSUM LODGE
Norwich, Norfolk, England
Weekend courses year-round

Founded in 1965, this residential adult education center offers more than 40 weekend courses on a variety of subjects for resident and nonresident students of all ages. In addition to courses in art, crafts, and writing, titles include Britain in the Roman Empire, an introduction to the archaeology of Roman Britain and the development of towns, public buildings, military establishments, temples, and cemeteries; and Antiquarian Books, covering scribes, bibles, 19th century illustrators, bookplates and bookmarks, and bindings. Sessions begin with Friday evening dinner and continue all day Saturday and until 4 pm Sunday.

Specialties: A variety of topics.

Faculty: Teachers and persons who are knowledgeable in their fields.

Costs, Accommodations: Tuition is £56, which includes meals and double occupancy lodging. Nonresident tuition is £48. A £10 nonrefundable deposit reserves a space. A two-thirds tuition refund is granted within seven days of course.

Location: A few minutes walk from central Norwich, Wensum Lodge is a former Victorian brewery site and includes the 12th century Music House, the oldest domestic building in the city. Norwich is a two-hour train ride from London with direct airline connections to Heathrow Airport.

Contact: Wensum Lodge, King Street, Norwich, NR1 1QW, England; (44) 603 666021/2.

WESSEX HERITAGE
Dorchester, Dorset, England
One to seven-day tours of southwest England

Established in 1988, this professional tour operator offers specialty tours that focus on literary figures, homes, gardens, and antiques of England's southwest region. Approximately six itineraries are offered from May to mid-October, some including "Grand Style" travel from or to London on the Venice Simplon-Orient-Express. Group size varies, depending upon tour, with a range of from 12 to 30 participants. Literary tours are planned to coincide with a celebration, such as Dame Agatha Christie's centenary or the 150th anniversary of Thomas Hardy's birth, and include participation in special events as well as visits to sites connected with the author and his or her writings. Antique tour groups visit antique shops, fairs, and historic homes where antiques are displayed.

Specialties: Literary figures, homes, gardens, and antiques of southwest England.

Faculty: All guides are residents of the area visited and have a specific knowledge and interest in the tour theme.

Costs, Accommodations: Costs range from $20 (day tour) to $1,900 (Grand Style six-day tour), which includes double occupancy accommodations (single supplement available), some meals, and all planned events. A 25% deposit must accompany booking with balance due 42 days prior to departure. Cancellation penalty ranges from 10% of cost (more than 90 days prior) to 50% of cost (from 14 to 29 days prior); no refund thereafter.

Contact: European Travel Management, 235 Post Rd. West, Westport, CT 06880; (800) 992-7700 or (203) 454-0090, Fax (203) 454-8840. Main Office: Wessex Heritage, St. Peter's, Cattistock, Dorchester, Dorset DT1 0JD, England; (44) 300 20671, Fax (44) 300 21042.

WESTERN ILLINOIS UNIVERSITY
INDEPENDENT TRAVEL-STUDY (ITS)
Macomb, Illinois
At least seven days in the U.S. or abroad

Established in 1970, Independent Travel-Study is available to persons wanting to combine travel with academic study and credit. Participants can earn two, four, or six semester hours of credit by completing course work designed to complement their own travel plans. They select one, two, or three study units (a study unit is a two semester-hour course) and work with an instructor on a one-to-one basis. Each study unit can be individually tailored to meet the needs and plans of the participant. Those traveling abroad can choose from 20 study units, travelers within the United States choose from 10.

Study units include Historic Landscapes, interpreting sites containing buildings and other physical reminders of the past; Literary Landscapes, studying the landscapes described in works of selected authors; Art: Mirror of Society, examining various art forms for clues to political and social change; and Regional Cultural Patterns, identifying and explaining the customs and products that give a region its unique character. Comparative Cultural Analysis allows participants to design their own unit of study. The program format includes advance reading with submission of reports, a trial observation prior to travel, an orientation session with a faculty member in the U.S. or Europe, written field observations, and a debriefing conference.

Specialties: Independent travel-study.

Faculty: Western Illinois University faculty members.

Costs, Accommodations: Tuition ranges from $131 to $140 per study unit. Students pay for their own travel, which must be a minimum of seven days for each unit.

Contact: Office of International Programs — ITS, Western Illinois University, Macomb, IL 61455-1396; (309) 298-2426, Fax (309) 298-2245.

WESTERN MICHIGAN UNIVERSITY (WMU)
Office of International Affairs
Kalamazoo, Michigan
Nine-day to six-week international programs

Western Michigan University's Office of International Affairs, established in 1981, offers a variety of field courses and seminars (that include academic credit) and study-tours (that may include optional academic credit) for students and adults seeking enrichment. All programs are limited to 15 to 30 participants.

The six-week summer **Oxford Seminar Program**, held in odd-numbered years since the early 1960's, features four weeks of classes at Oxford, nearly one week of study and guided travel in London and other parts of Great Britain, and a ten-day optional European tour of France, Switzerland, Austria, and Germany. Participants earn six semester credit hours in the course Modern Britain: Literature, History and Society since 1870. While in Oxford, participants attend daily lectures and discussion sessions in the social sciences and humanities and weekend excursions are scheduled to Scotland, Stratford-Upon-Avon and locations in Wales. The concluding European motorcoach tour includes visits to Paris, Lucerne, Innsbruck, Salzburg, and Rudesheim, and a Rhine cruise.

The three-week **Summer Institute on the Mediterranean World**, offered biannually since 1967, is a study-cruise to cities in Italy, Sicily, Egypt, Israel, and Greece. The Institute offers two courses, Ancient Mediterranean Civilizations and Medieval & Modern Mediterranean Civilizations, which each offer three or four hours of academic credit and include lectures, on-site archaeological investigations, and visits to important sites, monuments, and museums.

The 18-day spring travel-seminar, **Tropical Biology in the Caribbean**, offered annually since 1981, provides an introduction to tropical biology of both the terrestrial and marine ecosystems of Puerto Rico. Students live at various locations throughout the island while they explore the six terrestrial live zones — from a tropical rainforest in the mountains to a marine coral reef and mangrove islands. Four semester hours of credit in Tropical Biology are granted as well additional credits for independent study.

A one-month summer study-tour, **The Grand Tour of Europe**, scheduled biannually since 1988, offers an optional four credits and includes guided visits to major sites in Amsterdam, Paris, Geneva, Rome, Florence, Venice, Vienna, Rudesheim, and Frankfurt. Participants earn four academic semester credits or audit the course European Cultures and Arts. A 15-day summer tour of the **Soviet Union**, offered annually since 1986 and granting two semester hours of college credit, features visits to Moscow, Leningrad, Tbilisi, and Riga. East African study-tours include **A Kenya Adventure**, an annual 17-day summer safari offered since 1987, that features two to three days in each of the four major game reserves; and **Africa: Journey of Discovery**, an annual three-week summer study-tour held since 1989 and offering two graduate or undergraduate credits, that features visits to Kenya and Nairobi, a safari through the Maasai Mara and Aberdare mountains, a climb on Mt.

Kenya, and exploration of the coast at Malindi. Other study-tours include **An Egyptian Odyssey**, an 11-day spring tour and Nile cruise first offered in 1990, and **London**, an annual nine-day spring tour offered since 1976.

Specialties: Study tours to international destinations.

Faculty: All programs are conducted by Western Michigan University faculty members with expertise in the regions visited. Participants in the Oxford Seminar Program are taught by Oxford scholars in the social sciences and humanities.

Costs, Accommodations: Costs are approximately $3,149 for the Oxford Seminar, $1,075 for the European extension, $2,395 for the Mediterrean Institute, $1,650 for Tropical Biology, $2,889 for The Grand Tour, $3,495 for the East African trips, $2,500 for the tour of the Soviet Union, $2,345 for the Egyptian Odyssey, and $973 for the London tour. Deposit and refund policies vary.

Contact: Office of International Affairs, Western Michigan University, 2090 Friedmann Hall, Kalamazoo, MI 49008; (616) 387-3951, Fax (616) 387-3962.

WESTHAM HOUSE COLLEGE
Barford, Warwick, England
One-day to one-week courses from April-December

Established in 1947 as an independent educational trust and registered charity, this short term adult residential college offers more than 70 day, weekend, and one-week courses, primarily in literature, arts and crafts, and health and nutrition.   Typical   courses   include   Spanish   Literature, Shakespeare, and John Betjeman.

Specialties: A variety of courses, including literature.

Faculty: All courses are taught by individuals who are knowledgeable in their fields.

Costs, Accommodations: Day courses are £12.50; weekend and one-week courses range from £57 to £190, which includes meals and double occupancy lodging.

Location: Westham House College is an old country house situated on 50 acres on a bend of the River Avon, approximately a half hour train ride from Birmingham and two hours from the London Paddington station.

Contact: Jean Long, Westham House College, Barford, Warwick, CV35 8DP, England; (44) 926 624206.

WHEATON-IN-ENGLAND
Wheaton College English Department
Wheaton, Illinois

Eight-week summer program on campus and in England

Wheaton-in-England, an annual British literature study and travel program first offered in 1975, is sponsored by the Wheaton College English Department. The program begins with one week of on-campus residence, where the 30 to 50 student and adult participants meet and attend preparatory classes. Once in England, the group spends the first 10 to 14 days viewing the literary and cultural sites in and around London, followed by four weeks of study-in-residence at St. Anne's College of the University of Oxford. Approximately every third year the program also includes a period of study at Dublin's Trinity College. Course offerings, which are based on the specialties of the faculty leaders and offer 2 to 4 credit hours, may include such titles as Arthurian Romance, Shakespeare, Renaissance, Victorian Literature, and Modern British Literature. Students may enroll for eight or ten hours of credit.

Specialties: British literature.

Faculty: Wheaton College faculty members, all of whom are full-time members of the English department and hold a Ph.D in literature, and Oxford University lecturers.

Costs, Accommodations: Program cost, including round-trip airfare from/to Chicago, room and board, and planned excursions, is approximately $4,000 to $4,200. A $100 deposit, refundable until March 1, must accompany application with balance due in late spring. Students may enroll for 8 or 10 hours of credit.

Location: Weekend excursions from London and Oxford, which usually emphasize sites that are rich in literary lore, include Canterbury and Dover, Cambridge, Rochester and Penshurst, Winchester, Salisbury, Stonehenge, Tintagel, Bath, Glastonbury (the Arthurian legends), Haworth (home of the Brontës) and the Lake District (Wordsworth and Coleridge), Stratford-Upon-Avon, the C.S. Lewis home, and Blenheim Palace.

Contact: Wheaton-in-England, c/o Joseph McClatchey, Chair, Department of English, Wheaton College, Wheaton, IL 60187; (312) 260-3781.

WHITE MESA INSTITUTE
College of Eastern Utah
Blanding, Utah

Three to seven-day programs from March-October

Established in 1982, the White Mesa Institute offers 15 to 22 programs annually that explore the art, archaeology, astronomy, history, and culture of the four corners canyon country of Arizona, Colorado, New Mexico, and Utah. Each program is limited to 8 to 20 participants and rated according to level of difficulty, from 1 (vehicle support, little hiking, motel accommodations) to 7 (total backpacking, new camps almost every day, strenuous).

Many programs are co-sponsored by the Utah Museum of Natural History, the Colorado Archaeological Society, and High Desert Adventures. College credit is available from the College of Eastern Utah.

Programs include Chaco Canyon — A High Desert Adventure, an exploration of the meanings of the great kivas, complex road system, and Anasazi life in the canyon; Upper Canyon del Muerto, a camping trip with experts in the fields of rock art, archaeoastronomy, archaeology, and Native American cultures; Navajo History and Culture in Southeastern Utah, an opportunity to learn about Navajo history, art, and culture by interacting with the Navajo population of the communities of Navajo Mountain and Monument Valley; Zuni: Rock Art, Prehistory and Present Culture, an inside look at the world of Zuni Pueblo highlighted by visits to prehistoric sites and rock art panels; and Cultures of the 4 Corners, Past and Present, an overview of Anasazi ruins and life, featuring talks by scholars, meetings with artisans, and a viewing of the once-yearly Ute Indian Bear Dance at White Mesa Ute Reservation.

Specialties: The art, archaeology, astronomy, history, and culture of the four corners canyon country of the U.S. Southwest.

Faculty: The more than 20-member Institute staff consists of archaeologists, anthropologists, historians, astronomers, authors, and regional specialists.

Costs, Accommodations: All-inclusive costs range from $185 to $675. Lodging is in motels, dormitories, or tent. Tuition is additional. A $100 deposit must accompany application with balance due 30 days prior. Cancellations more than 30 days prior forfeit $50; no refunds thereafter.

Contact: White Mesa Institute, CEU/San Juan Campus, 639 West 100 South (50-1), Blanding, UT 84511; (801) 678-2220.

WHITNEY MUSEUM OF AMERICAN ART
New York, New York

One to ten-day domestic and international tours

The Whitney Museum of American Art sponsors a variety of tour and travel programs for its members, ranging from day trips to nearby art centers to weekend and longer trips in the U.S. and abroad.

Day trips to such sites as the Hudson River Valley, Brooklyn Heights, and Long Island City usually include guided tours of current museum exhibitions and architectural landmarks as well as visits to private collections and artists' studios. Weekend to one-week trips to such cities as Los Angeles, Santa Fe, Miami, and Charleston feature visits to private collections and artists' studios, special receptions and performances, and guided tours of museums and historic sites. International tours offer members of the Whitney Circle the opportunity to visit major private collections, artists' studios, museums, and galleries, and attend special receptions and performances.

Specialties: Tours with a contemporary American art focus.

Faculty: All tours are planned and conducted by knowledgeable guides and historians.

Costs, Accommodations: Costs, which include round-trip air or motorcoach fare, double occupancy deluxe accommodations, and scheduled activities, range from $100 to $200 for day trips, $650 to $1,650 for weekend and longer domestic trips, and $5,000 to $6,000 plus a contribution of $1,000 or more for international tours. Annual memberships begin at $50 for members, $1,000 for the Whitney Circle.

Contact: Membership Dept., Whitney Museum of American Art, 945 Madison Ave., New York, NY 10021; (212) 570-3641.

WORLD AFFAIRS COUNCIL OF PHILADELPHIA
Philadelphia, Pennsylvania
Five to seventeen-day domestic and international trips

The nonprofit World Affairs Council of Philadelphia offers eight to ten tours annually that feature visits to American embassies and informal talks with government and military officials, journalists, businessmen, and educators in order to provide a deeper understanding of the countries visited. Destinations are selected to reflect current critical political and environmental issues as well as the interests of members.

Specialties: Tours that feature briefings with government officials.

Faculty: Some trips are accompanied by a specialist in the area visited, who provides informal lectures and moderates meetings with officials.

Costs, Accommodations: Costs begin at approximately $2,500, which includes round-trip airfare, double occupancy first class lodging (single supplement available), meals, ground transportation, and scheduled briefings and activities. Deposit and refund policies vary.

Locations: May include Alaska, Antarctica, Argentina, Brazil, East Africa, Morocco, Southeast Asia, the Soviet Union, and Washington, D.C.

Contact: Travel Dept. World Affairs Council of Philadelphia, 206 S. Fourth St., Philadelphia, PA 19106; (800) 942-5004 *or* (215) 922-2900.

WORLD EXPLORER CRUISES — S.S. UNIVERSE
San Francisco, California
14-day summer cruises to Alaska

World Explorer Cruises' S.S. Universe, an 18,000-ton, 550-passenger vessel, offers eight summer cruises that feature such educational benefits as lectures, classical music concerts, and the opportunity to earn college credit. The itinerary includes nine ports, 44 optional shore excursions, and a lecture series consisting of courses in anthropology, geology, history, and oceanography. Passengers desiring academic credit (one unit per course) are required to attend all lectures and audio-visual presentations and write a short paper or design a course-related project.

Specialties: Anthropology, geology, history, and oceanography of Canada and Alaska.

Faculty: Lectures are presented by university professors and specialists.

Costs, Accommodations: Costs, including meals and shipboard activities, range from $1,695 to $3,595, depending on accommodations. Optional shore excursions range from $16 to $250. College credit through Chapman College in Orange, California, is $65 per unit. A $500 deposit secures reservation with balance due 60 days prior to departure. Cancellations more than 60 days prior receive full refund; thereafter cancellation penalty ranges from $50 (46 to 60 days prior) to 50% of fare (8 to 30 days prior); no refund thereafter.

Location, Facilities: Ports include Vancouver, Wrangell, Juneau, Skagway, Haines, Glacier Bay, Valdez, Columbia Glacier, Sitka, Ketchikan, Seward, Anchorage, and Victoria. Educational facilities include a 12,000-volume library.

Contact: World Explorer Cruises, 555 Montgomery St., San Francisco, CA 94111; (800) 854-3835 *or* (415) 391-9262, Fax (415) 391-1145.

THE YELLOWSTONE INSTITUTE
Yellowstone National Park, Wyoming
Two to five-day workshops from June-October

Founded in 1975 as part of the nonprofit Yellowstone Association, the Institute offers more than 80 diverse field courses and nature vacations covering the ecology, geology, astronomy, history, plants, and animals of the region. A variety of photography and writing courses are also offered as well as horsepacking and llama trekking, fly fishing, programs for young people (scheduled to coincide with classes for adults only) and families, and research field trips with park scientists, which provide opportunities to learn and collect data for investigations. Most programs are limited to 10 to 15 participants and many grant academic and teacher recertification credit through nearby universities.

Typical ecology courses include Ecology of Greater Yellowstone, Exploring the Yellowstone Ecosystem, and Fire Ecology, which features field trips to gather data at old and recent burn areas and to an on-going fire, if possible. Geology courses include Fire, Ice and Fossil Forests; Geysers, Mudpots, and Hot Springs, featuring a day of geyser gazing at Old Faithful; and Hydrothermal Systems & the Yellowstone Caldera, with lectures, discussions, and field trips relating to volcanic rocks, caldera cycles, and the development of hydrothermal systems. Astronomy courses (Yellowstone's Night Skies and Star Trails West) offer lectures, visual planetarium presentations, and nighttime observations and history courses cover Indian tribal migrations, fur trade history, the flight of the Nez Perce, and early exploration. Programs focusing on Yellowstone's birds, bears, insects, mammals, wildflowers, and plants, include Wild Edible Plants and Medicinal Herbs, Bear Folklore and Biology, and Mammal Tracking, with emphasis on interpreting natural history and animal behavior. Research projects include Pronghorn Antelope Research;

Plants, Fire, and Grazing, which examines the interaction between fire and large ungulate (elk and bison) grazing on plant growth; and Coyotes and Mountain Lions, a comparison of the population dynamics, foraging ecology, and social behavior of these and other large predators. Programs for young people and families include an Introduction to Hiking & Camping, Exploring the Park with a Ranger Family, and Three Days at Buffalo Ranch, which features daily hikes to observe wildlife and learn about plants, ecology, and the park's history; and supervised projects such as silkscreening, plaster casting, and mural painting.

Specialties: The ecology, geology, astronomy, history, plants, and animals of Yellowstone National Park.

Faculty: Specialists in the various aspects of Yellowstone, including biologists, naturalists, ecologists, entomologists, historians, botanists, geologists, astronomers, environmentalists, researchers, and photographers.

Costs, Accommodations: Tuition, exclusive of lodging, meals, books, course materials, transportation, and university credit, ranges from $20 to $400. Members (annual dues begin at $25) receive a $10 to $15 discount per class. Lodging in multiple-occupancy cabins (no plumbing or heating) is $7 per person per night and participants provide their own food. Full payment must accompany registration. Those who cancel at least one month prior receive an 80% refund; no refund thereafter unless space can be filled. Cost for academic credit ranges from $25 to $50, payable at start of course.

Location: Courses are held at various locations within the Yellowstone ecosystem. Most are conducted at the Institute facility known as the Buffalo Ranch, an historic facility situated in the Lamar Valley between the Northeast Entrance and Tower Junction, 19 miles west of Silver Gate, Montana.

Contact: Yellowstone Institute, P.O. Box 117, Yellowstone National Park, Wyoming 82190; (307) 344-7381, ext. 2384.

YOUTH & HERITAGE INTERNATIONAL
Paris, France
Nine and fifteen day summer course in Dauphine, France

Youth & Heritage International (Jeunesse & Patrimoine) offers two consecutive historic restoration courses during July and August. **Conservation of Architectural Heritage and Environment**, a nine- day course begun in 1977 and open to adults ages 20 to 35, is devoted to a study of the restoration of old buildings and sites. The program consists of lectures, guided technical visits to protected areas and edifices, and practical work sessions. Topics covered include legislation, conservation of ancient monuments, town planning and sites, problems of restoration, upkeep and revitalization, protection of rural habitat, interior decoration and furniture, and historic gardens.

The **International Historic Building Training Session**, a 15-day session that follows the previous course, completes the entire program. First offered in 1988, this introduction to the practical aspects of modern and traditional techniques of conservation and restoration seeks to develop international exchanges between future specialists. Trainees, who are divided into teams under the supervision of skilled craftsmen and regional Head Architects for Historic Monuments, are assigned in turn to workshops in stone cutting and masonry, woodwork, plasterwork, and paintings. Evenings are devoted to lectures and visits to restoration worksites.

Specialties: Historic conservation and restoration.

Faculty: Architects, curators, representatives of official and private organizations, and skilled craftsmen.

Costs, Accommodations: The fee for the nine-day course on conservation, which includes double-occupancy lodging, ranges from 2,200 FF to 2,800 FF. Fee for the 15-day historic building training session, which includes dormitory housing and full board, ranges from 1,500 FF to 1,800 FF.

Location: The 12th century St. Antoine Abbey in Dauphine, located between Grenoble, Valence, and Lyon.

Contact: Youth & Heritage International, 9, Ave. Franklin-Roosevelt, 75008 Paris, France; (33) 42 25 91 92.

ZOOLOGICAL SOCIETY OF SAN DIEGO WORLDWIDE TOURS PROGRAM
San Diego, California
Ten to seventeen-day trips in the U.S. and abroad

Since 1968, the Zoological Society of San Diego has offered travel programs for its members and presently schedules at least three different destinations each year. Typical itineraries include a Baja/Sea of Cortez cruise that features lectures and informal discussions; a two-week Alaska expedition with visits to national parks, scenic and historic areas, and museums; and a classic tented safari to Kenya, with visits to the major national reserves and parks. Groups range from 20 to 50 participants.

Specialties: Natural history, wildlife.

Faculty: Society representatives who are knowledgable about the area's animal and plant life, tour company scientific personnel, and special keynote speakers.

Costs, Accommodations: Land costs, which include double occupancy accommodations (single supplement available) and most meals, range from approximately $2,900 to $4,600. Deposit, which must accompany reservation, ranges from $300 to $800 with balance due 60 to 90 days prior to departure. Refund policies vary. Society dues begin at $42 for a single and $49 for a dual membership.

Contact: Worldwide Tours Program, Zoological Society of San Diego, P.O. Box 551, San Diego, CA 92112-1515; (619) 231-1515, ext. 4241, Fax (619) 231-0249.

II

APPENDIX

GEOGRAPHIC INDEX OF SPONSORS

Cuyahoga Community College,
120
Insight Travel, 21
Ohio University-Lancaster, 124

OREGON
English Literature Summer
Schools, 56
Modern English Literature &
Culture Courses, 104
Nature Expeditions International,
112
The Oregon Shakespeare Festival,
127
Oxford Heritage Study Visits, 130
Sitka Center for Art and Ecology,
152
Wilson & Lake International, 56,
104, 130

PENNSYLVANIA
Brandywine River Museum, 21
Edinboro University, 53
Fudan Museum Foundation, 72
North Museum, 119
Pennsylvania German Research
Society, 79
The Pennsylvania State
University, 133
The Philadelphia Museum of Art,
134
Pocono Environmental Education
Center, 137
Rosemont College, 162
Susquehanna University, 163
Travelearn, 169
University of Cambridge
Summer Study Program, 178
The University Museum of
Archaeology and Anthropology,
183
University of Pittsburgh, 135, 149
Villanova University, 162
World Affairs Council of
Philadelphia, 208

SOUTH CAROLINA
Clemson University
Alumni Association, 34
Francis Marion College, 170

TEXAS
Baylor University, 17
Cowboy Artists of America
Museum, 41
Lamar University, 94
Texas Camel Corps
(Witte Museum), 167
The University of Texas at Austin,
191

UTAH
Canyonlands Field Institute, 25
College of Eastern Utah, 206
Colorado River & Trail
Expeditions, 36
The Four Corners School of
Outdoor Education, 70
Southern Utah State College, 23
Utah State University, 196

VERMONT
The University of Vermont, 12
A Vermont Inquiry, 196
Volunteers for Peace, Inc., 198

VIRGINIA
The Colonial Williamsburg
Foundation, 34
The Cousteau Society, 139
Virginia Commonwealth
University, 197
Washington and Lee University,
201

WASHINGTON
International Bicycle Fund, 18
Intersea Research, Inc., 90
Journeys, 92
Olympic Park Institute, 125

GEOGRAPHIC INDEX OF PROGRAMS

ALASKA
Camp Denali/North Face Lodge, 22
Intersea Research, Inc., 90
World Explorer Cruises -
    S.S. Universe, 208

ARIZONA
Archaeological Conservancy
    Tours, 11
Canyonlands Ed Ventures, 25
Four Corners School of Outdoor
    Education, 70
White Mesa Institute, 206

CALIFORNIA
Farm Tours, Etc., 61
Field Studies in Nat'l History, 63
Point Reyes Field Seminar, 138
San Diego Natural History
    Museum, 147
Stanford University
    Alumni Association, 159
University of the Pacific, 186

COLORADO
The Aspen Institute, 15
Canyonlands Ed Ventures, 25
Colorado River & Trail
    Expeditions, 36
Conservation Summits, 38
Denver Museum of Natural
    History, 46
Dinosaur Discovery Exped's., 48
Four Corners School of Outdoor
    Education, The, 70
Tulane University
    Summer School, 171
White Mesa Institute, 206

DISTRICT OF COLUMBIA
Site Seeing Tours, 151

GEORGIA
Caretta Research Project, 26

HAWAII
Eye of the Whale Marine/
    Wilderness Adventures, 58

ILLINOIS
The Art Institute of Chicago, 13
Center for American Archeology, 27
Chicago-Europe Language Center, 30
Northwestern University, 121

INDIANA
Indiana University
    Mini University, 82

LOUISIANA
Tulane University
    Summer School, 171

MAINE
Norlands Living History Center, 118

MARYLAND
The Aspen Institute, 15
National Aquarium in Baltimore, 108

MASSACHUSETTS
Massachusetts Audubon Society, 101
Old Sturbridge Village
    Summer Field School
    in Historical Archaeology, 124

MICHIGAN
Leelanau Outdoor Classrooms, 96

MISSISSIPPI
Faulkner and Yoknapatawpha
  Conference, 61

MONTANA
The Glacier Institute, 77

NEW HAMPSHIRE
Dartmouth Alumni College, 45
Learning Weekends, 95

NEW MEXICO
Archaeological Conservancy
  Tours, 11
Canyonlands Ed Ventures, 25
Four Corners School of Outdoor
  Education, 70
White Mesa Institute, 206

NEW YORK
Adirondack Mountain Club, 1
Appalachian Mountain Club, 9
The Asimov Seminar of the
  Rensselaerville Institute, 14
Chautauqua Institution, 29
Cornell's Adult University, 40
Dire Wolf Nat'l History Tours, 48
Metropolitan Opera Guild
  Members Travel Program, 102
Museum of American Folk Art
  Explorers' Club, 106
The Museum of Modern Art, 107
The New York Botanical Garden,
  114
Omega Institute for
  Holistic Studies, 126
Wainwright House, 200
Whitney Museum of
  American Art, 207

NORTH CAROLINA
Adventures in Ideas, 2
Conservation Summits, 38

OHIO
Northern Ohio Archaeological
  Field School, 120

OKLAHOMA
Journeys Into American Indian
  Territory, 93

OREGON
The Oregon Shakespeare Festival,
  127
Sitka Center for Art and Ecology,
  152

PENNSYLVANIA
Penn State Alumni
  Vacation College, 133
The Philadelphia Museum of Art,
  134
Pocono Environmental Education
  Center, 137

TEXAS
Cowboy Artists of America
  Museum, 41

UTAH
Camp Shakespeare, 23
Canyonlands Ed Ventures, 25
Crow Canyon Archaeological
  Center, 42
Four Corners School of Outdoor
  Education, 70
White Mesa Institute, 206

VERMONT
Archaeology Field School at
  Mount Independence, 12
A Vermont Inquiry, 196
Conservation Summits, 38

VIRGINIA
The Colonial Williamsburg
  Foundation, 34
Washington and Lee University
  Alumni College, 201

WASHINGTON
Conservation Summits, 38
Olympic Field Seminars, 125

SPECIALTY INDEX

CULTURE,
HERITAGE & HISTORY

NATURE & SCIENCE

MASTER INDEX